THE REBBE'S DAUGHTER

Memoir of a Hasidic Childhood

Malkah Shapiro in her middle years

THE REBBE'S DAUGHTER

Memoir of a Hasidic Childhood

Malkah Shapiro

Translated, with an Introduction and Commentary by

Nehemia Polen

THE JEWISH PUBLICATION SOCIETY
Philadelphia
2002 / 5762

The Jewish Publication Society
2100 Arch Street
Philadelphia, PA 19103

Malkah Shapiro's work was originally published in Hebrew by Mossad Harav Kook,
Jerusalem, 1969 under the title סיפורים מחצרות האדמו״רים: מדין לרחמים. Shapiro
designated the section translated herein by the title קוזי׳ניץ.

Design and Composition by Book Design Studio

Manufactured in the United States of America

02 03 04 05 06 07 08 09 10   10 9 8 7 6 5 4 3 2 1

Library of Congress Cataloging-in-Publication Data

Shapiro, Malkah, b. 1895.
    [Mi-din le-rahamim. English]
    The rebbe's daughter : memoir of a Hasidic childhood / Malkah Shapiro; translated by
    Nehemia Polen.
       p. cm.
    Includes Bibliographical references and index.
    ISBN 0-8276-0725-3
    1. Shapiro, Malkah, b. 1895--Childhood and youth. 2. Jewish
girls--Poland--Kozienice--Biography. 3. Hasidim--Poland--Kozienice--Biography. 4.
Shapiro, Malkah, b. 1895--Family. 5. Hapstein family. 6. Kozienice
(Poland)--Biography. I. Title.

DS135.p63 S4298513 2002
943.8'4--dc21

Support for the publication of this book is made
with admiration, respect, and affection for
Professor Nehemia Polen,
by

THEODORE HERZL TEPLOW

and in memory of Rosalie Katchen,
a woman of great courage, wisdom, and gentility,
by

PHYLLIS AND MICHAEL HAMMER

In memory of Sima Schechter

Contents

Preface

On sabbatical in Jerusalem in 1985–1986, my wife and I were looking for some household items in a used furniture store called *Yad Sheniyah* (second hand). On a dusty shelf in an aged bookcase, my eye was caught by a Hebrew volume whose spine bore the name "Malkah Shapiro"; I was then working on a collection of hasidic homilies written during the Holocaust in the Warsaw Ghetto by a rabbi named Kalonymos Kalmish Shapiro. I picked up the volume, which bore the title *Mi-Din le-Rahamim: Sippurim me-Hatzrot ha-Admorim* (From severity to mercy: Stories from the courts of the hasidic masters). Leafing through it, I realized that Malkah Shapiro was the sister-in-law of the rabbi I was then studying and that the work was a memoir describing the lives of a family I was already quite familiar with. Although the book seemed to be a prop to illustrate the bookcase's functionality rather than an item displayed for sale, the owner was willing to part with it. I paid six New Shekels (about two dollars) and went home with my find.

I was taken by Shapiro, or more precisely by her literary persona: the eleven-year-old Bat-Zion. I was captivated by her innocence and vulnerability, her exuberance and inquisitiveness. I felt her terror as she peered out toward maturity and intuited the changes she would face. I knew of no work originating within the arena of Hasidism that depicted so vividly the world of a preadolescent, her inner angst, headstrong curiosity, and spiritual exuberance, or one that described the domestic life of a hasidic master's family from the inside. I envied the author's evident gifts of observation, memory, and literary description. As a father of three girls and as someone who had personally struggled with issues of spiritual maturation and who had negotiated his own uneasy truce between tradition and modernity, I was grateful for her candor. The thought came to mind that it would be wonderful to bring this literary treasure—a woman's perspective on Hasidism at the start of the twentieth century—to the attention of the scholarly community and the wider reading public. This would involve translating the work into English and providing an introduction and other reader aids not present in the original Hebrew. My prior work on Rabbi Kalonymos Shapiro would furnish me with essential background knowledge.

I began in earnest in the spring of 1994, with time provided by a research leave from Hebrew College and a Daniel Jeremy Silver Fellowship at Harvard University. The translation was concluded in 1998–1999, with the help of a National Endowment for the Humanities fellowship. In April 1999 I traveled to Poland to see Kozienice and the places described by Shapiro. Colleagues warned me that nothing was likely to have survived the war and that the trip would be a waste. But I knew that the topography, which plays such an important role in *The Rebbe's Daughter*, would still be there.

The flatness of the terrain during the two-hour drive from Warsaw to Kozienice was surprising for someone who had spent most of his life in New England. I knew the Vistula was a mighty river, but I was still breathtaken by its size and power. On its banks one finds old-growth trees, whose vast girth suggest an origin in medieval times. Kozienice itself is still a provincial town. The post–World War II apartment houses reveal the drab architectural legacy of state socialism, with featureless rows of concrete slabs. Only by wandering in back alleys could one find traces of old Kozienice: tiny houses and barns with low ceilings, small entranceways, and rough wooden exteriors; the remains of a water mill and copper foundry. The natural beauty had indeed survived: the birch trees, the stream with banks ablaze in wildflowers and cherry blossoms, the elegant grounds and serene footpaths of the Larski palace (partially restored after the war).

Indeed there were no Jews and hardly even a memory of the great hasidic master who bore the town's name and whose spiritual powers had once attracted Jewish and gentile visitors from all across Poland. The only trace of the Jewish community was the cemetery, whose location is clearly marked on municipal maps. Not one tombstone appears to have remained after the Nazi onslaught; but after the war's end, survivors returned to fence in the cemetery land, located on a sandy rise overlooking a lovely pond. A single monument now serves to commemorate all the town's Jewish dead. Shortly before my own visit to Poland, I spoke with a friend (an ophthalmologist with a layperson's enthusiasm for Hasidism) who had made the trip the previous year, in 1998. He told me that he found the monument covered with graffiti and that he had taken the initiative to purchase paint at a local hardware store. He returned to the cemetery and wrote on the monument, in English, "KOZHNITZ MAGGID LIVED HERE." He also wrote, in Hebrew script, *"Am Yisrael Hai"* (The people Israel lives).

When I visited in the spring of 1999, my friend's handwriting was still there. It was the only thing Jewish I found in Kozienice.

Acknowledgments

Many people and institutions contributed to the advancement of this project. Pride of place goes to Malkah Shapiro's family, whose members have been unfailingly gracious and helpful. These include the memoirist's daughters, Chava Drazin and Devora Silman; her granddaughter, Sima Schechter; and her son-in-law Rabbi Yehoshua Hutner. Among their many courtesies, they granted extensive interviews; provided letters, photographs and other precious family memorabilia; and (especially Rabbi Hutner) helped me in obtaining translation rights from Mossad Harav Kook.

My initial research was conducted during a leave granted by my home school, Hebrew College, spent as a Daniel Jeremy Silver Fellow at Harvard University. I am grateful to the trustees of the Silver Fellowship, and to all who welcomed me so warmly at Harvard, including Dr. Peter MachiZnist and Dr. Kimberley Patton. Dr. Elizabeth Rhodes (at the time a Visiting Lecturer at the Women's Studies in Religion Program at Harvard Divinity School) introduced me to the literature on women's spiritual autobiography.

The translation work was completed on a sabbatical provided by Hebrew College and supported in part by a National Endowment for the Humanities fellowship. The NEH fellowship also enabled a trip to Kozienice in the spring of 1999.

In translating a work such as *The Rebbe's Daughter*, one is always struggling to remain faithful to the original while producing an English text with its own literary integrity. The process is painstaking and cannot be rushed; there is a constant need to avert the gaze and then return with new eyes. At some point, the new eyes must be those of someone other than the translator. Among those who reviewed the English version in whole or part, were my wife Lauri; my daughters Sara Henna, Esti, and Adina; Diana Muir Appelbaum; Amy Bernstein; Rabbi Deanna Douglas; Dr. Judith Kates; Rabbi Lawrence Kushner; Susan Megerman; Dr. Lawrence Rosenwald; and Channah Schafer. Dr. David Assaf and Dr. Arthur Green read the Introduction and made helpful comments. My deep thanks to them all.

Dr. Menachem Rotstein shared his extensive knowledge of modern Hebrew literature and gave important insights into questions of genre, style, and vocabulary. At a later stage, he reviewed the entire translation. His help, always offered in the most gracious manner, has been simply indispensable. Shai Nathanson of Hebrew College spent many hours carefully reading the text, reviewing suggested translations, and answering specific questions. His interest in the work went much beyond the expectations of collegial courtesy and I am very grateful. Rabbi Bernard

Mehlman, my study partner in Midrash for many years, read a number of chapters with me, *havruta* style. I deeply appreciate the knowledge, wisdom, and literary sensitivity he shared. Among the people who answered specific linguistic questions were Tamar Aronson, Shula Bamberger, Dr. Louis Glinert, Shulamit Katznelson, and Dr. Yochanan Petrovsky.

Dr. Ellen Frankel, editor-in-chief of The Jewish Publication Society, grasped the significance of this project at its inception. Her astute advice guided me around many obstacles and pitfalls, and her editorial experience and wisdom were indispensable. Carol Hupping, publishing director at JPS, moved the book through the final stages to completion. My thanks to her, as well as to Candace Levy, Kristina Espy, and Emily Law.

During stays in Jerusalem to conduct research, Dr. Alon Goshen-Gottstein and Tamara Gottstein provided warm hospitality and logistic support. My brother-in-law Dr. Ranan Wolff assisted me with interviews, both in New York and in Israel. At a moment just before completion when things seemed stalled, Gloria Greenfield injected crucially important new energy and ideas. Yitzhak Meir Twersky graciously provided information on the genealogy of the Twersky family and the Chernobyl dynasty. Dr. Maurice Tuchman and Harvey Sukenic of the Hebrew College Library responded eagerly to all requests, as did Nancy Zibman of the Brandeis University Library.

The initial sketch of the family compound, based on my model constructed with children's blocks, was made by my daughter Esti. The final artist's rendering, which drew on Esti's work, was executed by our friend and relative Aviva Wolff Greenland. The Hapstein-Shapiro family tree is based on the version set in PageMaker by my daughter Adina.

The faculty and administration of Hebrew College have encouraged this project at every step and have provided a warm and stimulating intellectual environment. Special thanks are due to Dr. David Gordis, Dr. Barry Mesch, Dr. Gila Ramras-Rauch, and Dr. Sol Schimmel, who all offered valuable insights and suggestions.

Professor Elie Wiesel, who directed my doctoral dissertation on Rabbi Kalonymos Shapiro and *Esh Kodesh*, answered many questions about the functioning of the hasidic court. I am grateful for his help, and for his gracious encouragement of my work in general.

My wife Lauri inspired and guided this work every step of the way. Without her love and support, it would not have happened.

Several people thanked above are now deceased. These include Shulamit Katznelson; Chava Drazin, Malkah Shapiro's daughter; and Sima Schechter, Malkah Shapiro's granddaughter. Sima was a most worthy scion of the Kozienice lineage—a teacher and writer whose life was filled with Torah learning, joy, faith, and a spirit of giving. She was very enthusiastic about this project, assisting and encouraging me in every way. Our working relationship blossomed into a family friendship. In her final illness, she retained her sweetness, courage, strength, and sense of humor. This book is dedicated to her memory.

Introduction

It was a dense and fragrant time, like honey.
Mikhail Bakhtin

This book is the spiritual memoir of Malkah Shapiro (1894–1971), daughter of the Rebbe of Kozienice, a master from one of the most notable lineages in Hasidism. Focusing on her life when she was eleven and twelve years old, the author presents us with a memoir of a hasidic childhood through a girl's eye. It is the story of the awakening of a young woman, a Rebbe's daughter's coming of age. We follow her as she discovers who she is and the meaning of the world into which she was born. The author portrays her fears surrounding biological maturation and her impending marriage, at age fourteen; her introduction to the world of Jewish learning, especially textual studies; and her intense curiosity about the mysteries of hasidic spirituality and Kabbalah.

In addition to her own story, the author paints a vivid picture of her family and her father's hasidic court. The atmosphere is ethereal and dreamlike; the social and personal relations are mannered and deeply respectful, mediated by governing hierarchies of master–disciple and parent–child. In Shapiro's account, her entire family is committed to an ethos of integrity and compassion, shaping every waking moment with reverential, meticulous care. While the author's father, the tzaddik or Rebbe, is certainly a central figure, the women of the family—especially her mother and grandmother—hold key roles; and their personal and devotional lives are portrayed with depth and vibrancy. In addition to directing the household and performing acts of service, kindness, and charity, the women are also scholars of Torah, transmitters of sacred traditions, and spiritual exemplars of deep piety.

Shapiro paints a domestic landscape in which people are seamlessly in touch with their natural and spiritual environment. In this world, there is a harmonious balance between action and contemplation. The courtyard resounds with wordless melodies, Talmud-study chant, and moments of meaningful silence. Flora and fauna are personified, fully participating in the sacred rhythms and rituals. The air is heavy with fragrances of the forest, and spirits of departed ancestors.

The book preserves sacred family memories going back to the beginnings of Hasidism in Poland and the family's illustrious progenitor, the Maggid (preacher) of Kozienice (1737–1814). It is set four generations after the Maggid, in 1905, a year the author correctly perceived as a watershed year. At that time, elders were still alive who remembered the family's early patriarchs and matriarchs, some of Hasidism's founding figures; one could look back to the simpler, quieter world of nineteenth-century rural Hasidism, when faith reigned supreme. But 1905 was also a time in which the ineluctable pull of the twentieth century was to be felt in full force.

This is a learned text, filled with biblical, talmudic, kabbalistic, and hasidic allusions and direct quotations. The erudition is an integral part of the story, demonstrating that, in contrast to the stereotype of girls' education in traditional Jewish society,[1] the author was blessed with a thorough education in Judaic classics. But insofar as it focuses on the young eleven-year-old who haltingly and somewhat reluctantly advances in her studies, it highlights the distance between the innocent child and the astutely knowledgeable adult. It invites us to ponder how one was transformed into the other and how the first may still somehow reside in the second. While this theme is implicit in nearly every autobiography, in this case the poignancy is heightened by the knowledge that this child's world would be swept away by the events of the twentieth century: by the encroachments of modernity, by the Great War, and, most conclusively, by the Holocaust. Because the adult writer knows what the child does not, a subtle elegiac feel is never far from the surface.

Except for the last chapters, Shapiro chooses to tell her story in the voice of a third-person narrator. This literary technique—autobiography in the third person—allows Shapiro to maintain a distance between herself as empirical author and her childhood alter ego, whom she calls Bat-Zion. You will read more about this literary device and its implications later.

MALKAH SHAPIRO AND HER WRITINGS

Malkah Shapiro was born Reizel Malkah Hapstein on April 27, 1894, in the town of Kozienice, Poland, then a part of the Russian Empire. Her family was at the center of the tightly interwoven tapestry of hasidic nobility. Her father was Rabbi Yerahmiel Moshe Hapstein (1860–1909), the town's hasidic Rebbe, a descendant of the Maggid of Kozienice, one of the founders of Polish Hasidism. Her mother was Brachah Tzipporah Gitl Twersky (1861–c. 1930), a descendant of Rabbi Menahem Nahum of Chernobyl (1730–1797), a prominent early Master in Ukraine. In 1908, Malkah married her first cousin Avraham Elimelekh Shapiro of Grodzisk (1896–1967), a descendant on his mother's side of the Masters of Karlin-Stolin in White Russia. At the time of her marriage she was fourteen and her husband was thirteen. She went to live with her in-laws in Grodzisk, a town twenty-five kilometers southwest of Warsaw. During World War I the family moved to Warsaw. In 1926 she emigrated to the Land of Israel, living first in Haifa, then in Kefar Hasidim (a settlement near Haifa co-founded by one of her brothers), and finally in Jerusalem. She died in 1971.

In 1934 she began publishing stories, essays, and poems in various Hebrew-language journals. Three volumes of collected writings appeared in 1952, 1955, and 1969; and a volume of poetry, in 1971. Her most mature prose work is the 1969 volume *Mi Din le Rahamim: Sippurim me-Hatzrot ha-Admorim* (From severity to mercy: stories from the courts of the hasidic Rebbes), published by Mossad Harav Kook, an Israeli publishing house with a religious-Zionist orientation.

Mi-Din le-Rahamim comprises three distinct story collections. The first collection, titled *Kozienice*, consists of seventeen chapters centering on the author as a young girl, called Bat-Zion, in the hasidic milieu of pre–World War I small-town Poland. The *Kozienice* collection is about 150 pages, by far the volume's longest division. The second section—about 50 pages long, titled *Hasidim Mesaprim* (Hasidim recount)—is a collection of four unrelated hasidic stories. The third section is 60 pages long and is titled *Eretz Yisra'el* (The Land of Israel); it describes the author's early days in Mandatory Palestine, with a special emphasis on the village near Haifa known as Kefar Hasidim.

Our focus is the first group of stories, which is an independent work with a distinct literary character and a continuous narrative arc. It is presented here for the first time in English translation, under the title *The Rebbe's Daughter*.

FAMILY ORIGINS AND HASIDIC HISTORY

Malkah Shapiro/Bat-Zion was born into the world of Hasidism, the movement of Jewish religious revival that traces its origins to Rabbi Israel ben Eliezer (d. 1760), known as the Baal Shem Tov, an extraordinary mystical teacher and charismatic healer. The movement's next leader was Rabbi Dov Baer, the Maggid of Mezhirech (d. 1772), who combined dazzling spiritual intensity with depth of traditional talmudic learning. It was the third generation, largely the disciples of Rabbi Dov Baer, who carried the movement beyond its original territory. Soon Hasidism became a dominant force in almost all of the eastern European Jewish world.

The major concerns of Hasidism are simply stated. These include an emphasis on love of God, Torah, and Israel; ecstatic fervor in prayer and study; and a theology of divine immanence, the teaching that all the universe is permeated with God's Glory—the indwelling Presence of the Divine. The theology of immanence suggests that God could be found everywhere, in any situation and tends to infuse hasidic life with a sense of robust optimism and joy. Also important is the doctrine of the tzaddik, the Righteous One who, like Moses and the other biblical prophets, stands in the breach between God and man, mediating between the two, bringing his hasidim closer to the divine by their association with him. The sanctity and sublime elevation of the tzaddik's soul; the inexhaustible resources of his mind, heart, and spirit; and his ability to perceive and respond to the needs and inner lives of his hasidim, all fostered the belief that the tzaddik is another kind of human, a unique category of being who, if sought out in humble pilgrimage, would confer blessing by his word and holiness by his proximity.

There are no generic hasidim, only hasidim of particular Rebbes. One can be a Lubavitcher, Satmarer, Gerer, or Vizhnitzer, but one cannot simply be a hasid, unaffiliated and unattached. This pattern begins with the disciples of the Maggid of Mezhirech, each of whom staked out a certain territory—spiritual as well as geographical—within the Jewish world. The tzaddik Rabbi Elimelekh of Lyzhansk (1717–1787), for example, was instrumental in bringing Hasidism to southeastern Poland and Galicia. It is said that when Rabbi Elimelekh passed away, he bequeathed his eyes to the Seer of Lublin, his power of speech to the Apter Rebbe, his mind to Rabbi Mendel of Rymanow, and his heart to Rabbi Yisrael the Maggid of Kozienice.

Malkah Shapiro/Bat-Zion, born into the family of Rabbi Yerahmiel Moshe Hapstein, was a fifth-generation descendant of the Maggid of Kozienice. In order to understand her world, we must know more about her lineage.

The Maggid of Kozienice

Rabbi Yisrael ben Shabbetai Hapstein (1737–1814) was one of the founders of Hasidism in Poland. A master of Talmud as well as the practical and theoretical Kabbalah, he was famed for his ecstatic prayer and intense devotion to God. Sought out for blessings and amulets, which were reputed to assist barren couples in having children, his reputation attracted Christian Poles as well as Jews.[2] It is said that prominent figures from the Polish nobility such as Adam Czartoryski, Josef Poniatowski, and Prince Radziwill came to seek his blessing. He used his influence and prestige in Polish ruling circles to mitigate the effect of prejudicial regulations and to protect his people from outbreaks of anti-Jewish violence. The author of works in all areas of rabbinic literature,[3] he was active in sponsoring the publication of kabbalistic manuscripts. He transmitted his

teachings to scores of disciples, many of whom became leading figures of the hasidic movement in Poland and Galicia throughout the
first half of the nineteenth century. Among the personalities who
were profoundly influenced at an early stage in their careers by the
Maggid was Rabbi Isaac Meir (Rothenberg) Alter, the founder of the
famed Ger dynasty. The Maggid of Kozienice thus combined in one
person all the ideals of the early hasidic master: selfless devotion in
service of God and of other human beings; mastery of traditional
rabbinic literature; cultivation of a rich inner life of ecstatic prayer
and mystical practice; a reputation for paranormal powers, especially the ability to grant efficacious blessings; the mentoring of disciples and followers; and finally, saintly prestige and influence in
the gentile as well as the Jewish world, deployed for the benefit and
protection of his community.

After the Maggid

The Maggid died in 1814; he was survived by a son and two daughters. Along with the Maggid's son Rabbi Moshe Eliakim Beriyah
Hapstein (1777–1828), the older daughter, Pereleh (known as *Pereleh
der Maggid's*; d. 1849), was a pivotal figure in the family. Stories
about Pereleh's spiritual practices and paranormal powers abound.
It is said that hasidim came to her for blessings and that she com-
municated with the spirits of departed tzaddikim.[4] Pereleh's husband, Rabbi Avi Ezra Zelig, was a scion of the prominent Shapiro
rabbinical family; her son Rabbi Hayyim Meir Yehiel Shapiro of
Mogielnica (known as "the Seraph of Mogielnica"; 1789–1849) was
a popular tzaddik known for his fiery prayer and ecstatic spirituality. The Seraph's son, Rabbi Elimelekh Shapiro (1816–1892), followed his father as a major figure in Polish Hasidism.

As one traces the succession of the Maggid's descendants
through the nineteenth century and into the twentieth, one discerns
two parallel branches of the lineage: the Hapsteins and the
Shapiros. Time and again a Hapstein and a Shapiro would be
betrothed to each other, in a match of cousins that many hasidic circles favored. In one such match, the great-grandson of the Maggid,
Yehiel Ya'akov Hapstein (1846–1866), married his second cousin

Sarah Devorah Shapiro (1844–1921), the daughter of the afore-mentioned Rabbi Elimelekh Shapiro of Grodzisk. He was about fourteen years of age; she, about sixteen. The couple had two children: a son, Yerahmiel Moshe (b. 1860), and a daughter, Leah Reizel (b. 1862).[5]

In 1874, at age fourteen, Yerahmiel Moshe married Brachah Tzipporah Gitl Twersky of Loyev,[6] from the large and influential Twersky family of hasidic Rebbes, originating with Rabbi Menahem Nahum of Chernobyl, another prominent disciple of the Maggid of Mezhierech. In the 1880s, Yerahmiel Moshe became the Rebbe of Kozienice, filling the seat of his ancestors.[7] As a direct descendant of the dynasty's founder, his incumbency in the lineage's original location carried great spiritual authority and weight.

Yerahmiel Moshe Hapstein and Brachah Twersky had seven children, four girls and three boys: Hannah Goldah (c. 1885–1939), Aharon Yehiel (1889–1942), Rahel Hayyah Miriam (c. 1890–1937), Asher Elimelekh (c. 1892–1936), Reizel Malkah (1894–1971), Havvah (1896–1977), and Yisrael Elozor (1898–1966).[8] To the best of my knowledge they were all born in Kozienice. Malkah, the author of *The Rebbe's Daughter*, was fifth of the seven children.

SACRED SPACE: THE TOWN OF KOZIENICE AND THE REBBE'S COURT

Kozienice is a provincial Polish town situated near the Vistula River, about fifty miles southeast of Warsaw, in the Radom district. In 1909, its Jewish population was 4,700, which was 55% of the total population of 8,600.[9] The otherwise undistinguished town was famous throughout Jewish Poland as the home of the Maggid of Kozienice. Christian residents of the town as well as Jews revered the saintly memory of the great Master. The street he lived on and on which his house still stood was named Magitowa in his honor.[10] That house or *shtibel*—actually just a single room and a foyer—was revered as a shrine, preserved just as it was in his lifetime. As Shapiro describes it, "The canopied bed, upon which the Maggid slept; the upholstered chair upon which he sat; the high and narrow table, upon which he wrote the amulets and Torah esoterica: these all were still in their places. Silently they absorbed the laments of people who came to pour their hearts out in this sacred place."[11]

Everyone apparently believed that the spirit of the Maggid was still present in the room. On the eve of the Sabbath, Shapiro's father, Rabbi Yerahmiel Moshe, would enter the room with reverential awe, say "*Gut Shabbos*," and leave. At the end of the Sabbath, he would bring his violin and play the special Kozienicer melody for *Eliahu Ha-Navi*. During times of illness, the room would be used for prayers and the chanting of psalms.

Other places associated with the memory of the Maggid were his *beit midrash** and his synagogue. Just outside the town was the Jewish cemetery that held the Maggid's sepulcher (the *ohel*, or "tent"). The Maggid was buried there alongside the successive generations of male inheritors of his seat; the wives and other women of the family were interred nearby. The *ohel* would be visited for petitionary prayer at any time but especially on yahrzeits of family members.

Magitowa Street was the location of the family compound, a complex of buildings that housed the Rebbe's immediate family as well as a wider circle of workers, household staff, hasidim in permanent residence, guests, and visitors. The large numbers of hasidim who visited required a permanent staff of cooks, domestic workers, and service personnel of various kinds, who in turn required overseers and managers. The ultimate responsibility for the workings of the household and the staff rested with Shapiro/Bat-Zion's grandmother Sarah Devorah and, to a lesser degree, her mother, Brachah Tzipporah Gitl.

As described by Shapiro, the family compound had two courtyards: an outer and an inner. Significantly, the outer courtyard was "open"—that is, not entirely fenced in—whereas the inner courtyard was completely closed off, accessible only by a wooden gate that was kept tightly shut. The open courtyard included the *beit midrash*,

* Uncommon words and terms such as this are defined in the glossary in the back of the book.

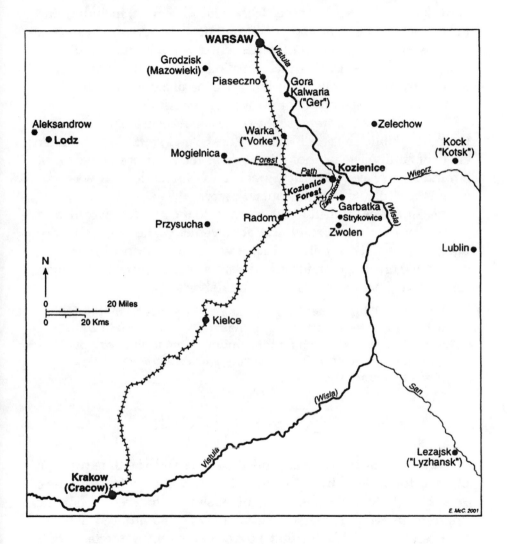

Kozienice and other hasidic centers in Poland, 1905

synagogue, and the Maggid's room. It also had two large kitchens (one meat and one dairy) and dining rooms, a wine cellar, horse stables, and a garden planted with birch trees. The inner closed courtyard held the residence of the Rebbe and Rebbetzin, including the Rebbe's study, the boys' and girls' residences, the servants' quarters, and a woodshed. In the courtyard's center was a bronze sundial on a small marble pedestal, which testified to the Rebbe's interest in astronomy as a religious discipline. (See the illustration of the family compound, based on Shapiro's written descriptions.)

The two courtyards represent two nested domains of association: the outer public circle of hasidim, guests, and staff, and the inner circle of family. The interior domain was hidden from casual view. An intimate place of delicacy, grace, and familial love, it was protected and isolated from the outside world.[12]

The court was attuned to the cosmos, to the spiritual world, and to human religious dignity and achievement. The place was not burdensome, not confining; rather it was centering, inspiring, energizing. No one there said *tzar li ha-makom*—"this place is too small for me." As Shapiro writes about the Rebbe's residence:

> Even the tall birch trees banging against the panes seem to want to break into the room; but they remain outside, covered in white, in the frozen garden behind the window. Here in this cozy pensive space, enveloped in whispering silence, here was the purpose of the universe.

TEMPORAL SETTING

The Rebbe's Daughter is set around 1904 to 1905.[13] The time was one of crisis for all Jews living in Imperial Russia, of which Kozienice was a part. In 1903, the Jews of Kishinev suffered a horrific pogrom, an event that shook Russian Jewry and aroused the conscience of the world. But that pogrom was only a foretaste of a much wider wave of anti-Jewish violence associated with the First Russian Revolution of 1905. The events of 1905, which forced Nicholas II to promise basic political rights to the Russian people,

THE FAMILY COMPOUND

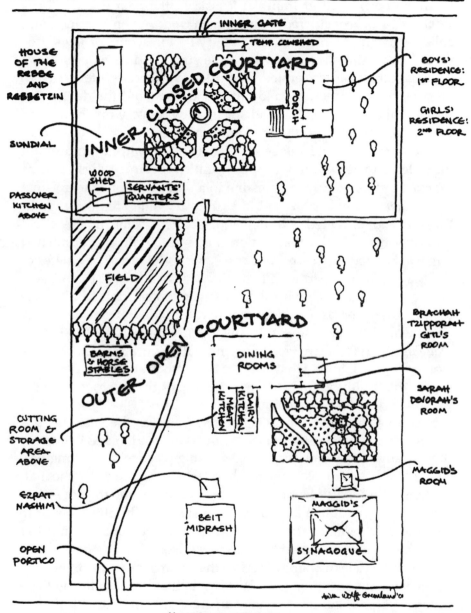

INNER GATE

TEMP. COWSHED

HOUSE OF THE REBBE AND REBBETZIN

INNER CLOSED COURTYARD

BOYS' RESIDENCE: 1ST FLOOR

GIRLS' RESIDENCE: 2ND FLOOR

PORCH

SUNDIAL

WOOD SHED

SERVANTS' QUARTERS

PASSOVER KITCHEN ABOVE

FIELD

OUTER OPEN COURTYARD

BARNS & HORSE STABLES

DINING ROOMS

BRACHAH TZIPPORAH GITL'S ROOM

DAIRY KITCHEN MEAT KITCHEN

SARAH DEVORAH'S ROOM

CUTTING ROOM & STORAGE AREA ABOVE

MAGGID'S ROOM

EZRAT NASHIM

BEIT MIDRASH

MAGGID'S SYNAGOGUE

OPEN PORTICO

MAGITOWA STREET

UNFINISHED BRICK HOUSE

adumbrated the fall of Imperial Russia in the next decade. Thus 1905 could be considered a watershed year, when the incipient collapse of the old order could already be foreseen. For Jews, this would mean the disappearance of the shtetl and its way of life, a process soon to be accelerated by World War I and its aftermath. To be sure, the new century held out much hope; but the dangers of the new age, both physical and spiritual, were very much in view. For Kozienice specifically, the modern period had brought economic stagnation and the seeds of decline, prompting more and more Jews to leave for the opportunities of large cities such as Warsaw or to emigrate to Palestine in a wave of Zionist idealism.

The memory of the Maggid of Kozienice, venerated throughout Poland, had provided a buffer against the erosion of the shtetl economy caused by urbanization and industrialization and had largely shielded the town from anti-Jewish violence. The shelter of the Maggid's aura had held firm since his death in 1814; but economic, cultural, and political forces were conspiring to alter the town's character as the new century unfolded. Eventually, the town would be swept away in sheer brutality. Setting *The Rebbe's Daughter* in 1905, then, positions the narration at a great divide, closing the curtain on what was for the author an idyllic period of serene tranquility, as ominous winds were beginning to invade the protected domain of the courtyard.

Shapiro also focuses on 1905 because that was the year she was about to turn twelve—the age of bat mitzvah. And, indeed, much of the narrative focuses on the changes taking place within young Bat-Zion herself. We are told of her embarrassment and terror at the maturation of her body.[14] Her parents urge her to assume the demeanor expected of an adult, a lady of the Hapstein family. She is about to lose the private inner space of childhood; her parents remind her that she is already betrothed and will soon marry her cousin Avraham Elimelekh Shapiro.[15] After their marriage in 1908, the couple eventually come to settle in Warsaw. In that urban milieu with its diverse religious culture, she encountered and studied with figures such as Hillel Zeitlin, a religious seeker and mystic fully acquainted with the diversity of both Western and Eastern spirituality.[16]

By 1926, she was in the Holy Land. She never returned to Poland; and during the last decades of her life, Jewish Kozienice no longer existed. So the year 1905 was the watershed year when the child Bat-Zion was about to cross the threshold into adulthood, the notion of adolescence not existing in that world. What Bat-Zion did not know, but Malkah Shapiro did, was that the act of leaving that protected courtyard on Magitowa Street was the act of entering a century unparalleled in upheaval and catastrophe. It is hardly a surprise, then, that the adult author wished to reenter in writing the child's world she once inhabited.

THE INNER SPIRIT OF HASIDISM
IN THE REBBE'S DAUGHTER

The Rebbe's Daughter must be read not only as autobiography but also as an elegy for a family and a way of life that has disappeared. Shapiro is deeply attached to her family and its values, portraying them in the most appreciative and complimentary light. This motive looms large especially in view of the general perception that Hasidism was in a state of decline at the turn of the twentieth century. Opinion was widespread that tzaddikim were interested only in enhancing the wealth and influence of their own courts and that the spiritual ideals and mystical practices of the movement's early period had been largely cast aside. It is sobering to read the strikingly bleak assessment in the *Universal Jewish Encyclopedia:*

> "The movement . . . has become weak and impotent. . . . External circumstances linked to internal corruption hastened the destruction of the movement. . . . [I]t is an empty shell the contents of which had been blown away by the wind, never to be revived again."[17]

It was not only outside observers who were pessimistic about the movement; in many cases, the sons and daughters of the leaders themselves felt that Hasidism had reached a dead end. One young Rebbe, Yitzhak Nahum Twersky, wrote a moving "confession" in 1910, bemoaning what he saw as the deterioration of Hasidism in his day.[18] This Rebbe, who was a contemporary and relative of

Malkah Shapiro, did remain within the hasidic fold, but other scions of famous dynasties simply abandoned the hasidic way of life.[19] This deterioration accelerated after World War I but was already being felt in the latter part of the nineteenth century and in the early twentieth century.

Implicitly, Shapiro writes to counter this view. In her depiction, her father's hasidic court is an oasis of true religion, a fountain of blessing to the community, indeed to all of eastern European Jewry. The spiritual practices are alive and vital; "truth" and "integrity" are the watchwords, the standards by which all actions are measured. The lives of her parents and family are characterized by self-sacrificing devotion to God and acts of loving-kindness. Widows, orphans, and unfortunates are welcomed at the courtyard and receive not only a handout but also dignity, a place to stay, and even employment. Far from amassing money, her father is utterly unconcerned with it: He gives away the donations the hasidim shower upon him, even to the extent of disregarding his own health and the legitimate needs of the household.

While others pointed to coarseness, superstition, and intolerance in the movement and its leadership,[20] Shapiro's writing portrays a very different reality. Her family life was characterized by nobility and refinement; it was steeped in wisdom and the very best of Jewish and general culture. Most of all, relationships were marked by infinite gentleness.

In *The Rebbe's Daughter*, every religious act is a work of art, to be performed not only with reverence but with delicacy and an aesthetic sensibility. Shapiro's Hasidism is a *derekh avodah*[21]—a pathway of divine service. This means that it is not enough to be punctilious in performance of the statutory commandments; every aspect of life must make a personal statement of sacredness and reverence. Everything one does must reflect one's personal religious signature and must be informed by one's own modality of honoring God and God's presence in the world. This is the fulfillment of the early hasidic teaching that one must know God in all of one's pathways.

Each hasidic dynasty had its own style. The style of Kozienice, as portrayed by Shapiro, is deliberate, reflective, contemplative, sober, dignified. Sacred times and ritual practices are not to be rushed through. Even to fulfill them joyfully, while important, is not enough. They are to be savored, entered into with all one's senses, with all the levels of one's being. For Shapiro, Hasidism means to take the time to experience deeply, to immerse oneself so fully that the waters of holiness seep through the very pores of the skin.

Here it is helpful to note that Shapiro's brother-in-law Rabbi Kalonymos Shapiro wrote a series of works on hasidic spirituality containing a graded series of exercises leading to greater levels of sensitization to holiness. The essential technique involves visualization of sacred scenes and training one's senses to become aware of the presence of the divine in the world. The system employs extended contemplative imagery.[22] Malkah Shapiro shares this same sensibility and wishes to immerse herself and her readers in the world of holiness that she knew as a child, by invoking a fullness and intensity of sensory description: the sights, the sounds, the smells of that life. Each bit of imagery is an element of an enveloping meditative structure.

Rabbi Kalonymos Shapiro was fond of quoting a hasidic epigram based on a creative reading of a fragment of Deut. 11:17, which reads in Hebrew "va-avadetem mehera." The standard translation is "[if you worship other gods] you will soon perish." But the hasidic reading parses the phrase as an imperative, a religious desideratum: "you must cause meherah (haste) to perish" or "you must banish haste." This kind of reflective Hasidism was becoming increasingly rare in the twentieth century, pushed aside by an urban Hasidism that was faster paced, more militant, and politicized. One of Shapiro's goals was the depiction of the older, rural Hasidism: more vulnerable, delicate, and contemplative.

All of this explains why in many passages "nothing happens." These passages are spiritual tone poems, meditative inductions, beckoning the reader to enter an ethereal, dreamlike world of holiness and tenderness.

The mood of The Rebbe's Daughter is lushly romantic. It should be recalled that Hasidism, at least in its early period, was a romantic movement, tending to an intensity, sometimes excessive, of

religious emotion and feeling. That was one reason why its oppo-
nents criticized it. In Shapiro's portrayal of Kozienice in 1905, this
early romanticism is very much alive.[23]

A key teaching of Kabbalah and Hasidism is "as above, so
below." In *The Rebbe's Daughter,* there is a profound correspondence
between the inner human world, the world of nature, and the cos-
mic/heavenly/sefirotic world. The natural world is personified
and celebrates the sacred times in harmony with the faithful in the
Rebbe's courtyard. There is a harmonious balance between action
and contemplation. People are seamlessly in touch with their
environment.

Shapiro emphasizes auditory experience as well as visual. The
sound of music is ever present, powerful, and redemptive; it
blends with the song of the birds. Melodies are punctuated by
thoughtful silences, providing opportunities for reflection and inte-
gration. The task of the hasidic master, the Rebbe, is to convey this
derekh avodah to the community, to form sacred space out of collective energies, as the entire congregation conspires—breathes
together—in holy rhythm.

In sum, *The Rebbe's Daughter* captures Hasidism as sensuous
experience.

CENTRAL FAMILY MEMBERS: FATHER, MOTHER, GRANDMOTHER

It will be helpful to say a few more words about the central members of the family. Bat-Zion's father, Rabbi Yerahmiel Moshe
Hapstein, is a saintly figure, far removed from the affairs of the
material world. His time is spent in prayer, study, and ministering
to the needs of the community, especially the poor. A deeply
learned and pious man, he has an unusual breadth of knowledge.
In addition to mastery of talmudic literature, he reads Rabbi
Saadiah Gaon's Bible commentary in the original Arabic, has an
active interest in mathematics and astronomy, and corresponds
with the *maskil* Hayyim Selig Slonimski on the subject of calendri-

cal calculations. A visible indication of his interest in matters astronomical is the sundial that he erected in the courtyard outside the family house. Shapiro makes a point of portraying her father's breadth of knowledge to suggest that, contrary to the stereotype, piety and wide-ranging scholarly interests need not be in opposition to each other.

In his daughter's loving portrait, Rabbi Yerahmiel Moshe does not engage in extended conversation; his words are brief and pregnant with meaning. His sayings and epigrams dot the pages of *The Rebbe's Daughter*. Although he is totally immersed in the world of study, he has a warm appreciation for the folk customs of Judaism. He is intolerant only of untruthfulness; any hint of deception elicits a quick response. In Malkah Shapiro's depiction, her father is characterized by inner dignity, radiant intelligence, and profound spirituality. Significantly, he encourages and fosters the religious and intellectual growth of his daughters as well as his sons. Tutors come to the house to instruct the girls in TANAKH and other texts of Torah as well as in secular subjects such as Russian, German, and history.

For all his many virtues, it is clear that Bat-Zion's father is detached from the affairs of the world. The practical responsibilities of the household fall largely on Bat-Zion's mother, Rebbetzin Brachah Tzipporah Gitl. In Bat-Zion's eyes, her mother is full of grace and beauty. She is tall, towering over the other women of the family. Pious and hardworking, she is proud of the spiritual achievements of the women in her family. When others attempt to minimize the significance of women's spirituality, she asserts her views strongly, despite her modesty and shyness. Yet she subordinates her position in the family to that of another female presence who dominates every aspect of the household's functioning: Bat-Zion's grandmother Sarah Devorah Shapiro.

Rebbetzin Sarah Devorah, the Rebbe's mother, manages the affairs of the household and makes all major decisions. She is appropriately respectful toward her son, who is, after all, the Rebbe, but Rabbi Yerahmiel Moshe treats his mother with the greatest reverence. She is constantly chastising him for endangering his health with a grueling schedule of study and service as well as extreme asceticism. A major point of contention is the question of building a new mansion to replace the elegant home that was destroyed in a fire around 1900. Rebbetzin Sarah Devorah, along with a group of loyal and generous hasidim, conspires to go ahead with plans for new construction, but Rabbi Yerahmiel Moshe does his best to subvert their intentions, believing that it is improper to build elaborate edifices outside of *Eretz Yisra'el.* Even when hasidim specify that donated funds should be used for his home, he immediately distributes these funds to the poor. Eventually, the new house does begin to rise, due to Rebbetzin Sarah Devorah's indefatigable marshaling of architectural, financial, and managerial resources. Speaking Polish, she works with contractors, artisans, and suppliers of raw materials; conducts labor negotiations; and deals with work stoppages and strikes. Everyone is in awe of her; she need only give one look in the direction of a group of chatting workers, and they fall silent and return to work.

Rebbetzin Sarah Devorah is a woman of elegance, culture, and refinement who prizes education and piety. Her knowledge of German and of delicate embroidery techniques comes from a tutor whom she had engaged from Hungary. She maintains excellent relationships with members of the Polish nobility; they respect her family heritage and cultural sophistication and share her aristocratic values rooted in an era that was fast disappearing. But the ambience of majesty and nobility that Sarah Devorah cultivates is grounded in devout piety and *yirat Shamayim* (fear of Heaven). In between her managerial activities she prays and recites psalms. The Rebbetzin's blessings are sought by Polish peasants as well as by hasidim.

Rebbetzin Sarah Devorah is a dynamic, enterprising, and courageous individual who confidently travels to the crown city of St. Petersburg for an interview at the Russian imperial palace. With a memory of events going back to the first half of the nineteenth century, she is the repository and transmitter of the sacred family traditions and foundational stories. She is powerful and assertive, qualities that are essential for her effectiveness in managing the household.

FROM KOZIENICE TO THE HOLY LAND

An important theme in *The Rebbe's Daughter* is the centrality of *Eretz Yisra'el* in the consciousness of the court. Visitors from the Holy Land are honored guests of the household, and holidays such as Tu B'Shevat are opportunities to celebrate the holiness of the Land. This motif helps explain Shapiro's own move to Israel in 1926. In contrast to many hasidic dynasties, the house of Kozienice seems to have been favorably disposed to the Zionist enterprise. As already mentioned, one of Shapiro's brothers was a founder of the village near Haifa known as Kefar Hasidim.[24] Two of her sisters and a number of other family members settled in the Holy Land around the time she did.

The disagreement between Rabbi Yerahmiel Moshe and his mother, Rebbetzin Sarah Devorah, about rebuilding the family mansion reflected the differences between the ascetic and other-worldly Rebbe and his more practical and goal-directed mother. But the Rebbe's opposition to the rebuilding project may signal something more fundamental. Perhaps he sensed that the days of Kozienice, and the kind of irenic rural Hasidism it embodied, were numbered. As noted, in the following few decades most of his own descendants either would emigrate to *Eretz Yisra'el* or would die in the Holocaust. In the narrative as well as in the author's life, there is a shift away from Poland to the Holy Land. This shift expresses a hard fact: For all that the Hapstein family, beginning with the Maggid himself, had vested the town of Kozienice with sacredness, in the end it was not enough to prevent the cataclysm. By virtue of the saintly personalities who made it their home, Kozienice had indeed been endowed with the qualities of sacred place. For generations, its boundaries had created a protected domain in which a quiet and unhurried Hasidism could flourish, luxuriating in holiness far from the pace and pressures of urban life. But Shapiro herself wrote in Mandatory Palestine and in Israel, and she knew her life was saved by her decision to leave Poland in 1926. Thus the love of her birthplace, so much in evidence in her writing, must have competed with a still greater love for the Holy Land, which was not only the land of biblical Israel but also the land where she found refuge, raised her own family, lived most of her life, and was to die. The dynastic center of the house of Kozienice, with all its hallowed structures, was to become a kingdom of memory.

THE WORK'S NATURE: THE GENRE OF AUTOBIOGRAPHY

Up to this point, my exposition has assumed the autobiographical nature of *The Rebbe's Daughter*. But this genre identification evidently eluded many readers of the Hebrew original, so the time has now come to examine this literary issue, explore the nature of autobiography, and explain the lack of understanding that attended the work's initial reception.

Shapiro provided no preface or introduction to the volume as a whole or to any of its sections.[25] This means that outside the body of the text, the only information available to orient the reader is the book's title and subtitle. The title *Mi-Din le-Rahamim* (From severity to mercy) is based on a well-known rabbinic teaching about the merit of tzaddikim, "righteous or saintly individuals." In Midrash *Bere'shit Rabbah* 33:3 (commenting on Gen. 8:1) we read that tzaddikim transform *midat ha-din*, "the divine attribute of severity or judgment," into *midat ha-rahamim*, "the divine attribute of mercy." This dictum was embraced by the hasidic movement in its ardent veneration of the hasidic Rebbe, who was known a tzaddik (in a more formal, institutionalized sense than in the midrashic source). So it is not surprising that Shapiro would choose this motif as the title of a collection of hasidic tales, in which a hasidic Rebbe or Rebbes must figure prominently. Precisely for that reason, the title does little to characterize the tales with any specificity.

The subtitle, *Stories from the Courts of the Hasidic Rebbes*, is still quite vague. It prompts associations with well-known collections of hasidic tales, like the celebrated work of Martin Buber. Such an association would be quite misleading, however. Buber's *Tales of the Hasidim* is an anthology of short, gnomic wisdom tales, brief bursts of illumination with little or no narrative thread connecting one story to the next. They are organized under the rubric of master and school in a loosely chronological schema. Each master's portrait is limned by the aggregation of insights rather than by a linear unfolding of narrative. In contrast, the chapters in *The Rebbe's Daughter* are arranged in a single story line, focusing exclusively on the household of one hasidic Rebbe at a particular time in history. Furthermore, again unlike Buber, Shapiro pays great attention to describing the physical appearance of her characters, the courtyard, the buildings, and the natural setting. It is also notable that women figure as major personalities, to a far greater extent than in Buber's *Tales* or any other collection of hasidic tales I know of.[26] For all these reasons, then, the title and subtitle are less than fully informative about the work's specific character.

There is one other feature of *The Rebbe's Daughter* that beclouds its real nature. The stories are written in the form of a standard third-person narrative, in which the identity of the narrator and that of the protagonist appear to be distinct. In fact, however, as noted, the work is autobiographical. The young protagonist Bat-Zion is the author herself as a child. Not only does Shapiro not directly inform the reader of this crucial point but she actually goes to some length in the early chapters to disguise it. To fully appreciate the significance of this, it is necessary to pause and examine the genre of autobiography.

The nature of autobiography has become a contentious issue in recent years, and even the existence of the genre is a matter of discussion. The commonsense definition—the biography of a person written by that person—seems clear enough. Questions arise, however, when one begins to examine works such as autobiographical novels, which present themselves as fiction yet seem to be deeply anchored in the experiences of the author's life. Conversely, many works of fiction present themselves as autobiographies but are not. Reflection on such examples has led some writers to suggest that there is no genre of autobiography and that the very idea dissolves in incoherence.[27]

My own thinking has been informed by the writings of the French critic Philippe Lejeune, who has written extensively and with great perspicacity on these matters. Lejeune defines autobiography as "Retrospective prose narrative written by a real person concerning his own existence, where the focus is his individual life, in particular the story of his personality."[28] Most important for Lejeune is the identity of author, narrator, and protagonist. The author is the person who has produced the text and who takes responsibility for it. When the author gives his or her proper name on the title page, and that name is identical with that of the narrator and protagonist in the text, then the author has entered into an "autobiographical pact" with the reader, signaling his or her intention to "honor his/her *signature*."[29] Lejeune is careful to consider special cases, such as pseudonym[30] and autobiographies written in the third person.[31] In his view, his general approach is capable of accommodating these and other special cases without undermining the category as a whole.

Now I'll consider three fundamental questions regarding Shapiro's hasidic stories: Is *The Rebbe's Daughter* autobiographical? If yes, is there any indication in the book itself? Finally, what difference does it make for understanding the author and her work?

Let me address each question in turn.

Is The Rebbe's Daughter *autobiographical?*

The name "Malkah Shapiro" does not appear in *The Rebbe's Daughter* after the title page, and the protagonist is called "Bat-Zion," so the identity of author as protagonist is not evident. However, Shapiro's family: mother, father, grandparents, brothers, sisters, aunts, uncles, and other relatives *are* mentioned by name in the normal, expected manner, often with appended titles, honorifics, and diminutives of endearment. The biographical facts about them that one gleans from *The Rebbe's Daughter* are entirely consistent with those available in other sources, including biographical dictionaries, tables, and charts of hasidic genealogy as well as articles in standard reference works such as the *Encyclopaedia Judaica*. There is much information about Shapiro's family in the memorial book of Kozienice,[32] a work of over five hundred pages in Yiddish and Hebrew.[33] Shapiro's brother-in-law Kalonymos Kalmish Shapiro, who is mentioned in *The Rebbe's Daughter*, was the subject of a previous book of mine.[34] Most important, the position of Bat-Zion in the family constellation is precisely the one we would expect for the author Malkah Shapiro as a child. All of this serves to encase Bat-Zion in an envelope of externally verifiable reference, suggesting that the author saw her protagonist not as a fictional character but as her literary alter ego.

In extensive interviews, Shapiro's children and other relatives stated unequivocally that Bat-Zion is Malkah Shapiro, that in fact Shapiro's third name was Bat-Zion. A reproduction of Shapiro's wedding invitation in another work—a biography of her oldest brother, Rabbi Aharon Hapstein—confirms this information. The invitation gives her name as Reizel Malkah Bat-Zion.[35]

Is there any indication in The Rebbe's Daughter *itself that the work is autobiographical?*

In the first fourteen chapters of *The Rebbe's Daughter*, the narrator speaks in the third person. However, in Chapter Fifteen the narrative voice switches to the first person (see the "Translator's Note" to that chapter). This change is coupled with a change from a contemporaneous to a retrospective position. That is, in Chapter Fourteen—which deals with pre-Passover preparations—the narrator speaks of the family as if situated in 1905: the father, mother, grandmother, and others are all very much alive; Bat-Zion herself is twelve years old. But in Chapter Fifteen, which continues the story line by moving forward to the seder celebration on Passover, the author speaks of "my father, his righteous memory a blessing"; "my mother, peace be upon her"; "my grandmother, her memory a blessing"; and so on. The continuity of story, coupled with the startling change in voice and temporal orientation to first-person retrospective, collapses the initial narrative posture and catapults the reader forward into the real time of the empirical author, writing in post–World War II Israel. The voice of the narrator has fused with that of the author, the adult woman living in Jerusalem. This device is somewhat reminiscent of Gertrude Stein's *The Autobiography of Alice B. Toklas*, in which the author disguises the work's autobiographical nature by presenting it as ostensibly written by her companion, not her. In the case of *Toklas,* the disguise is removed at the very end, when Toklas acknowledges that Gertrude Stein offered to write her autobiography, "And she has and this is it."[36] Readers of *Toklas* and *The Rebbe's Daughter* are informed by the end of the respective works that the narrator, author, and protagonist are indeed one and have been so throughout the entire work. This knowledge compels thoughtful readers to reassess the nature of what they have already read and to realize that the autobiographical pact—the author's commitment to tell the story of her life in her own way—has been in place all along.

Lejeune considers very important those works "in which one part of the text refers to the principal character in the third person, while in the remainder of the text the narrator and the principal character are [conflated] in the first person."[37] They are "true Rosetta Stones of identity," confirming that there can indeed be autobiographic narration in the third person. It must have been important for Shapiro as well, since she went to some length to carry out her plan. In Chapter Three, the narrator tells the story of how the protagonist Bat-Zion received that name: It was added as a protective talisman during a serious childhood illness. The narrator notes that her protagonist already had other names, but refrains from mentioning them. Again, in Chapter Eight, a certain devotional practice involving one's proper name is described and explained, but the narrator goes into detail only in regard to the final name Bat-Zion, passing over the first names in silence.

Let us reflect for a moment on the name Bat-Zion, "daughter of Zion." The name occurs often in prophetic literature as a figure of Israel personified. Whether in announcing impending doom or in envisioning the dawning of an age of deliverance and restoration, prophets often invoked "Bat-Zion" as a way of adding tenderness and intimacy to their addresses to the people. We may safely assume that Shapiro associated her name with well-known biblical verses that appear prominently in the synagogue service as the first line of *haftarot* (prophetic lectionary readings). One example is Zech. 2:14: *"Shout for joy, daughter of Fair Zion! For lo, I come; and I will dwell in your midst—declares the Lord."* The name Bat-Zion would have held special meaning for her, because it was added during her illness and, in accord with traditional belief, it redirected her fate from death to life.

It is thus clear why the name Bat-Zion held special significance for the author. But we must still understand why she initially suppressed her other names, thereby hiding the autobiographical nature of the work, and why the camouflage was eventually removed. Among reasons mentioned by Lejeune for adopting the third-person voice in autobiography are great conceit, religious humility, or a desire to place a modest distance between the author and an unsettling or embarrassing aspect of his or her past. In the case of *The Rebbe's Daughter,* the author describes an awkward, fearful child who is relentlessly hurled into physical maturity and adult responsibility. One can imagine that the painful frankness of her self-portrait may have prompted Shapiro to place some distance between her youthful protagonist and her adult self.

The child Bat-Zion is also characterized by innocence. Deeply spiritual and curious about all matters pertaining to religion, she is shut off from the outside world, completely enveloped in a self-contained realm of holiness and purity. Only gradually do external events (such as the political upheavals of 1905), begin to make themselves felt. One could hardly imagine a greater contrast than that between the idyllic world of small-town Polish Hasidism at the start of the twentieth century and the overwhelmingly violent events that the rest of the century was to unleash. World War I was itself a trauma of unprecedented proportions for the Jews of eastern Europe. But the memories of the Great War—its dislocations, disorder, and death—were to be swept aside by the second, larger, and much more total wave of destruction of World War II and the Holocaust.

Only in the last few chapters, where Shapiro switches to first-person retrospective, does she allow knowledge of the Holocaust to intrude. When she does, her tone changes dramatically. The radiant buoyancy of youth is replaced by heavy-hearted reflections of an adult trying to come to grips with the unimaginable. Most members of Shapiro's family who stayed in Poland perished in the

Holocaust. One sister who had emigrated to Palestine with her, actually returned to Poland for a visit in the late 1930s and was killed by an aerial bomb in the first weeks of the war. Referring to herself as "Bat-Zion" underscores the gulf that separates the child from the adult and points to the fact that only by moving to Palestine and becoming—quite literally—a daughter of Zion did Shapiro survive to write what was to be an elegy for her family and her childhood world.

So the point of transition from third to first person and from contemporaneous voice to retrospective is the point at which the empirical author acknowledges the horrific truth that the child did not know and could not imagine. The move from "Bat-Zion" to "I" is the move from innocence to dreadful knowledge. The shift in narrative perspectives is a way to give each position its due, without either one overwhelming or undermining the other. Implicitly, the work as a whole poses the questions of how the two positions coexist; how they might be reconciled, if at all; and how the author grasped the whole of her life and made sense of it. But these questions, while they hover just below the surface, are never asked directly.

Having established that The Rebbe's Daughter *is autobiography, how does it affect the understanding of the work?*

When one realizes that a body of writing that at first glance appears to be fiction is actually autobiographical memoir, one's evaluative criteria must change dramatically. It is not a question of truth versus fiction—both genres aim to reach a kind of truth in their own way—but of granting the author permission to envision and present her life in her own voice. Shapiro's evaluations and assessments are not more accurate or historically truer for being autobiographical. They are simply hers.[38]

Roy Pascal pointed out that every autobiography is a combination of "design" and "truth"—that is, conscious artistic molding coupled with fidelity to the stubborn circumstances of one's own past. The best autobiography "holds the balance between the self and the world, the subjective and the objective."[39] It is not a photographic reproduction of some alleged historical truth but an effort at self-understanding, an attempt to reach a comprehension of how one has arrived at one's place in the world. It contains elements of wonder and puzzlement, and it is always incomplete, because life itself is incomplete.[40] It never quite comes to closure, and what is most important is often left unsaid or is told—as Emily Dickinson would say—"slant," that is, by indirection.

Because the development of her own young self is everywhere a central concern, what Shapiro wrote is autobiography, not mere reminiscence or even memoir. As Pascal put it, autobiography gives "that unique truth of life as seen from the inside," which "can be written only by men and women pledged to their innermost selves."[41] One major preoccupation of *The Rebbe's Daughter* is to show that the family cultivated the innermost self of its members and that the parents fostered the development of that innermost self in their children, including Bat-Zion. Shapiro's principal concern in *The Rebbe's Daughter* is to explore how her upbringing predisposed her to become precisely the kind of person for whom nothing is more important than inner truth.

In every respect, then, *The Rebbe's Daughter* satisfies the generic criteria for autobiography. To go further and be more specific, this is a work of spiritual autobiography, essentially concerned with matters pertaining to the spiritual life. It is helpful to think here of concentric circles. In the innermost circle is the protagonist Bat-Zion and her challenges at the onset of adolescence. But Shapiro/Bat-Zion was a part of a loving family of venerable lineage that treasured every aspect of Judaism. Their actions are imbued with a pervasive sense of delicacy and reverence. Her family members, women as well as men, shower meticulous care upon matters of the spirit. They cultivate the interior life and seek higher states of awareness. Even the debates in the family revolve around spiritual issues. The anxieties and worries are spiritual, and the discussions are informed by categories of Torah and ethics.

Each expanding circle—the extensive staff of the hasidic court, the townspeople, the peasants of the surrounding countryside—is influenced in an attenuated but still significant way by the powerful religious personalities at the center. Even the world of nature is attuned to the rhythms of the courtyard. The environment is alive with metaphysical and kabbalistic forces. Humans and nature resonate in unison to celebrate the sacred days.

The Rebbe's Daughter is not a work characterized by dramatic plot turns and crises. Whatever tensions emerge are depicted in muted tones and are resolved, if at all, without a moment of tumultuous climax. Instead, the author presents a landscape of serene domesticity and reflective spirituality. Many extended passages are actually literary meditations, which aim to call forth a sacred moment from the past, convey it, and prevent the dispersal and evaporation of the holiness in the face of the corrosive effects of forgetting and the pressures of profane existence. The author imparts multisensory texture to her depiction of sacred moments. Both the visual and the auditory senses are invoked to conjure up the palpable feel of sacred time.[42] In her portrayal of the ambience of everyday life, Shapiro draws us into the serene power and delicate beauty of the vanished world of her youth.

Finally, *The Rebbe's Daughter* is an exemplar of women's spiritual autobiography. It focuses largely on the lives of women: Shapiro herself (as Bat-Zion), her sisters, mother, grandmother, several aunts, and her great-great-great grandmother Pereleh, daughter of the Maggid of Kozienice, a powerful, charismatic religious leader in her own right. Shapiro depicts the women of her family as excelling not only in acts of service, kindness, and charity but also as scholars of Torah, transmitters of sacred traditions, and as holy individuals who strive for elevated states of inner piety.

Most discussions of Jewish autobiography have focused on works by men.[43] A study by Alan Mintz examines the autobiographical writings of Mordechai Ze'ev Feierberg (1874–1899), Mica Yosef Berdichevsky (1865–1921), and Yosef Hayyim Brenner (1881–1921). All these works share a common pattern established by the first modern Jewish autobiography, that of Solomon Maimon: a childhood confined by the heavy constraints of piety, then a religious crisis and a break with family and tradition, followed by an attempt to live in a world void of religious faith. This attempt is usually painful and often ends in frustration and failure.

The life dilemma of these individuals is captured by the title of Mintz's work: *"Banished from Their Father's Table": Loss of Faith and Hebrew Autobiography.*[44] The father of the title refers to God as well as to the biological father.[45]

By contrast to the autobiographies of these Jewish men from the Hebrew Enlightenment (*Haskalah*), however, Shapiro projects an overwhelmingly positive attitude to her childhood, her family members, and her community. She stresses continuity with her origins rather than discontinuity; and she tries to show that, despite the geographical and existential distance she has traveled from Kozienice, she was not "banished from her father's table."[46]

Caroline Walker Bynam noted that "when women recount their own lives, the themes are less climax, conversion, reintegration and triumph . . . than continuity."[47] Rather than crisis and conversion, there is a deepening and intensifying of what one always was. What Bynam says of the life of Beatrice of Ornacieux might have been written of Shapiro's portrayal of Bat-Zion: "To an astonishing extent, hers is a life in which 'nothing happens,' at least if we expect to find a social drama."[48] Of course, in Shapiro's later life much does happen in terms of disruption and dislocation: the move to Warsaw and big-city life, World War I, a wrenching departure from Poland to Mandatory Palestine, a slow and difficult acclimation to *Eretz Yisra'el,* the death of siblings and other family members in the Holocaust. These events undoubtedly had a profound effect on her inner life. But if they ever precipitated a religious crisis, Shapiro does not tell us about it. She portrays her inner soul as continuous with that of the eleven-year-old girl we meet in these pages.

Perhaps one reason why Shapiro chooses to depict herself as not banished from her father's table is that she never quite sat there in the first place. For there is another side to Shapiro's portrayal of the role of women in her family. Despite her emphasis on their achievements, she also discloses an element of struggle regarding women's place and religious aspirations. Without ever being overtly critical, she does point to tension surrounding women's access to the sacred domains of hasidic experience.[49]

In one revealing incident, Bat-Zion's mother mentions the name of a woman ancestor who was celebrated as a scholar of Torah. A certain hasid parries her point by bringing up another woman who excelled in acts of charity. In that instance, Bat-Zion's father intervenes, underscoring and affirming his wife's original point: "It is true that there is no greater character trait than kindness to others, but there is also virtue when a woman studies Torah for its own sake." Throughout the work we are introduced to family matriarchs who were true spiritual leaders and Torah scholars, but the author finds ways to indicate that such leadership met with overt or subtle resistance.

As she moves from childhood to young adulthood, Bat-Zion herself begins to experience the limitations of a young woman in the world of Hasidism. The book's very first scene sets a consistent pattern: "Young Bat-Zion . . . ran from the dining rooms to the outer door of her brothers' residence." That is, she moves from the women's space in the family compound toward the men's—where her brothers were studying Talmud with their father. She catches tantalizing snatches of talmudic passages, but she is quickly whisked off to bed. In this scene, as in others throughout the work, she is at the threshold looking in, yearning to gain admittance. In another scene, she stumbles across a kabbalistic diagram of the spiritual worlds that arouses her curiosity and interest. Her father expresses approval of her efforts to understand the chart; but one of her brothers tells her, "In those gardens and in those rivers, a young woman has no right of entry."[50]

And then there is the disclosure in the last chapter that Shapiro/Bat-Zion's birth in 1894 was not met with unalloyed joy: Her grandmother Sarah Devorah was hoping for a boy, in order to name the new baby after her own illustrious father who had recently passed away. Once again, this troubling knowledge is counterbalanced by the assurance that Shapiro's father accepted his new daughter with warmth and love, but the matter obviously continued to weigh on Shapiro throughout her life. She writes that she always lived with anxiety about whether she was fulfilling the expectations her family had for her.

Estelle C. Jelinek observed that while male autobiographies tend to project a self-image of confidence and orderly progress toward a goal, women's autobiographies tend to display self-doubt and a search for understanding.[51] They are often irregular, disconnected, and fragmentary.[52] Jelinek's observations are remarkably consistent with what we find in *The Rebbe's Daughter*. In addition to the manifest self-doubt just mentioned, there is indeed a fragmentary quality to the narrative. Some important events—such as the fire that engulfed the old family mansion in 1900—are never introduced to the reader in a coherent fashion but appear in snatches throughout the book.[53] The pattern that Jelinek points out in Stein's *Toklas:* "incremental repetition"—in which facts are presented in "bits and pieces at different points in the narrative"[54]—describes Shapiro's style precisely.

In sum, the awareness of *The Rebbe's Daughter* as women's spiritual autobiography is indispensable for hearing Shapiro's voice and allowing her work to speak to us.[55]

CONCLUSION

In the last chapter, the author provides a window into her state of mind as she called forth her memories and, perhaps, as she wrote. We read there:

> At times the sights and sounds come back to me of that sublime atmosphere in the Maggid's synagogue, filled with its holy congregation all wrapped in their prayer shawls; women in the women's gallery weeping; and both men and women together, focusing their hearts upon our Father in Heaven and proclaiming His sovereignty over the world. At those moments, the image of the prayer leader appears before my eyes, wrapped in his tallit, dancing before the Holy Ark as he sang the sacred march. I imagine even the birds flying from the tinted glass windows in a blaze of colors to the double vault at the top of the building, adding their voices to the singing holy congregation. . . .
>
> Sometimes on a Sabbath eve as we sing the prayer melodies, I feel myself back in the room of the Maggid's wife the tzaddeket,

which in my day served as the women's prayer room. . . . I imagine myself between my sisters. . . . I'm standing next to grandmother, the Rebbetzin Sarah Devorahleh of blessed memory, . . . and next to my mother, the tzaddeket Brachaleh, her righteous memory a blessing. . . . Sometimes I am taken by the feeling of being caught in that unbroken chain. Whether it exists in reality or just in my imagination, it nevertheless gives me both pain and occasional comfort.

Shapiro's writing is an act of conjuration, an attempt to revive the vanished world into which she was born.

Most essential, *The Rebbe's Daughter* is the spiritual autobiography of a woman of faith who as a young girl awakened to religious consciousness at a time of crisis. It offers a fascinating glimpse of the frustration and exhilaration that attended her struggle to discover herself in the world of Hasidism. There are few voices comparable to Shapiro's in the literature of Hasidism or in Jewish literature as a whole.[56] For decades, many Hebrew-readers did not understand this work as her own story. It is a privilege to bring *The Rebbe's Daughter,* in its proper literary context, to the attention of the English-reading public.

Nehemia Polen

Some Words about the Translation

This book was originally written in Hebrew, but my translation succeeds only insofar as it enables the reader to forget that fact. As stated in the introduction, Malkah Shapiro constantly draws on biblical, rabbinic, and kabbalistic materials. Her language is reminiscent of poetry in the density of its images and the complexity of its literary allusions. Sentences are long and intricate; descriptive passages are lushly romantic. Nearly every noun is nestled in a cluster of adjectives or a concatenation of subordinate clauses. The tone is tender and reverent, the pace slow and measured, the register elevated and dignified, all of which mirrors the aristocratic hasidic life Shapiro intends to limn.

My aim is to allow Shapiro to speak in her own voice, giving the reader a sense of the original, yet in a text that breathes naturally in English. The translator must on the one hand strain to hear the author's voice, putting his ear to the page, feeling the author's breath. On the other hand he must put the book aside and exhale the words anew, in English.

Now to a few specific translation issues.

Much of Shapiro's Hebrew narration is written in the present tense. This no doubt reflects Shapiro's entry into a reverie of remembrance, the enchanted time of childhood that remained eternally present in her heart. The present tense was intended to conjure moments of ethereal grace, signaling Shapiro's immersion in a dreamlike state where temporality is subjectively transcended.

That having been acknowledged, it remains true that the continual use of present tense does not work well for narration in English. While my initial translation followed Shapiro's tenses faithfully, each subsequent draft moved incrementally to a more natural voice for an English-language memoir. The final version retains very little of the Hebrew's present tense; most of the narration has been transferred to the past or past imperfect. In the end, considerations of readability and narrative clarity were determinative, but I hope that Shapiro's style still beckons the reader to enter her contemplative reverie.[1]

In referring to her parents and other family members, Shapiro repeatedly employs honorific terms, titles, and other flourishes—"her father the Rebbe," "her mother the Rebbetzin," "his righteous memory a blessing," "his soul in Eden." Furthermore, the Rebbe and Rebbetzin are always addressed in the third person, rather than the second person. I have decided to track this aspect of her style faithfully (with very few exceptions) in order to convey a sense of this world's ambience, so concerned as it was with honor, rank, propriety, and familial devotion.[2]

Finally, no Yiddish words appear in Shapiro's Hebrew text. Yet Yiddish often hovers in the background, determining speech rhythms and special terms. One example is *"yehudim yafim,"* which is a direct translation into Hebrew of the Yiddish expression *"sheine yidden,"* referring to Jews of impeccable piety and religious devotion who serve as inspiring exemplars for the community. In such cases, it seemed best to translate back to the Yiddish rather than present a calque, which would be a source of puzzlement and confusion.[3]

Nehemia Polen

Whispers of a Kislev Evening[1]

A cold wind blew and penetrated the courtyard, making the lantern's flame on top of the pole flicker up and down. Young Bat-Zion wrapped her head with a small woolen scarf and ran from the dining rooms to the outer door of her brothers' residence.

She entered the foyer, which was bathed in the dim light of a kerosene lamp hanging on the wall. There she came upon a small group of hasidim who were conversing in hushed tones. Suddenly the outer door at the other end of the foyer opened and a man wearing a fur hat, his neck wrapped in a wide woolen scarf, entered jubilantly.

"The lighting in the streets of Kozienice could certainly be better. Unless I've gotten lost, it seems I've finally stumbled upon the court of the Rebbe,[2] Rabbi Yerahmiel Moshele,"[3] he called out, apparently having just gotten off the wagon from the railway station.

Bat-Zion quietly opened the door to the inner room where her father the Rebbe was studying Talmud and Codes with her brothers by candlelight. As she entered, she felt a slight shiver go through her body. The cold was leaving her and a sweet warmth was settling in. A select group of devoted hasidim stood pressed together around the table, blocking the light of the candles sitting in silver candlesticks. She could not see the faces of those seated at the table. Only the melammed* Reb Elazar Berish, a thin short man, came into view at the end of the bench, swaying broadly while listening to the class.

Bat-Zion tiptoed through the shadows and came to the back room where the old servant was putting logs into the stove. She sat down facing the stove and gazed at the thick logs that had caught fire and were turning into flaming chunks. The captivating voice of her father the Rebbe broke the cozy silence, instilling in her such a feeling of awe that she was afraid to move a limb, even though the only one in the room was the servant. The tall oak clock, painted red, sounded its *tick-tock* incessantly, as if striking against the holy serenity. Her ears picked up the veiled, hushed tones of her father the Rebbe's sweet voice:

> "The Hanukkah lamp may be kindled until the Tarmodians can no longer be found walking on the street."[4] "[The eyes of the Tarmodians are bleared] because they live in sandy places."[5] Our ancestor the holy Maggid of blessed memory explained that "their eyes are bleared, closed, unable to see the radiance of the lights which come down from heaven."[6]

She did not quite grasp the meaning of the words, but she sensed a whiff of the spirit of Hanukkah in them.

The logs blazing in the stove threw off sparks and crackled loudly. Suddenly, she saw small, strange creatures with bleary, bloodshot eyes jumping together with the sparks from the stove's open door and spraying her with their flaming breath. Bat-Zion dozed off.

"What are you doing drowsing here?" called Yashkar-Ber, the Rebbe's personal attendant,[7] who happened to come into the room. "Roll up those curls from your glowing face, Bat-Zion, say good night, and go to sleep."

Yashkar-Ber grasped her arm and turned toward the door, pulling her in tow. Bat-Zion woke up as she was tugged along. The fire in the stove burned low and the few embers whispering amid heaps of ash darkened her mood a bit.

Passing through the inner room, she didn't dare to approach her father to say good night as she usually did. She would have to tunnel through the group of intimates who were standing huddled around the table, listening to the exposition on Talmud and Codes. Her father chanted the words in rapturous tones, pausing occasionally to interject ethical teachings. Accompanied by the attendant, Bat-Zion left the foyer and came to the small closed courtyard surrounded by ancient buildings, now immersed in cold darkness.

The tall birch trees[8] shook their white, snow-drenched limbs, frightening her. The lantern hanging on a building wall had been blown out by the wind and the entire courtyard was bathed in darkness. The only light penetrating the courtyard came from the lit entryway to her parents' residence. She heard the sound of heavy coughing accompanied by hurried steps coming from the pathway. She recognized the footsteps of the Litvak aide, who often brought the concerns of the household members to her father the Rebbe.

Bat-Zion climbed the snow-heaped wooden stairs to the girls' residence. Her older sisters were out at that moment. Just her younger sister, Havaleh, was there, lying on the sofa in the middle room, fast asleep. At her side was old Nanny Sarah, also overtaken by slumber, her right hand clutching the young girl's closely cut hair.

For a while Bat-Zion stood gazing at Sarah, the nanny she had loved from early childhood, and smiled to herself. A few short years ago she had also enjoyed lying down like that, just like her little sister, falling asleep listening to the stories and lullabies of the nanny, who would rock her head to help her drift into slumber. She had been a child full of fears, and sometimes she would cling to those hands, just skin and bones, grabbing on to her skirt to prevent the nanny from leaving. She just loved everything having to do with Nanny Sarah, especially her birthplace, Zwolen, since it was near the family's estate, Strykowice.[9]

3

Without waking Nanny Sarah, Bat-Zion passed to the adjacent bedroom. She dozed off and then woke up thinking of the estate's ponds, which supplied fish for the holidays, and the manicured gardens, where teas would be held on summer evenings.

The full moon rose from the frozen rooftops of the courtyard, and the sapphire light filtering through the frost-covered windowpanes imparted a dreamy appearance to her sisters' tall beds and headboards and to the mirror table in the corner of the room. A jumble of images now floated through her half-asleep mind. It seemed as if the apples produced by the trees brought as saplings from Italy to the estate had grown as big as the rubber ball that she once had as a child in the house that had gone up in flames. That house made of fine finished wood had abounded with light and joy, but now. . . . The building's frame stood there across Magitowa Street.[10] She wondered how it would ever be finished, since finishing it would just make father upset. The Jewish people had many troubles, and everything pertaining to the house was trivial, trivial. . . .

The wall clock struck midnight. After having fallen asleep, she was awakened again by the weeping of distressed women behind the windows of their house, their voices mingling with the wind howling and blowing wildly outside. She knew what the weeping was all about. It came from women who cried in anguish near her father the Rebbe's windows, so that the tzaddik might arouse God's mercy for a sick child.

When the voices outside were finally still, her ears caught the breathing of her sisters, asleep in their beds. She remembered that the days of Hanukkah were approaching, days of joy and redemption, with their Hanukkah lights. A sense of contentment came over Bat-Zion, and she slipped into sleep.

The morning light of the day before Hanukkah shone through the double windows of the girls' residence. Flowers were etched in frost on the panes, and the red wildflowers scattered on artificial moss on the windowsills appeared to be bathed in dew. The small bedroom, whose walls were decorated with embroidery hand-made by the girls, seemed to be all aglow in the sunlight filtering through the ornate windows. Even the potted lemon and fig trees in the guest room peered contentedly from their tall, narrow three-legged stands. Bat-Zion was in a happy mood and didn't even notice the woman from *Eretz Yisra'el* reciting psalms and weeping profusely, a sight that would normally arouse a feeling of tightness in her heart.

Bat-Zion began picking up the linen clothes spread over the carpet. Finished just the night before, they were intended for the daughter of the woman from *Eretz Yisra'el*, who was soon to be married. As she wiped the tears from her eyes and put away her prayer book, the woman called out, "Isn't it time for you to say good morning to your parents? You haven't braided your hair and you haven't put on your white pinafore. Have you already said your Benedictions for Torah Study?[11] Don't bother with this now."

"You're right," said Bat-Zion respectfully, even though she was hurt by the reprimand. Her full face reddened a bit, like a child who had misbehaved and received a punishment.

Bat-Zion began hurrying to prepare to greet her parents. She looked around the room to find something upon which to focus and concentrate. She always tried hard to remove all distracting thoughts from her pounding heart whenever she went to salute her father the Rebbe. Her sisters had preceded her a short while ago, so she went down by herself from their residence. She descended the wooden stairs with great care, quite unlike her usual manner of jumping down and skipping steps.

The frozen air of the closed courtyard, which seemed as if seized in deep thought, was crowned in serenity by the snow-covered rooftops of the old buildings glistening in the sunlight. The tall white birch trees hid the two-story structure housing the boys' and the girls' residence, as well as the bronze sundial that shone on its marble pedestal in the center of the courtyard.

"How different this morning is," Bat-Zion noted with wonder. "It seems a day like every other, yet it has a Hanukkah hue."

"Make way for the young lady," Yashkar-Ber the Rebbe's personal attendant called as he passed quickly between the hasidim standing in the hallway in front of the Rebbe's door.

Bat-Zion entered the room of her father the Rebbe. She stood by the door adjoining the room of her mother the Rebbetzin and waited until her father paused from his studying. She appreciated the opportunity to wait and hoped it would last a long time. Her father studied standing, his pale face sunk in the book he was leaning over. From time to time an "Oy, Oy" would burst out from his lips as if coming right from his heart, in pain. Cotton wicks from the Holy Land sat on the table, and the white cotton peeped out of its coils like an infant in diapers. The old silver lamp in the shape of flower stalks and palm branches, a family heirloom, sat next to the piles of coils, crowning the eloquent stillness with a royal splendor.

The door opened quietly and people from *Eretz Yisra'el* entered, together with a group of devoted hasidim, rousing the Rebbe from his text. He closed the sacred book with a kiss, placed it with the other books in the tall bookcase, and took out a large *Humash* with the commentary of Rabbi Saadiah Gaon[12] in Arabic. The Rebbe turned to Reb Naftali of Safed and to Eliezer of Tiberias and, smiling warmly, asked them "Do you have a clear grasp of Rabbi Saadiah's comments to *Parashat Va-yeḥi?*"[13]

"No, Rebbe, our knowledge of Arabic is limited to the spoken word," Reb Naftali replied, and old Eliezer added, "Our Rebbe knows written Arabic much better than we do."

After the Rebbe had pored over his *Humash* and explained the Arabic commentary, the elderly servant Pesach David entered suddenly and began complaining loudly, "Our Rebbe does not permit us to lock the woodshed door at night, and now we have no firewood—it has all been stolen."

"Don't be foolish," the Rebbe responded with a smile. "Whoever came to take the wood was no doubt cold, and he came at night because he was too embarrassed to come during the day."

At a break in the discussion Bat-Zion approached her father, seated in his armchair. She kissed his hand in good-morning salutation, and her father responded with a kiss on her forehead and asked her if she had been sleeping until now. She lowered her face with embarrassment and smiled anxiously. Her father the Rebbe turned to Reb Moshe the ben-tovim and to the others present and said, "One who rises at dawn on a weekday tastes the taste of the lower Garden of Eden;[14] one who rises at dawn on the Sabbath day tastes the taste of the supernal Garden of Eden. But this is only true for someone who engages in Torah study and good deeds and does not turn his heart to idleness."

Silence prevailed in the low-ceilinged room until the Rebbetzin Brachaleh entered. She stood at the threshold of her adjoining room and said cautiously, as if hesitating, "According to the stories we've heard, Aunt Peseleh, daughter of our grandfather Rabbi Elazar of Kozienice, would rise early to study Torah. The same is true of my aunt the tzaddeket Hannah Havvah of Chernobyl,[15] the sister of my holy grandfather Rebbe Aharon—she was a learned scholar, a *talmidah hakhamah.*"[16]

Reb Moshe the ben-tovim said, "Yes indeed, Hannah the daughter of Rebbe Moshe the holy Maggid's son, would rise after midnight in order to patch the socks of the resident[17] hasidim; when they woke up, they found their clothes mended and they had no idea who did it."

The others softly chimed in, "That is character, that is holiness."

The Rebbe turned to them and said, "It is true that there is no greater character trait than kindness to others, but there is also virtue when a woman studies Torah for its own sake."

A smile flitted over the Rebbetzin's aristocratic face, for her words had been accepted. Out of modesty, she stepped back a bit. Bat-Zion approached her mother and kissed her hand in morning salutation. When the Rebbetzin's lips touched her daughter's forehead, she said with concern, "Your forehead seems hot and your face is flushed; I think you have a fever."

Bat-Zion answered, "I have no fever, the frost made my face cold and I got red." Gazing at her mother's worried face, she thought contentedly, *It's almost as if I never noticed how attractive Mother is, especially with that lovely white silk kerchief she wears in the morning.* Bat-Zion followed her mother to the adjoining room, which was divided by a screen covered with multicolored fabric. There her mother had a hurried discussion on important plans for the day.

The sound of chopping wood echoed loudly in the courtyard as Bat-Zion left her parents' residence. Near the garden in front of the servants' room stood a wood chopper swinging an ax into the heart of the log that lay before him. The sound of his heavy breathing between each swing cracked the courtyard's frozen air. He threw the cut logs into the nearby shed, which gave off a fresh forest smell. On the other side of the small gate leading to the open courtyard stood a wagon filled with logs. The driver loosened the reins of the horses; they neighed and raised their legs—they wanted to gallop, as horses of the nobility do. These were riding horses from the estate, but they had been brought here for the winter and the wagon driver was using them as draft horses. He had harnessed them to a simple peasant wagon in order to bring firewood from the forest.

"Forgive me, ma'am. I didn't notice that a young lady was here," the wagon driver, Frank, said when he saw Bat-Zion. He removed his cap, held it against his ear, which was red from the cold, and scratched the side of his head in a shy manner.

The horses neighed again. Their voices resounded with the raucous *caw-caw* of a massive flock of ravens that were covering the frozen rooftops of the residences and service buildings. The open courtyard, almost clear of people, seemed as if it were enjoying the fresh air and the cold wind that struck the white rooftops, with the birds upon them, and the frozen branches of the trees.

Wrapped in her warm coat, Bat-Zion leaned against the wagon loaded with firewood for a few moments; she listened to the sounds floating in the clear cold air and blue sky. The sweet cadences of Torah-study chant rose from her brothers' rooms as well as from the *beit midrash* next to the sacred room of the Maggid, which had retained its holiness for over one hundred years.[18] From the kitchens adjacent to the *beit midrash*, one could hear the conversations of workers busy at their tasks.

Suddenly the air filled with the coarse voices of a group of hasidim who had come through the closed courtyard's small gate. Bat-Zion recognized the voice of the guest who had arrived the night before, when her father the Rebbe was studying Talmud with her brothers. This tall man was the hasid Moshe Hayyim, a friend of the family from the district capital Kielce. Walking with his companions, he spoke excitedly, gesticulating with his hands, until he was met by another group of hasidim who had come from the open pathway in front of the *beit midrash* at the other end of the courtyard.

"*Shalom aleikhem*, Jews from Lodz the manufacturing city, from Lublin the city of the Seer,[19] from Radom, Kielce, and other Jewish locations," Moshe Hayyim called, stretching out his hand to the approaching men. Some of the visitors were wearing fur coats; others wore plain coats with woolen scarves wrapped around their necks.

"And why didn't you mention the name of my town Zwolen," Mr. Eichenbaum interjected critically. He was a tannery owner who had arrived for Hanukkah with the good news that his young brother Samuel had been released from conscription at his draft examination.[20]

"Your business is tanning. You know what the Talmud says about going into a tannery,"[21] answered Moshe Hayyim jokingly.

"If a person's deeds are good, then a sweet fragrance can come even from a tanner," responded Samuel. The paleness of his face peering from his blond beard testified to much physical suffering. His eyes had a hard look; and even when he smiled, they appeared dim. This young man, who worked in the processing of hides and who had hopes of starting a substantial business, was known as a gentle soul. Nevertheless, the fund-raising emissary from *Eretz Yisra'el*, Velvele the short, said, "Good deeds, you say? How much have you contributed to the fund for *Eretz Yisra'el* since you were spared from the brutality of the wicked one, from the hands of Esau?"[22]

The young man responded gently, "First of all, we must go to our Rebbe's house to pay our respects, for all this good has come to us by his holy merit."

Velvele added, "Exactly as I said! Let us go into the sanctum[23] and see how things will turn out. Your first contribution will certainly be to the fund for *Eretz Yisra'el*."

"Velvele knows his business," said Reb Eliyahu Hayyim of Lublin, a beloved hasid and ben-tovim. "You know our Rebbe directs contributions to *Eretz Yisra'el* first and foremost, while the fund for this court remains empty."

"The first contribution is to *Eretz Yisra'el*, the second to the tithe and to the families of bnei-tovim and the poor in general—and then what about the needs of this very house? The daily difficulties of the household are known only to us, close friends of the family. It's good that we've all come to lodge here together for Hanukkah." Moshe Hayyim spoke these words forcefully, running his hands through his sparse beard.

"You are right, we want to obtain deliverance by means of our Rebbe's righteousness and by his prayers, but we are not concerned about the upkeep of the house," several voices broke in. Amid feelings of consternation, they moved toward the building, whose plastered roof was crumbling with age. "In the end, we will have to explain to the community of the hasidim that it is our responsibility to concern ourselves with the worldly needs of the household and not just with other-worldly matters. Perhaps we can come up with strategies to lessen the burden of worries that weigh upon the Rebbetzin, the tzaddeket Brachaleh, long may she live, in providing for the household and all the families that depend upon it."

As the group approached the wagon to continue their conversation in private, Bat-Zion slipped away to the girls' residence in the closed courtyard. It was already time for the melammed to come for a Bible lesson.

Before she had a chance to take off her coat and warm her hands by the stove, Reb Aharon the melammed entered the girls' residence. As always, his pale face had turned blue from the cold. The hairs of his beard and his little earlocks glistened with frost. He untied the heavy scarf from his neck, removed his coat, and clapped his hands together for warmth.

"Ah! Ah! It's paradise here," he said as he bent over the small bookcase between the flowerpots and took out a Book of Isaiah.

"Hoi goi hote, am keved avon" [Ah, sinful nation! people laden with iniquity!],[24] his voice chanted the Hebrew words with fervor as his pupils sat at the table, which was covered with a plush red tablecloth, and opened their books.

"You've lost your appetite for study, Bat-Zion," Reb Aharon said, stopping the lesson. He turned to Bat-Zion, who had seated herself completely in the sun peering through the window, the pane awash in melting ice. Above the window, a flock of sparrows approached a nest.

"Look, Reb Aharon," said Bat-Zion, "the sparrows are benefiting from the work of the swallows who built the nest but left it for the winter."

"After the lesson you can talk all you want about the birds," the melammed reprimanded her.

"Then let's learn another chapter," she said with a laugh as she looked upon the leaves of the lemon tree being warmed by the sun.

"That's right," said her sister Hayyah Miriam, whose head was buried in the book. "Let's learn one of the chapters of consolation;[25] today is the day before Hanukkah."

"Yes, of course," laughed Reb Aharon. "There is more value in the casual remarks of our Rebbe's daughters than in the Torah wisdom of tutors."[26]

He began leafing through the pages of the book, and Bat-Zion was delighted at the pause in the lesson, so that she could think about Hanukkah. The samovar for the melammed, put up by the old nanny in the outer room, had come to a boil, shaking the small table on which it stood.

The maid came with a message from the Rebbetzin; the girls and the woman from *Eretz Yisra'el* were to come to lunch in the dining room in the other courtyard. After lunch they would have the opportunity to assist the workers in the two adjacent kitchens with

11

their Hanukkah preparations, especially with those fragrant and delicious latkes.

The sun of the day before Hanukkah[27] was low in the west; the moment of sunset had arrived. Bloodred clouds appeared on the horizon. They gathered in formation to meet the approaching sun. They captured her, hid her, and imparted a damp redness to the overcast air. The entire town of Kozienice was wrapped in a reddish mantle spread over its old houses frozen between bare chestnut trees and its streets teeming with Jews dressed in warm clothing, hurrying to the synagogues at this time of the afternoon service.

The courtyards of the Maggid, surrounded by ancient buildings—home for his descendant and successor the tzaddik Rabbi Yerahmiel Moshe and his family—drank the flaming elixir of sunset to intoxication and were covered in the deepest secrets. The roof of the stable at the end of the open courtyard had caught on flame. The necks of the thickly entangled bare trees in the garden were bedecked with crimson too, as if they had stolen some trace of the sun's mysteries. The many hasidim scurrying through the long courtyard to the old *beit midrash* were lost in contemplation. Under their breath they sang snatches of the Hanukkah hymns. They were not permitted to profane the sacred melodies by singing them at other than the proper time, but they could not contain themselves. Some rubbed their hands together to restrain their emotions as they ran.

Bat-Zion stood deep in thought, leaning on the sundial stand at the center of the closed courtyard. It seemed as if the bronze pointer on the white marble was about to reveal secrets to her. Mysteries were hiding there in that sundial, set up by her father. It was not only the love he had for astronomy and geometry that led to his interest in sundials; nor was it mainly the reason, known to the entire community, that they assisted him in determining the times for sacred service. There were many unknown reasons, mysteries that her young mind could not grasp, concealed in the sundials.

Suddenly, she lost her train of thought and stood there in confusion. Her father the Rebbe had left his room and was walking briskly as he always did at a time of sacred service. His attendants and the visitors from *Eretz Yisra'el* hurried after him as he walked out to the *beit midrash* in the open courtyard.

Darkness overtook the day. It swallowed and lapped up the dusky red hues of the sunset, and the courtyards plunged into black.

During prayer services, the girls would usually go to the *ezrat nashim* adjacent to the *beit midrash* in order to participate in the congregational recitation of *Kedushah* and *Barekhu*, but this time Bat-Zion didn't go. It was hard for her to leave the courtyard, which, although most of its buildings were now empty of people, still murmured and whispered. She often sensed whispers such as these. At times they frightened her, especially during dark nights, but now they didn't bother her at all. The blowing wind, cold and penetrating though it was, somehow brought warmth to her body, and good tidings as well.

She went up the wooden staircase to the porch in front of the girls' residence. The rooms on the upper story were dimly lit. The old nanny was busy with bedtime chores. She lit the stove, made up the beds, and cleaned the lamp glasses. Bat-Zion did not want to startle her by entering. She peered through the frost-covered windows and saw the old woman going to and fro, doing her work.

After a while the courtyard woke up. Her father the Rebbe entered his room. In her brothers' residence the lamps were lit and the room began to stir with life. Her mother the Rebbetzin, accompanied by the old household manager, went to the servants' room where the Passover pots were stored, in order to prepare goose fat for the coming Passover.[28]

Then things quieted down, and the courtyard once again returned to silence. The only sound was the faint clanging of pots coming from the servants' room.

13

The dark blue skies that had descended upon the closed courtyard began to fill with clouds. Some of the them converged, but some broke apart to make way for the shining stars to peer through. The courtyard harbored the mighty wind seeking to shatter the partitions of corporeality, to cast them down in order to connect to the Will of the blessed Creator, so that wonders and miracles would happen as once of old.[29]

Outside the Rebbe's residence, a number of human shapes could be discerned, bent over, trying to listen in. They peered through the cracks in the door shutters of the silent house. Snatches of their whispered words reached Bat-Zion's ears. She knew that these were veteran hasidim who yearned to take part in this exalted moment, before the kindling of the Hanukkah lamps.

After the evening service the Rebbe went to his room to study and pray and to engage in sacred *yihudim*, meditations on the forms of the Divine Name. His personal attendant brought him bedclothes. He changed quickly and rested briefly in bed. Then he got up and washed his hands in the ritual manner. The attendant provided him with other clothes, which he donned very quickly. Accompanied by the attendant, he left his house wearing a fur coat lined in satin, without buttons, heading for the *mikveh*, the ritual bath of the Maggid, in the lower part of town. He hurried down the hill, which was covered with drifts of snow, wearing open slippers over his white socks. Silence pervaded the dark hillside. Hanukkah lamps, which householders had already lit, peered from the small windows of the houses on the hillside. On top of the hill were houses of finished wood belonging to gentiles, nestled in snow-covered gardens.

The Rebbe did all these preparations with exceptional vigor. When he returned, he once again washed his hands ritually and began arranging the wick and the oil. The wick came from a coil of cotton sent to him from the Holy Land. It was made expressly for Hanukkah kindling, and for it the Rebbe had paid a high price. The olive oil was also sent from the Holy Land. The average hasid was not permitted to come to the candle lighting; besides family members, only the most worthy could be present at this time.

When the Rebbe left the courtyard, Bat-Zion came down from the loft and went through the courtyard, which was steeped in the aroma of frying oil, to the servants' quarters. She stepped quietly, as if fearful of disturbing the holiness permeating the courtyard filled with holiday smells. The floor of the servants' room had been washed spotlessly clean and was covered with golden sand; polished copper pots glistened on the wide bench and the square table, both of finished wood. The household manager, the elderly and pious Malkah, dressed in a white linen smock, was taking copper pots filled with boiling oil from the stove and setting others in their place. Bat-Zion's mother the Rebbetzin divided the liquid and the congealed oil into three parts: one for Passover, one for Hanukkah, and one to be distributed to the poor. She was immersed in her work, quietly praying. "May it be Your will that we will be found worthy to partake of the sacred offerings in the Holy Temple in Jerusalem," her lips whispered with intense devotion.

"In honor of Passover; in honor of Passover," the voices of her mother the Rebbetzin and the elderly household manager gently rang out, as they worked in the middle of the room, amid the steamy, tantalizing aromas.

Pausing momentarily from her work, the Rebbetzin turned to Bat-Zion, "Why aren't you resting, my daughter? A young girl should not be up all night; your mind won't be clear during the kindling of the Hanukkah lights."

Bat-Zion did not have the boldness to say that she wished to help out with the work, but the old woman sensed this and said, "You no doubt want to help out for the holiday. If so, you may place the congealed oil in plates."

As Bat-Zion sat down on the bench and began working, the fragrant steam from the boiling pots reached her nose, leaving her pleasantly intoxicated. Her eyes were overcome by sleep.

"Hanukkah lights! Hanukkah lights!" the servant's joyous voice rang out in the rooms adjoining the *beit midrash*.

When Bat-Zion woke up, she was lying curled up on a narrow sofa in her grandmother's room, where they had brought her, half-asleep. She loved this sofa in the corner of the room under the clothes rack. She often enjoyed the pleasure of napping during long evenings while the grownups were busy with their work. As she drowsed, she would overhear tales of Jews from *Eretz Yisra'el*, tales of latter-day descendants of tzaddikim and of veteran hasidim.

In the semidarkness of the empty room, one could sense the warmth of people who had been there before. On the square table stood a nickel lamp, covered with a plush green lampshade; it gave off a dim light. The tiny flame convulsed like someone about to give up the ghost.

"What are you doing napping, Bat-Zion?" Hayyim'l's joking voice frightened her.

No stranger to suffering, Hayyim'l was nevertheless a proud individual. His ancestors were veteran hasidim, part of the inner circle of her father the Rebbe's ancestors. Everybody loved Hayyim'l, especially the members of the Rebbe's court, and most especially the children.

"You ought to be working on your bow," he said, attempting to rouse her. "Your bow is sticking up like rabbit ears!"

"Don't make fun of me, Hayyim'l! I must have missed the Hanukkah candle lighting," she said playfully, buoyed by his joking voice. She ran to the door while fixing her hair, glancing at the mirror on the wall.

She left by way of the dining room to the footpath, which was filled with the women of the household. The women were crowded near the open door of the empty dining room to make way for the hasidim running on the path from the *beit midrash* through the open courtyard on their way to the closed courtyard for the candle lighting.

"Is this how you're taking care of your children?" Bat-Zion's grandmother, the Rebbetzin Sarah Devorahleh turned to her daughter-in-law, pointing to Bat-Zion. "Look, Brachaleh, she's still half-asleep. Her velvet dress alone won't keep her from getting cold, and those white pinafore skirts won't warm her either."

A frown appeared on the younger Rebbetzin's prominent forehead, imparting an extra measure of grace to the kindly expression on her noble face. She bent over a bit so as not to accentuate her height in the presence of her mother-in-law, who was very short, and whispered to her daughter, "You're no longer a baby who needs supervision in matters such as this. If you were diligent in your studies, you would have remembered the verse, *"Cold drafts are in the way of the crooked; one that watches himself will be far from them."*[30]

"I'll get some warm clothes right away," old Nanny Sarah said, wishing to spare the younger Rebbetzin any further embarrassment. She entered the kitchen, brought out a wide woolen shawl, and placed it on Bat-Zion's shoulders. As the kitchen doors opened, clouds of steam from the boiling pots burst forth.

CHAPTER

Hidden Treasures of Hanukkah

The winds blew noisily in the courtyards, covered in darkness and wrapped in a veil of secrets, enclosing the sublime awe of hasidim hurrying to hear the blessing for Hanukkah lights from the mouth of the Rebbe, the tzaddik, Rabbi Yerahmiel Moshe.

The rooms of the open courtyard and the old *beit midrash* were now empty of people and seemed to follow along silently, illuminating the crowds of running hasidim. The air in the open courtyard swirled with white snow that heaped up in piles. The pole at the entrance to the footpath was bedecked entirely in white and the ladder leaning on it, wrapped in a white tallit, climbed up to the roof of the loft where straw awaited the horses.

The tangled branches of wood, lying in haphazard heaps in the frozen garden nearby, alternately contracted and stretched out, rolling naked in the snow, as if in penance. The lantern sat in fear and terror on top of the modest pole; taking blows from the trees, its flame flickered and flashed. Like a concealed eye it squinted and signaled from distant antiquity to the quivering air of the courtyard. It signaled to the iron door of the old cellar, which peered out from the brick building covered with moss from age.

Walking in the courtyard, Bat-Zion's grandmother the Rebbetzin Sarah Devorahleh turned to the women and said, "Master of the universe, say 'Enough!' to Israel's many troubles, in the merit of our holy ancestors." Bat-Zion's mother, the Rebbetzin Brachaleh, sighed frequently, and her face turned pale. All of this brought to Bat-Zion's mind stories she had heard from some very old hasidim:

> In this vaulted cellar the Maggid built a secret hiding place for tormented, persecuted Jews who had fled from the oppressor at the time the Polish people rebelled against the wicked Russian regime.[1] They tied Jews, young and old, to the tails of mighty horses, belonging to mad squires, and dragged them through the streets. Even Russian officers participated in horrific outrages against the Jews. The door to this cellar preserves the hidden sighs of the oppressed. The small room of the Maggid, groaning in its old age under the weight of its patched cover, snow-covered white, stands witness, raising up all the prayers that the Maggid offered in his room; it raises up the mighty cry of pain of a tormented and hounded people.

Bat-Zion was overcome with sadness as these thoughts assailed her. Then the covered sleigh on its runners by the closed stable reminded her of chaperoned trips through the snow on pathways in the pine forest. When she noticed that the snow was making her hair wet and was falling softly on her face, she felt a wave of contentment.

The closed courtyard was still, listening silently. A powerful wind brought the snowflakes from lofty, distant worlds; they had been gathering for thousands of years, frozen on a stiff template of divine judgment in skies beyond the horizon. The stars, acting as messengers of mercy, tore the clouds and gazed upon the marble sundial that gestured from the center of the closed courtyard. The clouds jostled one another in the sky; the heavy clouds pursued the light clouds, the light pursued the heavy, and the snow fell and melted.

Hasidim crowded into the Rebbe's old residence and peeked through cracks in the portico's shutters at the tzaddik standing on the threshold between the posts of the inner doorway. A sable *shtreimel* crowned his head, and his face, exuding a royal splendor, radiated the light of faith. His face turned pale from heroic efforts of his soul, almost expiring at its moment of triumph.

The Rebbe leaned over and kindled the Hanukkah light in the old silver menorah with the wax candle in his hand. The blessing sang itself on his lips: ". . . Who has performed miracles for our ancestors in those days, at this time." In that stillness, the blessing was drawn out, the notes and words held so long that his spirit almost left his body. The notes continued to travel, breaking into the closed courtyard's mysterious darkness, until the wind carried them away and they expired, disappearing into the distant heavens.

Bat-Zion, who had been silent until now, was overwhelmed by her raging emotions. She leaned over to her little brother, Yisrael Elozor'l, who stood motionless among the other family members, his blue eyes fixed on the Hanukkah lamp. She kissed his curled earlock, soft as strands of silk. Startled and flustered, he eyed her furiously. He was not able to utter a sound, lest he desecrate the holiness of the moment. But he stared at her indignantly as his hand played silently with his gold-banded hat.

Excitement hit Bat-Zion, who had come to the kitchens adjacent to the old *beit midrash* like a storm attacking stillness. There was hectic activity in the meat kitchen. Streams of sparks were flying about and fiery flames poured from the oven's open jaw, licking the damp vapors swirling from the pots on the stovetop. As the women worked they engaged in lighthearted conversation, and their ringing voices cut through the steamy air. Young girls in aprons were using feather brushes to apply beaten egg whites on cakes in molds. Elderly women in hair nets were kneading dough and frying latkes on the stove. The poor widow Hayyah-Sarah tried to lend a hand in honor of Hanukkah. Her little son Shmerele, drowsy eyes half-closed, hung onto the hem of her skirt. The Rebbetzins were fully involved, entering and leaving frequently by way of the dining-room door adjacent to the kitchen, where bnei-tovim families waited for their portions of food. While the Rebbetzins supervised the entire job, they also assisted the workers in their tasks.

The pungent smell of garlic from the dressed geese entered Bat-Zion's nose. Their skins had been removed to make fat for Passover, and the birds were arranged in copper pans, ready to be roasted in the hot oven after the loaves of challah were done. *Goose flesh is vulgar*, Bat-Zion thought to herself disdainfully in order to suppress her appetite that had been stimulated by the pungent odor. *Father never tastes goose, perhaps just a bit during the Hanukkah dinner; it seldom appears even at the women's table.*

"Come and enjoy some fresh raisin cakes," said old Nanny Sarah, carrying a mold filled with cakes just out of the oven, still soft and puffy, as she bumped into Bat-Zion. Sarah was on her way to a room where she was preparing dairy foods and boiling coffee for the members of the household and the hasidim. Bat-Zion sat down and ate some cake that the nanny had brought to the table. Her little sister, Havvaleh, sat down at her side on the wide bench of planed wood. She was really hungry and the cake tasted delicious. She pinched her sister playfully on her plump dark cheek, and she hugged the scrawny neck of the old woman. "I don't have time now to play around with you, my dear," the nanny said, breaking away.

Bat-Zion sat down, her head dizzy. A spirit of contentment passed through the quiet, cozy room filled with joy and excitement. The young servant Shlomo was going in and out of the room, dimly lit by the sleepy flame of a small kerosene lamp. He poured cups of steaming tea from the samovar in the corner of the room and coffee from the pots for the *sheine yidden*[2] who held permanent residence in the *beit midrash*. Even the horse driver happened in, wearing a high velvet hat that came down over his forehead and ears. Totally covered in snow, whip in hand, he kept banging his feet together. Bat-Zion was again reminded of those sleigh rides and left the room in a good mood.

The conversation flowed quietly in the dining room's warm air, which took on a dreamlike appearance from the light filtering through the pink-colored glass over the kerosene lamp on its china base. The old beams covered by decorative wallpaper absorbed the constant *tick-tock* of the ancient wall clock. They listened silently to the sounds and echoed them back into the room. The powerful aroma of tea steaming in the shining cups placed before the seated guests rose in a swirl of vapor above the old square table covered with a shiny oilcloth. The Rebbetzin Brachaleh rose deliberately from the divan at the head of the table and leaned over the china lamp; she adjusted the flame.

"May there be light for Israel as in the days of Mattathias ben Yohanan the Hasmonean High Priest," she said, as she stood among the inner circle of hasidim, who were drinking tea and telling stories of tzaddikim and hasidim.

"In every generation that is blessed with tzaddikim, there is indeed light," Reb Elimelekh son of Pinhas said enthusiastically as he wiped the sweat from his forehead with the sleeve of his black caftan.

"But where are the righteous women who bring redemption to Israel, as did the courageous Judith[3] in her day?" the Rebbetzin asked with concern. She turned to her daughters, who were playing dreidel at the end of the table with the apprentice girls and girls from the town's respected families: "So, girls, you be the Women of Valor, and the redemption will come through you."

"Rebbetzin, you know the talmudic saying, 'If the earlier generations are angels, we are humans,'"[4] Reb Elimelekh said, looking at the girls who, in embarrassed confusion, began laughing and whispering to each other.

Just as the oldest daughter, Hannale, got up to respond to her mother's words, her shining face red with the excitement of the festival, the Rebbetzin added, "I can't agree with the words of Reb Elimelekh. I knew women in the court of my holy grandfather from

Chernobyl who were great in wisdom and in piety. One example is my aunt Hannah-Hayyah the tzaddeket, whose accomplishments were renowned. And everybody knows about the miracle that was brought about by the merit of a righteous woman. My dear daughters, you've surely heard the story from old hasidim."

The Rebbetzin began quietly telling the story. Her black velour dress highlighted the serious expression on her face, while the black muslin kerchief covering her embroidered hairpiece imparted a gracious modesty. "Here's the story," she said:

Before the passing of the Maggid, the gentiles conspired to attack and exterminate the Jews—young and old, men and women—on the night of Yom Kippur. The sun was about to set, the night of the *Kol Nidrei* service was about to arrive, and the gentiles gathered around the town. The petrified Jews attempted to hide. Pereleh the Maggid's daughter rose and summoned all the women of Kozienice: "Let us go to the synagogues on this holy evening and pour out our hearts to Heaven; let us not annul the sanctity of this holy day." All the women of the town listened to her. They filled the *ezrat nashim* of the great synagogue where the Maggid was chanting his Heaven-shattering prayers. There was a great cry at the time of the *Kol Nidrei* prayer. Hearing the cry, the gentiles became terrified of the Jews and they fled in disarray, crying out, "Mercy! Help! The Jews are upon us!"[5]

The elderly household manager had come in with latkes fried in oil. She waited until the Rebbetzin had finished her story and then placed a tray of steaming latkes on the table, their fragrance filling the room. They caught the attention of the hasidim, who praised their appearance and taste. Reb Elimelekh also enjoyed them, his penetrating eyes smiling. As he heaped extravagant praise on the latkes, the old woman, who was leaning against a chair, quietly sighed in pious satisfaction that the hasidim were enjoying them. And even the Rebbetzin gave a subdued smile. The outer door opened and the Rebbe entered, accompanied by his attendants and the man from the Holy Land.

"So you're playing dreidel?" he asked with a loving smile. "If a person arranges his life to turn on an axis of good-hearted intentions and integrity, then this elicits a corresponding movement from the Cause of All Causes, resulting in a turn of events toward a life of compassion and contentment."[6] He concluded his brief remarks and then turned to the adjoining room, which was his mother's.

As people left in groups for the room of the older Rebbetzin, the dining room began to empty out. That dreamlike space, its old covered beams still reverberating with the conversation, hovered in contemplation. The girls from the town remained standing in their places, crowded in by the kitchen door. Bat-Zion, who had snuggled up to the lit stove in her grandmother's warm room, listened to the sounds of the conversations in the two adjoining rooms and to the whispering of the intermittent silences.

The Rebbe saluted his mother who rose to welcome him. The *sheine yidden* and the hasid Rabbi Hersheleh got up also.

"Your face is so pale, my son. You are totally disregarding your health," she reprimanded him. "You're up all night as if it were daytime.[7] Your community needs you. Where will all this lead?"

"It will lead to the end, but the end is the start of something good." He spoke with a smile, but he was suppressing anguish, and he fell silent.

His mother also stopped talking, her face clouding with worry. Her long eyelashes fell, covering her blue eyes; and the area between her thick eyebrows was creased with deep furrows. Finally she let out in a whisper, "Follow your path, my precious son. May Heaven grant you strength and endurance."

The elderly rabbi Reb Hersheleh, a veteran devoted hasid, stood mute, sighing frequently.

The light projected by the stained glass in the nickel oil lamp covered the palpable silence. Like mighty gates of a royal palace, the double windowpanes, etched with frost, blocked the tumult of the outside world. Even the tall birch trees banging against the panes seemed to want to break into the room; but they remained outside, covered in white, in the frozen garden behind the window. Here in this cozy pensive space, enveloped in whispering silence, here was the purpose of the universe.

Bat-Zion, who was standing by the hot stove, began to feel tired. The woman from the Holy Land next to her glanced at Bat-Zion severely, urging her to keep her eyes open. Her dear friend Hayyim'l happened into the room and tried to amuse her. After the Rebbe had left the room, Hayyim'l began telling a wondrous tale about what happened to him once when travel was hazardous and evil spirits wished to attack him in the gentile village nearby. Hayyim'l was accustomed to experiencing miracles as he journeyed to sell his wares in the cold days of winter and the sunny days of summer.

It was now midnight. Songs were ringing out from the old *beit midrash* of the Maggid, filled with veteran hasidim. After the Rebbe had kindled the Hanukkah menorah, adjusting the wick with the old silver tongs, he began singing psalms and songs of praise; the hasidim joined in.

The wick from the Holy Land, which had been made with holy *yihudim*, caught flame, ascending from the pure oil. The *beit midrash* was afire in songs of praise and melodies, rising with the candle flames in silver candlesticks on long tables. The notes of the Great Hallel[8] and other psalms flowed under the beams of the low ceiling. They traveled out and enveloped the courtyard and its buildings and trees, which were seized by nocturnal slumber.

"Praise the Lord; for He is good, His steadfast love is eternal."[9] *"I extol You, O Lord, for You have lifted me up, and not let my enemies rejoice over me."*[10]. The verses left the Rebbe's lips with pure soul-notes like the embroidered golden threads that precede sunrise, beaming warmth and light to the human silhouettes.

The ambience of the *beit midrash,* bathed in an ancient light and saturated with melodies drawn from the Primordial One, warmed the spirits of the hasidim. They stood jammed together, listening, spontaneously breaking out in response to the verses. The sacred service flowed on.

The Rebbe began playing a melody on the violin. The notes trembled and quivered, streaming out, overflowing and breaking barriers, enveloping the room like the current of a river, uniting in holy longing with the song that bursts out of the heart of the hasidim: "*A psalm of David, a song for the dedication of the House.*"[11] The room shook, as if the space itself was singing. The sacred service flowed on.

The notes of the melody combined with the pounding of feet as the hasidim joined hands and began to dance in unison, swept away by a storm of spirit. The dancers circled round, linked together, hand in *gartl*, hand in arm. The eyes were closed; only the heart was open.

The Rebbe stilled the wondrous violin. With the silver tongs he adjusted the Hanukkah lamp. He began dancing; he leaped with the others; his mouth uttered songs of praise incessantly. The shadows of the dancing hasidim pranced on the whitewashed walls, which, worn with age, told wondrous stories of bygone generations.

The press of emotions brought Bat-Zion to the point of collapse. Her young imagination took off like an eagle flying in the Heavens, rolling about like a fish swimming in the ocean waves. They carried her, weak and pale, to the girls' residence.

CHAPTER

Daily Life on the Verge of Redemption

The morning after the first night of Hanukkah, Bat-Zion woke at daybreak to the chirping of the birds. The sun melted the frost on the upper windowpane, and through the clear glass she could see a few birds flying from a snow-covered birch tree to the nest they had built above the window of the girls' bedroom. The faint chirping that penetrated the room was telling her something; it rang in her ear like a forgotten song. Her head was dizzy, and much as she tried to recall the events of the night before, she was not able to.

The multihued frost flowers glistened on the windowpanes like knives' edges. As she shut her eyes and buried her head in the warm pillow that caressed her with its white embroidered edging, she remembered that today was Hanukkah and that during the previous night's singing, she had been so moved that she literally fainted. Bat-Zion felt a cold sweat cover her body. Just as she began to wonder what it might mean, old Nanny Sarah entered, her frail hands carrying a pitcher of water, a basin, and towel.

"Time for *netilat yadayim*. I've already made coffee," the nanny said quietly, lest she wake up Bat-Zion's little sister, who was still sleeping in the next bed.

Bat-Zion wanted to amuse her beloved nanny with an impish smile as usual, but she wasn't able to. With a heavy heart she stretched out her hands and the old woman poured water over them. When she entered a second time with a pot of hot coffee, she said to Bat-Zion in a terrified voice, "Young lady, you have a fever; your face is on fire!"

She placed the coffee on a chair and quickly left the room. After a few moments she returned, accompanied by Rebbetzin Brachaleh. The Rebbetzin was still wearing her morning outfit—a white flannel blouse and pleated brocade skirt—and her head was covered with a white kerchief of fine silk that befitted her radiant face. The custom in the family was not to wear wool, for fear of sha'atnez.[1] After her came Yakht, the trusted friend of the family, who had a candy store on the outskirts of the town near the palace gardens of the local nobleman, the Russian general.

The Rebbetzin leaned over her daughter, touched her warm forehead with her lips and felt her pulse. "You've definitely caught a cold, you know that you refuse to dress up warmly when you go out to the courtyard," the Rebbetzin said in a tone of deep worry.

Yakht, a woman of advanced age, took off her black woolen coat and knit kerchief that covered a ribbon-decorated headdress. She said, "It's no doubt Ayin ha-Ra, the Evil Eye. People's eyes are almost always upon her."

The woman from Safed the holy city, a guest who was being put up in the girls' residence, came in carrying a prayer book. "Rebbetzin, she's stubborn. A young girl of this age does not need to be in the beit midrash while the hasidim are dancing," she said, as she raised an admonishing finger toward Bat-Zion. Without responding to this pointed remark the Rebbetzin sat down on her daughter's bed, and as she gazed at the young girl's flaming face with furrowed brow, her lips whispered the prayer "May the angel who redeemed me from all evil—bless the children."[2]

In the meantime, Yakht was preparing to fumigate[3] against the Evil Eye. She opened the stove's iron grating, raked the burning embers with a small shovel, removed a glowing coal, and placed it on the firepan. Then she tore off threads from the blouse of the woman from Safed and placed them on the coal. She also took threads from the Rebbetzin and the nanny, sheared some fringing from her kerchief, and added them all to the firepan. The two older daughters, who had come into the room, turned over the sleeves of their blouses, checked and found some loose threads between the seams, and added them to the incense offering on the firepan.

"Shall I call Doctor[4] Hayyim? He's always an angel of mercy for the children," said Nanny Sarah to the Rebbetzin, who had risen from her seat, untied a small bag that was on the bureau, and taken out several hyssop stalks.[5] Then she added them to the flame that was burning in the firepan. Yakht moved the firepan in circles around the bed. A fine smoke began to rise up, and Bat-Zion took deep satisfying breaths of the hyssop vapors rising in the smoke.

As the women were busy performing the incense rite, they heard footsteps coming up to the loft. The door to the outer room opened; it was the Rebbe, accompanied by his sons and some veteran household members, their tallit and tefillin bags under their arms.

The Rebbe approached the bedroom and stood at the inner door. The woman offering the incense stopped deferentially, shrinking back in apprehension. But the Rebbe encouraged Yakht to continue: "Go ahead, go ahead; an activity performed in true faithfulness surely finds favor in God's eyes."[6]

As the flame turned the burning materials into ashes, he approached the bed. After pausing for a few moments in deep thought, he sighed and said, "From now on it is time to be a grown-up. My dear daughter, you must examine what you do. You ought to take up skilled crafts like your sisters."

As he spoke, he pointed to china trays filled with wax fruits standing on the table covered with an embroidered tablecloth in a corner of the room. "Nevertheless," he continued, turning to his two older daughters, who were standing silently at the table, "we must mark them with a sign that distinguishes them from real fruit, so that we not be guilty of deception; someone is liable to violate the prohibition of 'YOU SHALL NOT COVET.' "

He took a small scissors from the table and made a tiny cut in a pear and an apple that appeared to be covered with dew, until the yellow wax appeared.[7] The youthful, fair face of the oldest daughter, Hannah Goldale, turned red. Hayyah Miriam'l bowed her dark-complexioned face, framed with black braids; in bewilderment, she began plaiting the braid that had fallen on her ear.

As the ice melted from the windows, the bedroom got brighter and brighter. But a certain tension was introduced with the arrival of the Litvak melammed, cane in hand. He turned to the Rebbetzin and said in a critical tone: "Isn't the girls' work with the fruits just a waste of time?" As he spoke, he coughed and choked on his words.

"That's not right at all, Elazar," the Rebbetzin, stung by the remark, responded indignantly. "It is skilled work demanding wisdom that keeps one's mind active and averts boredom."[8]

"Is there indeed wisdom in that work, dear Mother?" whispered the young Asher Elimelekh, the son with the dark eyes whose gaze bespoke intelligence.

"For you, your laboring in Torah study is your wisdom," the Rebbetzin answered with a smile of satisfaction. After a moment, a trace of worry clouded her face as she looked at her oldest son, Reb Aharon Yehiel'sh,[9] whose handsome bearded face was enveloped with a certain sadness. He blurted out, as if to himself: "We do engage in Torah study, but do we fulfill *'And thou shalt meditate therein day and night'*?"[10] A deep silence settled over the warm air of the heated room. Only the chirping of the sparrows penetrated the closed windows, sounding like the faint rustling of a silver chain.

After a few moments, the Rebbe looked up from the sacred book he was perusing, as one of his hands lovingly hugged the shoulder of his youngest child with the golden *peyos*, Yisrael Elozor'ke, whose soft blue eyes looked about pensively. The boy tried to suppress a smile as his sister looked upon him merrily, curling the locks of her chestnut hair in her typical manner.

As the Rebbe strode hastily across the doorway his voice rang out in a rapturous tone, "It is worthwhile to engage in crafts to come to the realization that there is no Craftsman like the blessed Creator, and that He bestowed of His wisdom upon us.

"And regarding your uncertainty, my son, about the value of your studies: If you focus your intentions Heavenward as you study, with the help of God you will achieve the desired end, and the Torah's light will infuse you, thus fulfilling '*And thou shalt meditate therein day and night.*'"[11]

Before leaving, the Rebbe took the cup of coffee, which was still full, and raised it to Bat-Zion's lips, adding lightheartedly, "Let's hear how you recite the blessing *shehakol*,[12] and we'll know if your head has cleared up and you're ready to receive the redemptive lights of Hanukkah that are evoked at this season, now just as long ago!"[13]

Bat-Zion drank the coffee thirstily. It seemed to her that the echoes of the beautiful Psalm verses set to music that ring out on the nights of Hanukkah—"*I will exalt you, Lord, for you have drawn me up. . . . You have preserved me from my descent to the pit*"[14]—were accompanying the voice of her father, whose face was radiant with a kind of supernal joy difficult to comprehend. It also seemed that the sun, shedding its burden of clouds from time to time, was directing its rays onto the potted lemon and citron trees with a fierce persistence.

She began to be troubled by the thought that tonight she would not be able to take part in the sacred singing, which raises one's spirit to the highest Heavens.

When her little sister Havvaleh came to kiss her father the Rebbe's hand in good-morning salutation, Nanny Sarah followed and asked again insistently: "Our holy Rebbe, shall I perhaps call Doctor Hayyim?"

Addressing his daughters, he responded firmly, "Your Nanny Sarah will no doubt do the right thing," and left hastily to the next room, where a group of devoted hasidim were waiting to accompany him to the *beit midrash* of the Maggid.

At sunset's dim light, there were only three people remaining in the girls' loft: old Nanny Sarah, Doctor Hayyim, and Elazar the assistant, the Litvak who served as melammed. Together they reminisced about wonders and miracles effected by prayers of tzaddikim in times of trouble.

The reddish light filtering through the double windowpanes mixed with the white hues of the carpeted floor and the room's warm air appeared to be completely dipped in red wine. Even the embroidered pictures with their white flowers were decked in red.

Bat-Zion, who was not yet permitted to go out in the cold of the night, paced restlessly inside the girls' rooms. She knew that the entire household was seized with the joy of anticipation for the Hanukkah lighting. Only in this room was there an atmosphere of sadness—the result of their conversation. She had no need to listen to the story they were all discussing, about the miracle of how she, Bat-Zion, had survived her childhood illness. Once again, as so many times before, they spoke of the diphtheria that had spread among the children, and that she herself had contracted. She knew the story by heart:

That night her cradle stood in the great living room of their old house, the house that was later destroyed by fire. Midnight had passed; the rooms were almost empty. Even in the great prayer hall there was barely a minyan; they had all gone with her father the Rebbe to prostrate themselves on the graves of his holy ancestors in the sepulchre of the Maggid, the holy patriarch of the Kozienice lineage. Her mother the Rebbetzin left the living room sobbing. She found Miriam, a young woman from *Eretz Yisra'el* who was staying as a guest and, taking her handkerchief that had come from the Holy Land, placed it on the sick child's crib as a talisman. Her mother the Rebbetzin, accompanied by her grandmother, her aunt, and a number of other women, spent the entire night at the cemetery prostrating themselves. The air was filled with words of supplication from the Psalms and prayers for mercy on behalf of the child. Within the sepulcher of the Maggid, illumined by many candles and oil lamps, her father the Rebbe added the name Bat-Zion to the two names she already had.[15]

"All night long I stood watch by her crib," Nanny Sarah burst out tearfully, seated next to Doctor Hayyim on the upholstered sofa, wiping away her tears with the hem of her wide apron.

"Even now we must keep it a secret that I participated," said the assistant who was standing near the door.

"All three of us took responsibility for the decision," answered the doctor quietly as he patted his bald head. "The act of putting my hand into her throat was risky. We might have lost the girl's life in an instant but for the Rebbe's supplications for mercy."

Listening intently, Bat-Zion stood by the bureau with many drawers. She gazed at the multicolored bird in the cage, which Doctor Hayyim had brought her. She noticed that tears had begun to roll down her cheeks. They were not telling the whole story now, but she knew it all anyway. Doctor Hayyim had taken action on his own initiative, without the knowledge of the old physician Zhurzhinsky, who had despaired of saving the little girl. He manipulated her throat after midnight when no one was home, using as his helpers Elazar the assistant and Nanny Sarah, swearing them to secrecy, fearing that he would not be successful. But when her father the Rebbe and the others came back from the cemetery, the child opened her eyes.

The bird in the cage began pouring out her evening's song; it appeared to Bat-Zion that in those trills she was hearing supplications from the cemetery long ago. Her melancholy deepened as the rays of setting sun intensified, as if her compassion had been aroused for that little girl and her parents' home.

And perhaps she was feeling a twinge of regret that she did not pass away while still a child, when she was pure, without sin, and she would have gone to Paradise to sit with Serah bat Asher and her melody,[16] and to be together with the Matriarchs.[17] Now she was getting more mature by the day, and her sins would certainly increase. Even now she caused the entire household to worry right in the midst of Hanukkah, just because she did not have the good sense to control her emotions. She felt a kind of terror in her heart, like the feeling she had had when, due to her maturing, the seamstress lengthened her short dresses. She remembered the words of her father the Rebbe: "From now on it is time to be a grown-up. You must consider the consequences of your actions."

She started feeling better when she heard hushed voices coming from the Inner Sanctum of the closed courtyard, where preparations for the kindling of the Hanukkah lights were being made. She recalled the words she had heard in her bedroom as she woke up that morning: "The lights of redemption shine with bountiful blessing during the days of Hanukkah in these days just as in times of old." In a short while those sparks of redemption would rise up and spread their glow from the small flames in the silver menorah, with oil from the Holy Land, along with the earth-shaking melodies accompanying the blessings and songs: "Who hast performed miracles for our ancestors in those days at this time."

In the Girls' Suite

On the second night of Hanukkah, Bat-Zion was not yet permitted to leave the girls' suite in the loft, but she did go down to her parents' residence in the inner courtyard to hear the blessing of the Hanukkah lights from her father the Rebbe. On her way back, wrapped in a heavy woolen shawl, she paused and stood alongside the loft's snow-covered banister.

She had been moved by that warm, mystery-laden ambience that suffused the ancient room when her father kindled the lights. As he stood before the menorah, the lines on his high forehead had stood out more than usual under his sable *shtreimel* and his face beamed an uncommon light.

Those present—veteran hasidim, visitors from *Eretz Yisra'el,* and members of the household (her brothers, her sisters, her grandmother the older Rebbetzin, and her mother the younger Rebbetzin)—stood in deep silence, swaying to the inner prayers of their hearts. The holy books filling the shelves of the high bookcases reaching up to the ceiling beams and piled up on the table responded mutely to the blessing uttered in holy ecstasy, intense to the point of the soul's expiration. The wicks' flames joined in also, rising up and telling about the miracles and wonders in those days, in these times. Her mother the Rebbetzin stood in her velvet coat

over her long festive dress, a lace veil covering her gold-embroidered headdress, her face expressing deep emotion. Her prominent
forehead creased in concentration, and the dimples on her cheeks
deepened.

Snowflakes began falling in abundance from the clouds. Stars
covered and uncovered themselves in patches of sky. For all that
Bat-Zion wanted to focus on worthy thoughts, petty musings kept
coming to her mind, and she was not able to push them aside.

She recalled another time when heavy reddish gray clouds had
gathered, piled up in the sky. Overcoming her fears of a flood that
would inundate the earth as in the days of Noah, she had trailed
after her Nanny Sarah when Sarah went to visit her own daughter,
who lived in a house full of children but otherwise bare. After that
they went to visit the feldsher, Doctor Hayyim, who had set himself
up in the open square market. His wife, wearing a wig arranged in
a high coiffure, stood by her husband as he shaved the beards of the
peasants who had brought produce from their villages to the market.

Bat-Zion was angry at herself for allowing her musings to profane the sacredness of this moment, especially since they distanced
her from the important goal she had been hoping to attain. "From
now on it is time to be a grown-up. You must consider the consequences of your actions," her father the Rebbe had said with a loving smile that morning when he had come to visit her in the girls'
loft. She safeguarded those words in her heart.

Her breathing stopped when she heard the hushed sound of people returning from her parents' wing of the compound. It seemed
to her as if her brothers, accompanied by the *gabbai* and the
melammed Reb Elazar Berish, were reprimanding her as they
entered the boys' residence on the first floor. She imagined all of
them admonishing her—her oldest brother, Reb Areleh, with his
gruff voice; the young Reb Asher Elimelekh'l, with his mellifluous
voice; and the youngest, little Yisrael Elozor'l, his blue eyes filled
with tears, saying, "Sister, why do you worry us so!"

She was overtaken by anguish for a number of moments, until they slipped into their rooms, hurrying to fulfill the mitzvah of Hanukkah lights, each one with his own menorah, as was the custom. She continued standing by the snow-covered banister near the pillar. Not one of the people quietly traversing the courtyard noticed the young girl all wrapped up in her large, heavy gray shawl, standing silently. Although her heart was pounding—she was once again breaking the rules, standing there unobserved at a time when she was not supposed to be outside—she did not move.

Notes of a joyous melody began to break out from the wooden structure tucked away at the end of the dark courtyard near the garden of frozen birch trees. Her father, in holy ecstasy after having kindled the Hanukkah lights, was singing Psalm 91, *"O you who dwell in the shelter of the Most High and abide in the protection of Shaddai."* It seemed to her that rays of luminescence accompanied the notes, hiding in the bluish darkness of the night air drenched in snow.

The flames that her father had kindled in the silver Hanukkah menorah, an heirloom of his holy ancestors, wandered between the frozen white gabled roofs of the old buildings, dreaming in their slumber of eternal redemption. They flashed from distant worlds through patches of sky toward the pointer of the sundial in the center of the closed courtyard. They shimmered and sang in burnished radiance and then disappeared together with shooting stars over the frozen trees.

She wondered whether the wars of the Jews were now being fought in Heaven with arrows and catapults, as in the days of the Maccabees when the mighty were delivered into the hands of the weak and the wicked into the hands of the righteous. Bat-Zion rubbed her forehead with snowflakes. Blinking her eyes, emotions of pleasure and fear coursed through her in tangled confusion.

The Hellenists who sacrificed a pig on the altar of the Holy Temple in Jerusalem were undoubtedly like those barefoot murderers who fell upon the Jews in Russian towns and killed them. At that time, her entire household had been shrouded in mourning and weeping. Even here in the town of her ancestor the holy

Maggid, it once happened that drunken hooligans came on their holy day, in wagons swelling with the sound of snorting pigs, carrying sticks to beat up Jews.

Those gloomy thoughts were swept away by the sound of singing, the melodies rising and falling in supplication, contrition, and triumph. *"You will tread on cubs and vipers; you will trample lions and asps."*[1] From early childhood, a fearfulness had lodged in her heart as a result of the many terrible events she had heard about. Whispering the psalm verses again and again, she felt the fearfulness evaporate, and self-confidence and courage gradually entered her soul.

This past week she had been studying the Book of Judges with her melammed Aharon Gutman. Like Samson from Judges, she would rip to pieces a predatory beast such as the wolf that once appeared in the forest near their estate, Strykowice. That time the gentile workers ran after it and stoned it. Once they also found a viper in a field of the estate. Then again, she didn't see it; maybe it was just a common snake? But her grandmother the Rebbetzin had indeed seen a truly dangerous viper, in the zoo in Petersburg the capital, after an audience she had been granted at the Russian royal palace.

Bat-Zion recoiled from her thoughts that were unworthy of this time, and she focused again on the psalm melody. The lion and the viper: They undoubtedly represented the Hellenistic oppressors of Israel who were vanquished by Mattathias the Hasmonean and his sons. And Judith the righteous heroine killed the serpent Holofernes, as her dear mother had read the story to them in the evenings before Hanukkah.

And now? Now heroism illumined these hasidim running, hurrying, swerving through the inner courtyard, to get close to the ecstatic devotion of their Rebbe, Rabbi Yerahmiel Moshe, an ecstasy unto death. Darting forward, using the lower porch of the boys' residence for cover, they sighed silently, straining their ears to take in a bit of those notes of confidence and courage, so that they would be able to endure the harsh decrees of the government and survive the afflictions of exile.

"Because you took the Lord—my refuge, the Most High—as your haven."[2] Her father was clinging to our Father in Heaven, entreating Him to protect our people and deliver them from all the troubles of the exile.

Surely angels of mercy were bringing that heart-song Heavenward. They were flying on the gray-black clouds and on flames, like the flaming sparklers used at wedding celebrations. Maybe the angels were carrying the Messiah on their wings, who would bring us there, to the wholly good land of our forefathers, whose oil was illuminating the Hanukkah lamps even now.

The notes of the soul-melody continued pouring out: *"For He will order His angels to guard you, wherever you go. They will carry you in their hands, lest you hurt your foot on a stone."*[3] The blue darkness, sparked with light from the rooms of the Inner Sanctum, legacy of the Maggid of Kozienice, murmured: *"I will be with him in distress; I will rescue him, and make him honored."*[4] It murmured assurance that the God of Israel would deliver His people from all obstacles, from all the troubles of exile, and would bring the redemption to Israel.

Despite the cold piercing her face, Bat-Zion stood transfixed for a long time, plunged in a sea of emotion to the point of tears by the warm flowing melodies that swept her away.

When the holy melodies were stilled, disappearing into a divinely hidden canopy, she heard another sound, the whispered conversations of a group of people approaching the stairs to the loft. She hurriedly went inside. Wrapped in her shawl, she sat on the upholstered sofa in the corner of the room. Overcome by slumber, sweet dreams came to caress her.

Half-asleep, half-awake, Bat-Zion sat in the corner of the room in the girls' loft. The room was tastefully decorated. A simple spotlessly clean colored rug covered the wooden plank floor; embroidered hangings, hand-made by the girls themselves, were on the walls. Suddenly, her sisters arrived, accompanied by a group of women guests.

Upon entering the room, her oldest sister, Hannah Goldeleh, lit a flame in the china lamp with the pink lamp glass and looked around to see if everything was in order.

The guests, still in the outer room, shook off the snow from their hats, hung their coats on wooden clothes hangers and took off their overshoes. As they entered the middle room gaily, Bat-Zion—still wearing her heavy shawl—slipped away into the outer room. She sat and listened to their loud conversation, suppressing her laughter.

The three daughters of Tuvia the tavern keeper said in unison, "We've come to you on the wings of the wind!" Tuvia was a respected householder whose residence and tavern stood by the town's municipal buildings. Taking seats around the polished brown wooden table covered with a lace tablecloth, their conversation streamed into the spacious room with its four windows framed by drapes of fine white fabric.

The oldest of the group, the Crown Rebbetzin Tovaleh,[5] adjusted the high hairdo of her curly blond wig, set her gold-rimmed glasses on her short nose, and began leafing through the Russian journal she had brought with her. "There are good descriptions of the lives and manners of the Russian nobility in this issue," she said, turning to the Rebbe's two daughters, who were busy welcoming their guests. They removed the lace tablecloth from the table, spread out an embroidered linen tablecloth handmade by the girls, and set a serving tray with cakes before the guests.

Hannah Goldeleh said, "There is much decadence in the lives of the nobility, but not in the Russian people as a whole. They have the quality of integrity; that is our family tradition going back to the days of our holy ancestors."

Old friend Yakht, who was wearing a Turkish shawl over her woolen coat, had come along with the other guests. She sighed and said, "There was once a time when it was possible to learn something from the manners of the nobility, but nowadays the plague of anti-Semitism has spread among them and drives them to acts of madness. They even evade paying their debts to Jews."

Etka, Tuvia's daughter, said: "I have some familiarity with the topic of anti-Semitism. I read the *Novoe Vremia,* the newspaper popular with the wives of officials.[6] It is filled with the poison of hatred against Jews. The paper injects that hatred into the Russian people as a whole and the Russian aristocracy in particular." A bitter smile appeared between the lines of her face that, weighed down by childlessness, always looked sad.

Devorah of Safed had just come from the Rebbetzins' rooms in the other courtyard. She said, "Isn't today Hanukkah? Why are we talking this way? The miracle of Hanukkah was brought about by women."

Old friend Yakht responded, "Yes, we need miracles now as well, and thank God we have great righteous women in the house of our Rebbe the tzaddik: the younger Rebbetzin Brachaleh and the older Rebbetzin Sarah Devorahleh. All activities in this holy house are for the sake of Heaven." She took out a small box tightly wrapped in tissue paper from her coat pocket and said, "Since it's Hanukkah today, why don't the girls play dominoes?" Removing the dominoes from the box, she spread them on the table.

"It's a pity that you're not allowed to play cards,"[7] said the tall, pretty young woman Raheleh. She went on in praise of other games, ending dismissively with an ironic smile, "Well, dominoes is also a game."

As those seated around the table began playing dominoes, Raheleh got up from her chair and went to the silver-framed mirror in the corner of the room. Straightening out the smartly pressed white collar of her silk blouse that perfectly set off her delicate features, she smiled contentedly.

All that time Bat-Zion was experiencing bewilderment. Since she had begun to mature she found herself feeling intensely bashful, so although she was attracted by the spirit of gaiety in the room with the guests, she could not bring herself to go in. She stayed in the outer room for a long time, assisting the apprentice girl in preparing the samovar for tea. Esther Reizel, the energetic apprentice, lit small twigs, placed them on coals in a flat metal plate and opened the room's outer door. A strong draft blew into the room and the coals, catching fire from the twigs, emitted sparks all around. The two of them lifted up the coals with tongs and put them inside the highly polished copper samovar.

Bat-Zion enjoyed her work. As she was taking out cups from the cupboard hanging on the wall, Nanny Sarah came in with her sweet little sister Havvaleh, wearing a cashmere coat with a brown cashmere hat on her head. Bat-Zion looked with pleasure at her young sister, this little girl whose long locks had just been shorn and whose outfit enhanced her attractiveness.

It was only a few years ago that she wore an outfit just like that one. Joy always filled her heart when she wore the cashmere coat topped with a cape decorated with a black fur stripe. One time she felt such elation that she threw herself down on the rug. Her mother the Rebbetzin and her sisters were afraid that she had fainted, but when they ran to help she jumped up and giggled until they all joined in the joke.

Polishing the cups with a dish towel, Bat-Zion felt a longing for years past. When the apprentice girl teased her for not applying herself to her work, she left the outer room and entered the room where the guests were. She was wearing a pressed white apron over her holiday dress. Those seated were so engrossed in their game of dominoes that they didn't notice her come in. Wanting to join, she stood hesitantly and wondered which person to approach. Should she approach her sister Hannah Goldale who sat opposite her wearing a wig of brown silk hair,[8] dressed in a pretty velour dress? Her bright face, so young and lovely, was overlaid by a tinge of sadness. Seeing that brought gloomy thoughts to Bat-Zion. Her oldest sister had already suffered much in her short life, and Bat-Zion was afraid of rubbing up against her wounds.

Or should she go to her sister Hayyah Miriam'l, her head graced by those black pigtails? But her attractive dark-complexioned face had taken on a serious cast ever since her betrothal to a young man of noble character, her true mate, a descendent of their great-

44

grandfather Rabbi Elimelekh Shapiro, the Rebbe of Grodzisk.[9] Bat-Zion hesitated to disturb her during the game.

She's getting more and more distant from me, we're growing farther apart, Bat-Zion thought, feeling a pang in her heart.

How much she misses having a friend to ease her torment, her piercing heartache! Now as for Rachel daughter of Tuvia, she had loved that girl so much when she was young! After she recovered from diphtheria, she would wake up at night awash in tears, calling for Rachel daughter of Tuvia. They would send someone urgently to get the girl, and when Rachel came and took her in her arms she would quiet down. To this day, she would be reminded and teased about those times.

Why then, was she so diffident toward her now? She even blushes when Rachel talks to her! She is more comfortable when she meets Rachel's sister, the Crown Rebbetzin Tovaleh, who is already forty years old. It's a puzzle. But wait—Tovaleh is looking at her through her glasses, she undoubtedly wants to say something interesting. . . . Bat-Zion tried to bring to mind her friends who were not here now, who were just thirteen, just two years older than she was, but she was distracted by a volley of hand clapping from the players: Racheleh had won the game. The excitement grew when the apprentice girl came in, gaily carrying a large tray with the cups of steaming hot tea, with its bracing fragrance and sparkling color, along with hot latkes still sizzling in oil.

Just then Doctor Hayyim arrived. He walked straight to Bat-Zion who was standing by the mirror with her head bent, smiling to herself. He asked how she was feeling and checked her pulse. None of those seated had noticed her until now, and they all turned to look at her.

"You really caused us to worry this morning, dear, and now you're still awake!" said old Yakht, a bit embarrassed at not having noticed her before.

"Bat-Zion, how did you manage to hide all this time so that we didn't notice you!" the others joined in. They went up to her and stroked her curls, smiling warmly.

"Now that you're a healthy young lady, it's your responsibility to take care of my bird," said Doctor Hayyim. Bat-Zion was astonished to realize that she had forgotten completely about the canary that she loved so much, dozing in the cage facing her.

"And you, Ladies, kindly attend to the potted plants," said the doctor to her sisters.

"Indeed you're right, we have to thank you for the cactus," Hannah Goldeleh responded, lifting up the pot whose sapling had sprouted what looked like a prickly hedgehog and showing it to the group.

"My wife is already working on a new sapling for you. You know my wife is virtuous; she even sits and reads the *Tzenah-urena*[10] all day on Sabbath," said feldsher Hayyim jokingly, to which those present nodded their heads smiling. The only exception was Nanny Sarah, who had come into the room after putting little Havvah to sleep in the adjacent bedroom and whispered with a touch of sarcasm, "Virtuous!"

The guests, who were duly impressed by the potted lemon, fig, and orange trees on tall stands and had politely expressed amazement over the cactus, now turned back to the table. Bat-Zion sat down between her sister Hayyah Miriam'l and old Yakht. She felt indebted to Yakht for her concern about her health earlier that morning as well as for performing the incantation against the Evil Eye together with Devorah of Safed, who had previously scolded her. Her sister gave her some overturned dominoes from the box and she placed her hand over them to hide them from the other players.

She got pleasure out of counting the black dots called popeyes on the yellow ivory tiles and began to join in the game. While she lost twice in the short time the game continued, she was still in a happy mood when it came time for the guests to leave. Escorted out by her sisters, they all said good-bye with the warmest of feelings.

After the room had emptied, Bat-Zion felt overcome by tiredness, but she didn't fall asleep because the air was still filled with a spirit of liveliness, the fragrance of perfume, and the aroma of fried latkes. And Nanny Sarah was still there, sitting and dozing by the lit stove; the sight of her ribboned headdress falling over her forehead imparted a humorous touch.

As she gathered the tiles scattered between the empty teacups, the individuals who had just left passed through her mind. She spoke with them, nodding to each one as if she were still there. Now she could speak with them freely and without anxiety. In fact, she had a number of questions that she wanted to address to the daughters of Tuvia.

Why, for example, did they not have a good relationship with the granddaughters of Yerahmiel the lumber merchant? Those girls were Bat-Zion's friends. Why did they speak disparagingly of their family's great wealth? Yerahmiel's granddaughters were pretty, their clothes were of the best material and well tailored. Was it that they spoke the language of the gentiles among themselves? In the past, those friends would often visit her and her sister Hayyah Miriam'l on Sabbath and festival days. Until recently, they would dance the waltz and the polka together. But recently she didn't enjoy being with them at all.

As she walked back and forth in the room, her reflection stared at her from the mirror in the silver frame, and it did not make her happy. Her wavy chestnut hair didn't seem to suit her light complexion that was now flushed. The golden blond curls of her friend Ronya, Yerahmiel's granddaughter, would have suited her better. And the velvet dress she was wearing: Right now she didn't like it one bit. But most distressing of all was that her eyes looked like they were peering out of a dream.

She stared at the mirror for a few moments and then turned toward the glass cabinet hanging on the wall, filled with decorative objects. A number of gifts were displayed that she, her sisters, and her brothers had received when they were little. There was a silver wagon that she had received from her aunt Rebbetzin Leahnu of Parczew,[11] and other small silver items from her uncle Rabbi Yisraelnu of Stolin.[12] Now here was the bee-shaped ruby brooch that she had received from a certain gentile lady they had met in the flower garden at Carlsbad by the Milbraum medicinal springs, a place where the harp, trumpet, and violin play continuously. "Permit me, Madame," the elegantly dressed lady had said to her mother the Rebbetzin, "to present this gift to your child, who resembles you in your royal features, like the matriarchs of old from the Book of Books."

And there were the ruby-inlaid earrings shining in the cabinet, a gift of the hasidic women of the Kosman family from Mishiev who had accompanied her mother the Rebbetzin to the old cemetery in Carlsbad. But the ring she received from one of her aunts, she had given as a gift to Ronya, her friend with the golden curls whom she loved so much. Perhaps her warm feelings toward Ronya were due to the fact that she was a member of the Prosk family, from whom grandmother the Rebbetzin Sarah Devorahleh had purchased the Strykowice estate.

She could hear the labored breathing of Nanny Sarah on the other side of the stove, which was filling the room with a pleasant warmth; and she remembered how her nanny took them on hikes through the fish ponds in the estate where her grandmother raised carp.

Early Friday mornings in the summer, she would accompany her sisters as they went to catch fish in honor of the Sabbath. The fish jumped about and sprayed water on the grass where they sat while they enjoyed the fresh air, laden with the sweet smells of the meadow and the orchards. Afterward, Nanny Sarah took her to the nearby town of Zwolen, her birthplace, to buy sweets for the guests who would be coming to the estate for the Sabbath. On the way, they met a group of beggars going to the estate, where they were accustomed to get dairy products and spend the night. They traveled by foot for two miles on the paved highway between the oak trees. Livery horses were grazing in the pasture nearby, their carriage empty. That Friday was a long day and the sky was all blue. It seemed that Sarah was young then, but now as she gazed at her nanny, it pained her to notice that her face had many wrinkles and signs of aging.

Bat-Zion's tiredness intensified. The potted saplings that stood motionless on their stands and on the end table, the bird drowsing in the cage, and the nanny's breathing that filled the room—all of this rolled over her like a soporific fog. Not wanting to take leave of those fields, the gardens, the animals, and the other delights of the estate, she tried to continue her imaginary excursions. But she was tired, so she let go of her thoughts with the consolation that tomorrow during the day there would definitely be discussions about Strykowice, because the tenant-farmer Shammai from the nearby village Policzna had arrived at the court today. Her grandmother the Rebbetzin had business to discuss with him about the harvest, and that would bring the spirit of their country estate into their home in town.

Musical notes began echoing out from the old *beit midrash* where her father the Rebbe had come to sing the psalms for Hanukkah evenings, and Bat-Zion was enveloped by a sublime spirit of exaltation. It seemed to her that she was flying to worlds of splendor holding wonderful fragrances, far superior to the fragrances of those fields on the estate. A thought entered her mind. Perhaps what she sensed was the fragrance of the Holy Land, in whose atmosphere her dear father lives. She took a short, drowsy breath and found her lips murmuring the psalm verses with the melody she knew by heart: *"I extol You, O Lord, for You have lifted me up. . . . I cried out to You, and You healed me."*[13]

All the world seems to be celebrating, Bat-Zion thought many times on that last day of Hanukkah called Z'ot Hanukkah.[14] As everyone was so busy with sacred tasks, she was not supervised carefully, and Bat-Zion was able to stroll about as she wished through the courtyards.

On that day, the sun came out only a few times. The sky was mostly gray, with a bit of blue and red. Snow fell on the roofs of the old houses, on the barn and stables, on the fences and the trees. It fell into piles along the ridges of the flowerbeds. The hasidim, wrapped in warm scarves around their necks, had been walking busily through the courtyards from early morning. They came from the synagogue to the open courtyard, from there to the closed courtyard and back again. Some of them were coming from the bathhouse in the lower part of town, ice droplets glistening from their earlocks and beards. Some of them had tallit and tefillin bags under their arms; others were carrying their copy of a talmudic tractate. Once the service began in the old synagogue and the words of prayer began to ring out, the courtyards started to empty, left alone to bathe in the white snow. Bat-Zion had the sensation that she was swimming in a sea of snow with no need for the sleigh that stood and listened to the horses' neighing from the stable. The notes of the melody sounded diffuse, as if they came to her from the other end of the world, from the sun sawing its way through the sky,[15] tearing the clouds and revealing its shining face, making the snow sparkle like millions of diamonds. When the sun wrapped itself in purple, Bat-Zion went inside to the women's rooms, where intense preparations were under way for the festival meal that was about to begin. Servants were going back and forth to the synagogue, which was swept up in sublime yearning, in song and words of Torah.

The dark air of the women's rooms and the adjoining kitchens was awash in vapors of roasted meat and foods baking in the oven, melting the frost on the windows. The Rebbetzins assisted by a number of women were supervising the distribution of foods from the caldrons and preparing the fried dishes, the vegetables, and the thirteen roast geese served at the Z'ot Hanukkah festive meal. The geese were carefully set aside in a separate area of the table so that they would not be mixed with other food, nor would their number be augmented or diminished until their time came to be served. (There are thirteen divine attributes of mercy.)[16]

Their work not quite completed, the Rebbetzins went to the *ezrat nashim* of the synagogue, followed by the old kitchen supervisor. Her face streaming with sweat, her flower-and-ribbon-decorated black headdress dripping black drops on her forehead, she left the pans of roasted geese on a wide bench and accompanied the Rebbetzins and their entourage.

The daylight of Z'ot Hanukkah was slipping away. The small *ezrat nashim,* once the bedroom for the Maggid's wife, was filled with the women's sighs, which vanished along with the dim light filtering through the frosted windowpanes. The psalms and chants poured forth as the eighth day's light came to closure. This was the climactic moment when all the holiness and joy of the eight days of miracles came together, in accord with the notion of "last in actual realization, but first in thought."[17] Exultation burst out willy-nilly from that reddish farewell light, reverberating in the men's section by virtue of the powers of first and last things till almost midnight.

It seemed as if the many candles on the long table were glowing with the light of inflamed souls. The old silver menorah with the carved flowers stood before the Rebbe, who was seated at the table with his sons and hasidim. Its wicks, kindled the previous evening, were still aflame.

The yellow lights veiled in mystery rose above the heads of the hasidim and into the *ezrat nashim.* There, too, candles had been lit, in two silver candlesticks placed on the table where the Maggid once wrote his amulets.

That same exultation swept over Bat-Zion, who was seated on the old ladies' bench near the lit stove. It seemed that she had grown up quite a lot since that first night of Hanukkah when she burst out in dancing and fainted during the service of sacred song. Since the fall harvest festival of Sukkot until Hanukkah, the days had wept with rain and the nights had alarmed her with the sounds of crying, coming from unfortunate souls pouring out their hearts as well as from young men summoned for conscription in the Russian army who recited psalms night and day. But now the lights of Hanukkah had come, illumining the darkness all of a sudden. Those lights had completely flooded over her, and from then on they never left her.

And now she heard sweet music ringing out. Her father the Rebbe was accompanying the sacred service on his violin. "From eternity to eternity, You are God"[18]—her father's mystic melody of yearning burst out, unfolding without end. The entire golden-hued space of the room was overtaken by a rush of prayer, and the vapor of voices billowed up like clouds of glory. At this moment, they were entering the inner chambers of their Father's house, the palace of the Sovereign whose kingdom is forever.

After the notes of the melody came an extended silence, the still small voice.

Now singing once more: the thrilling tones of *"I extol You Lord, for You have lifted me up, and have not made my foes to rejoice over me."*[19] And again the notes of the violin entered, joining in the songs of liberation and redemption. Finally they reached the sacred song "All creatures high and low testify that God is One and His Name is One. . . ."

It seemed that the entire world was uniting, drawn away to the hidden One. In her mind's eye, Bat-Zion began to see tracts of land, towns, and villages that she had visited when her mother took her to her own father's court on the banks of the Dnieper River in White Russia.[20] All these territories linked up with the fields of the family estate, coming along with the entire community to the dedication of the altar, there—there in the Holy Land. . . . Didn't she dream at night that the Messiah, the righteous Redeemer whose name she often heard, was coming together with a throng of people, by way of the grain fields of their estate?

Bat-Zion felt a pain in her heart. Just as she was about to break out in tears she hurriedly left the room. She ran to the girls' loft. No one was there at the moment and that frightened her a little. It seemed as if hidden figures were hovering around her. The middle room was lit with a small flame filtered through the decorated glass on the china lamp. The bird slept curled up in its cage, and the saplings stood silently in their pots. She looked at the embroidery table, the sewing machine, and the small bookcase. Tomorrow would be a regular weekday; she would have to apply herself to her studies with more passion.

She remained in that state of apprehension and dread for a number of minutes. The holidays, days of celebration, had passed. Now she was to be a grown-up. She held back her tears.

The Ambience of Eretz Yisra'el

On that cold, clear day, the snow-covered rooftops cracked as if stretching their frozen limbs. While the events of the day were minor and did not affect any essential issue of the Rebbe's court, they nevertheless generated great excitement within the household.

The gathering of a number of people from *Eretz Yisra'el*, some of whom were about to return there, colored the day's light with a sad and sentimental cast. The family's middle daughter, Bat-Zion, was now eleven years old, but her inherent emotional intensity had not diminished, and she was seized with a feeling of spiritual awakening such as she had never experienced before.

The bedroom in the girls' loft, still semidark in the dim light of early morning, already reverberated with the gasping sobs of Devorah of Safed, a guest who for various reasons had been put up in the girls' residence over a year and a half ago. That day she was scheduled to return to Safed, and it seemed as if all the hardships of her travels were about to burst from her heart in a storm before she went back to the Holy Land.

Bat-Zion's eyelids were still closed, but her heart was beating strongly in response to the room-filling sound of Devorah of Safed pouring out her soul in psalms. Confused feelings of terror and joy coursed through Bat-Zion. Opening her eyes wide, she gazed at the doorway to the adjacent inner room, where some people were moving about.

As the morning light got a bit brighter and she shook herself awake, she was able to make out a third figure in addition to the prayerful Devorah of Safed and Nanny Sarah, who was opening the stove door to remove the coffeepot. It was the slight figure of Nehamaleh of Jerusalem, who had arrived a while ago and who was now going to take the place of Devorah of Safed in the girls' residence.

"I've finally found a place to rest after my wanderings away from home," Nehamaleh broke out in a soft, subdued voice. She carried herself modestly as she walked and said very little, in order not to sin by improper utterance.

Devorah of Safed began to open her heart to her. "You, dear, have found a place to rest, but I must leave this holy house, and who knows what's in store for me on the road till I return to my home in the Holy Land."

Finishing her words, she wiped her swollen eyes with her white handkerchief, which she took out of the pocket of her neatly pressed pleated dress, and blew her nose. When her spirits picked up a bit, she got up from her seat on the upholstered sofa near the eastern window, whose frozen panes reflected pinkish flashes of dawn, and began attending to her belongings piled up between the flowerpot table and the sofa.

Bat-Zion washed her face and neck with cold water from the china pitcher on the washing table and felt a pleasing freshness throughout her body. Her mood continued to improve as she smelled the fragrance of roses from the soap she used for washing, called Beauty Secret.

This must surely be the way the air smells in Eretz Yisra'el, she thought, since it was a land where roses grew. And residents of the Land would often send rose honey to her household as a gift.

The door to the inner room was partly ajar, and as she dried her face with a soft towel and whispered the Morning Blessings, she looked with pleasure at the activities in progress. Bat-Zion's two older sisters were assisting Devorah of Safed in packing the wedding clothes for her daughter, who was engaged to be married. Bat-Zion's oldest sister, Hannah Goldeleh, had already put on her pink flannel blouse with the high collar that set off her fair face so handsomely. She was wearing a brown silk wig on her head, pulled tightly with ruby-inlaid combs.[1]

With great dexterity Hannah Goldeleh folded the blouses, which she herself had embroidered. She had devoted many weeks to the lace flowers decorating the collar and was happy they had come out so beautifully and would no doubt befit the lovely bride. Even though she had never met her, her mother Devorah had described her daughter, and the image of a beautiful woman floated before her eyes.

"May the merit of your good deed stand you in good stead; you performed the mitzvah of enabling me to bring my daughter Gitl to the marriage canopy in dignity," said Devorah emotionally as she folded the silk cloth that was set aside for her daughter's wedding gown. Bat-Zion's mother the Rebbetzin Brachaleh had shaped the fabric into the form of a woman's gown. At that moment another of Bat-Zion's sisters, Hayyah Miriam'l, was handling the baggage of Nehamaleh of Jerusalem, whose quiet sighs blended with the patter of tears from Devorah's eyes as they fell on her daughter's garments.

The dark-complexioned face of Hayyah Miriam'l looked worried as she put Nehamaleh's suitcases in the corner of the room between the sofa and the flowerpots, where Devorah's belongings had been, and one could notice creases on her forehead below her braids.

Bat-Zion hurried to the inner room in order to help with the packing of Devorah of Safed's belongings. She began with the big wicker basket, putting in the pearl and coral embroidered velour blouse, a gift from her grandmother Rebbetzin Sarah Devorahleh, who had embroidered it many years ago, as well as her oldest sister's red velvet dress, decorated with ruffles and ribbons. With enthusiastic, rapid movements she grabbed the white yarmulkes that the women from Israel had crocheted for her brothers and threw them in the wicker basket, together with the coil of red laces that were on the oval mirror table.

"You're just as wild as you were three years ago, Bat-Zion, but now you should be a mature young woman," Nehamaleh burst out, uncharacteristically, in reprimand. "I compassed the tomb of our matriarch Rachel seven times with those laces; they are a tried and true talisman for healing illnesses, God spare us!"[2]

Her face crimson, Bat-Zion walked in embarrassment toward the outer door, head bowed. But her path crossed that of her mother the Rebbetzin who had just entered the room, accompanied by Miriam of Jerusalem, a dear friend of the Rebbetzin's family for many years. Also accompanying the Rebbetzin was a young woman from *Eretz Yisra'el* and her baby, recently arrived from Vienna, where the child had undergone medical treatments for his eyes in the excellent clinics there. She had come to the girls' residence to say good-bye, for she too was set to leave that day.

When she entered the room, the Rebbetzin had caught Bat-Zion in her moment of disgrace. She gave her an indignant look, and when Bat-Zion kissed her mother's hand in good-morning salutation, her mother reprimanded her quietly. "Dear Daughter, if you will keep in mind, when you go to bed and when you rise, that good manners are even more important than the study of Torah,[3] you will not come to desecrate sacred objects or to humiliate other people."

"Rest assured that before she reaches the age of marriage, she will be cured of her childish capriciousness," old Nanny Sarah intervened with the young Rebbetzin Brachaleh, trying to spare the girl any further scolding.

The Rebbetzin listened in silence. Then she turned to the women from *Eretz Yisra'el* and began conversing with them.

The stove, which had been lit since the day before and was just stoked by the nanny, spread a pleasing warmth in the large inner room decorated with tasteful simplicity. The light flowed through the frost flowers on the windowpanes on the east- and west-side windows, highlighting the moss and the artificial flowers that the girls had placed between the double windows. The painted tree roots on the wallpaper seemed real and alive, as did the framed embroidered flowers hanging on the walls. The potted saplings—lemon, orange, and cactus, together with small wildflowers—beamed joyfully from the two tripods and from the sloping tiered hutch. The canary began to stir, jumping from side to side in her cage on the chest of drawers, and she let out a sweet silvery trill. The women's conversation, suffused with longing for what had vanished, glided like a quietly flowing stream. The younger Rebbetzin, who was head and shoulders taller than the women around her, stood before the open wicker basket and expressed satisfaction over the way the linens and clothing had been arranged in a neat and orderly fashion. In her hands were the white yarmulkes that the women from *Eretz Yisra'el* had crocheted for her sons. She examined the coral threads interwoven in the pattern and said that the women from *Eretz Yisra'el* are skillful and wise, just like our foremothers in the Book of Exodus, who wove the curtains of the Tabernacle with blue and purple threads.

"It appears, Rebbetzin Brachaleh, that you are also highly skilled in this craft," said Nehamaleh of Jerusalem, who had been born in Stolin and who, in her youth, was a friend of the older Rebbetzin's daughters. "I remember," continued Nehamah, "that your dear mother-in-law Rebbetzin Sarah Devorahleh asked the expert instructor she had brought from Hungary to Stolin to teach her and her daughters—Leahnu, Feigenu, and Havvahnu—the craft of crocheting intertwined with pearls."

"That's correct," answered the Rebbetzin. "It was in the gazebo in the fruit orchard. I was busy working on crocheting and embroidery, along with my dear sisters-in-law. Those skills my mother-in-law, long may she live, inherited from our foremothers. The instructor Zlotki was teaching similar techniques to the apprentice girls. She, too, undoubtedly drew her knowledge from an ancient source, for that young woman from Hungary was God-fearing and modest even though she was fluent in German and taught that language to my sisters-in-law and me."

The Rebbetzin was silent for a few moments and then continued quietly: "I regret that I did not have the privilege to learn much from my mother the tzaddeket, for she passed away at a young age in Chernobyl. And as for skill at handicrafts, there is no doubt that our wisdom flows from our ancient heritage rooted in the Holy Land. From there it finds a home in our courtyards."

By the time the Rebbetzin concluded her words, she was speaking in ecstatic tones, as if revealing a hidden mystery.

Devorah of Safed seconded her words: "What you say is absolutely right, dear Rebbetzin, like Torah from Heaven. Confirmation comes from the passing of my revered father, Reb Naftali. At the time that my father, peace be upon him, prepared to emigrate to the Holy Land, he went to receive a departing blessing from your family's ancestor, the tzaddik Rabbi Elazar, the grandson of the holy Maggid of Kozienice. The tzaddik said to him that when a worthy individual wishes to emigrate to the Holy Land, even if he does not die there, his soul eventually makes its way to *Eretz Yisra'el*."

"How prescient were the eyes of the tzaddikim. In fact your father Reb Naftali, peace be upon him, died in Kozienice on a trip on which he was serving as a fund-raising emissary from *Eretz Yisra'el*," the Rebbetzin whispered, seemingly to herself.

Miriam of Jerusalem spoke up enthusiastically as she rolled back the edge of her white kerchief on her forehead: "If that's true for simple persons of integrity, then it's certainly true of your holy ancestors; their holy souls are undoubtedly in *Eretz Yisra'el*. And there's something else I must tell you, Hannah Goldale my dear friend," Miriam continued, squeezing with her left hand the arm of the Rebbe's oldest daughter, which she interlocked in her own. "You should know that all your holy ancestors, and ours as well, are there in the Holy Land with us. My grandmother the tzaddeket, of blessed memory, saw the holy Seer of Lublin[4] and the holy Jew of Przysucha[5] walking to the Western Wall. And my mother, long may she live, has had dreams in which she saw the tzaddikim of Kozienice, Stolin, and Chernobyl in the holy sites of *Eretz Yisra'el*."[6]

The Rebbetzin sighed, and as she took from Miriam a model of Rachel's tomb carved from olive wood, she said in a sad tone, "Our Patriarch Jacob buried Mother Rachel on the road to Efrat in order that the Children of Israel would entreat for mercy at her grave as they were taken into exile."

Devorah of Safed stifled a sob and began leaning over the basket again. Miriam of Jerusalem turned her head to the Rebbe's daughter, whom she was clutching. Her eyelids, swollen from the burning rays of the sun in *Eretz Yisra'el* and from weeping over the burdens of her life, had been healed by the doctors in Vienna, but now they seemed to puff up anew.

The younger Rebbetzin turned toward the younger woman from *Eretz Yisra'el* who had not participated at all in the conversation because she was taking care of her child, feeding him some cereal that Nanny Sarah had placed on the table. She said that in her opinion it was important to apply the cream from the Viennese doctor to the child's eyelashes and to put drops in his eyes before the trip. Even though the child's eyes had cleared up and there were no signs of inflammation, the winds on the journey might, God forbid, harm them.

"Thank you for your kindness," said the young woman, her blue eyes smiling in gratitude. After she finished putting the last spoonful of food in the baby's mouth, she began looking in her satchel for the medicines.

Having taken the infant in her arms and given him a toy bell, the Rebbetzin called to her daughters to observe the child's clean outfit and his white pants, which his mother had skillfully sewn from torn diapers while on their journey.

Bat-Zion listened silently to the sound of the infant's playful cooing, which blended with the soft jingling of the toy in his tiny hand;
and, immersed in thought, she returned to the black mirror table
carved with leaves and flowers. There between the small china
vases were the red laces with which Nehamaleh had compassed
the tomb of Mother Rachel. The model of the tomb with camel and
rider carved in olive wood was also there on the table.

The chorus of soft tones from the toy bell, the cooing of the baby,
the patter of clothes falling on the wicker basket, the gentle silvery
notes of the canary in the cage—all of these seemed to blend together now with that mysterious conversation her mother the Rebbetzin
had with the woman from *Eretz Yisra'el*, which had taken place a
short while ago, and she fell into a kind of dream reverie.

Her hand grasped the model of Mother Rachel's tomb, and a bittersweet melody rose up from the recesses of her soul. It was the
melody that Bat-Zion heard every year from her brothers' rooms
downstairs. Her heart tightening, she began humming quietly,
"when I was returning from Paddan, Rachel died...." [7] She noticed her
reflection staring at her from the oval mirror with the silver frame
and, embarrassed, she stopped immediately. With the help of the
mirror, she touched up her hair and fixed the velvet collar, which
set off the fresh rosy complexion of her cheeks. Gazing at the room
and its bustling activities in the mirror, the commotion brought her
back to the days of her childhood.

It had been a long time since such a large number of men and
women from *Eretz Yisra'el* had happened to come together. In the
old house, destroyed by fire, there were often many guests from the
Holy Land, and their joking and singing filled the house with
much gaiety. She still remembered the Purim play that Miriam of
Jerusalem had staged in their house. Bat-Zion was five years old at
the time, and they dressed her up as King Ahasuerus since he was
a foolish king, and a five-year-old would fit the part perfectly. How
wonderful those days were; how the decorated drawing rooms in
that house glowed. How the house, situated on high ground, stood
out with its small turrets. And how endearing were the people
from the Holy Land....

But even now, even now—even though everything seemed to be emptying out with all this hasty packing—there was still something festive in the warmth of the air, in the expression on her mother's noble face and the faces of her sisters. Even Nanny Sarah's withered face seemed to have regained its youthful freshness.

And this was definitely true of those wonderful women from the Holy Land. All of them, with their white kerchiefs on their heads and their bright outfits, had faces that beamed with inner joy, despite the sad tone of the conversations and the sighs that could be heard in the chorus of sounds. . . .

Bat-Zion was overtaken by longing, but she didn't know if the sad melody playing within her was for the women who were about to leave, for their old house illumined by the enchanted light of her childhood, or for the road to Efrat that she longed for, which was riddled with holes like a sieve. . . .[8]

When the wagon driver entered, hood over his head and long whip in his hand, things were still not completely ready. The apprentice girls had just now brought food for the journey from the kitchens in the open courtyard.

The fish dried over straw in the baking oven and the yellow cheese that the older Rebbetzin had prepared at the Strykowice estate were the kinds of foods that would last for many days on a land or sea journey. The young servant Shlomo packed the food in a leather satchel he had brought. He was the son of pious Malkah and trustworthy Beryl, who were supervisors at the estate. He secured the large wicker basket with iron bands and helped the wagon driver to take it out by way of the open doors and down the stairs, along with the bags of the young woman and her baby.

That baby, whose blue eyes peered out intelligently from his woolen swaddling clothes covering him from head to toe, was passed from hand to hand between the apprentice girls and the Rebbe's daughters. Each one wanted to have the privilege of a few moments with the baby from the Holy Land. Bat-Zion smelled his robust, plump cheek and thought, *This fresh smell is like the smell of roses in the air of Eretz Yisra'el.* Even though the frost pierced her face she felt a kind of warmth pass over her, as if she were at that moment in the warm atmosphere of *Eretz Yisra'el.* As she went down the wooden staircase covered with packed snow, her hands laden with luggage, she felt no desire to slide down the icy steps all at once, as she always did on cold days.

The voice of her mother the Rebbetzin cracked the frozen air, filling her with added excitement. "May we all be privileged to ascend with dignity to our Holy Land, speedily, in our day," she said prayerfully, with rapturous intensity.

"With our righteous Messiah, with the righteous Redeemer," responded the older Rebbetzin Sarah Devorahleh, who had come from her rooms in the open courtyard to say good-bye, accompanied by a number of women. She was wearing a velvet coat with a silk kerchief over her gold-embroidered headdress.

"May we merit the redemption so that you all will come. It's hard to say good-bye, dear Rebbetzins, dear daughters," said the women about to begin their journey.

A frozen, heavy silence pervaded the air brightened by snow sparkling on the rooftops as the Rebbetzin ordered the opening of the rarely used inner gate that stood between the wooden residence of the Rebbe and Rebbetzin and the two-story building of the boys and girls. The sound of the gate's creaking blended with the dull sound of the wheels of the public-transport wagons dragging over the ice-covered ground.

The peasants' public-transport wagons, seats covered with straw, carried the townspeople to the Garbatka train station, a distance of about thirteen miles[9] from the town. The wagons were perfectly suited to survive forest trails in winter, obstructed as they were by tree roots and mounds of ice. The wagons were filled end to end with travelers, men and women bundled up in warm clothing. The fur hats on the men's heads, their coats, and the woolen scarves with which the women wrapped themselves were all bathed in a frosty powder, and it glistened in the tepid sun peering through the smoking chimneys of the houses.

"You're responsible to get us from here to there; the train won't wait for us," complaining voices shouted from the wagons approaching the gate, which led to a side street thickly settled with bnei-tovim and communal officials.

"As for the train—I take full responsibility. Not to worry, folks, not to worry," called out the wagon driver as he blew into his clenched hands to warm them, his broad shoulders pushing the gates wide open. Just then the Rebbetzins brought the women from *Eretz Yisra'el* inside to the Inner Sanctum to receive the Rebbe's blessing.

When they exited, they were accompanied by the old man Eliezer from Tiberias, who had spent many days in the Rebbe's house. "If you please, dear Devorah, please tell my family about my wonderful accommodations in exile. Tell them not to worry about my welfare," the old man said with a wink. Peering from his white beard, his face shone with a youthful glow; this was because he used to bathe in Sea of Galilee at Tiberias all year long.

"And one more thing," called out the Litvak assistant Elazar, who served as secretary, to the two women who were about to board the wagon. "Remember to tell our people in the Holy Land to send fruits for Tu b'Shevat.[10]

"Yes, yes, thistle and fennel seeds," added the old man from Tiberias.[11]

Finally the wagon driver, who had been waiting a long time since coming to take the luggage, swung his whip and pointed the horses toward Magitowa Street.

The women from *Eretz Yisra'el* were seated bundled up in their warm clothing with other passengers on the front seat of the wagon, which was cushioned with straw and a large woolen rug. They could not calm down after the good-byes and the kisses, and for a long time Devorah of Safed's sobbing echoed in the frozen blue air. The Rebbetzins whispered the Priestly Benediction[12] as they fulfilled the mitzvah of seeing off one's guests by taking a number of steps into the side street.[13] That tightly closed courtyard, which was breached when the inner gate was unlocked, seemed to have been thrown open to all the winds of the world, converging on a certain point, the nexus of *Eretz Yisra'el*.[14] Everything in these holy courtyards—the court of the tzaddik, the Rebbe Rabbi Yerahmiel Moshele, the incumbent Rebbe occupying the seat of his ancestor the holy Maggid Rabbi Yisrael in Kozienice—revolves around that point.

It seemed as if the small courtyard with its old buildings and its tall birches standing frozen before the two-story building, including the sundial pedestal near the Rebbe's residence—everything here looked with anticipation toward the open road on the other side of the gate, which led far, far away to the Holy Land. . . .

"Well, after all is said and done, it's going to be dreary now in our rooms; it's too bad that Miriam of Jerusalem will be lodging in grandmother's house and not with us, instead of that short-tempered Nehama," Bat-Zion whispered in the ear of Miriam'l her sister.

Miriam covered her ear with a lock of hair, because her pursed lips were still whispering the blessing, *"May the Lord bless you. . . ."* She directed a censorious stare at Bat-Zion, whose chestnut eyes filled with tears.

Sabbath of the Song[1]

Bat-Zion left the inner courtyard utterly contented, and the ewe that jumped out of its pen and licked her hand made her even happier. She gazed at the flock of sparrows resting on the snow-covered rooftops. *They're like guests invited to a feast*, she thought to herself. *Today is Sabbath of the Song, Shabbat Shirah, and we'll be sharing our Sabbath foods with them.*

When she reached the dining room in the outer courtyard, her mother greeted her with a puzzled "*Nu?*" The sacred book *Sha'arei Ziyyon*[2] lay open in her hands, and she was not able to interrupt her devotions to ask Bat-Zion why today she had come earlier than usual. When Bat-Zion approached to kiss her mother's hand she saw that her soft eyes were soaked in tears.

Her grandmother was also still holding her *Sha'arei Ziyyon* to which they turned each day before morning prayers, saturating its pages with tears over Israel's exile and the exile of the *Shekhinah*. Both Rebbetzins were still wearing their satin dressing gowns, their heads covered with white silk kerchiefs.

The rays of Sabbath sun filtered through the frost-covered double windowpanes, sheathed in holy tranquility. The warm air cast the small dining room in a diaphanous veil of mysteries. The long table was covered with a white tablecloth, upon which rested silver candlesticks that the maid had not yet had an opportunity to remove.

The kitchen door opened frequently and the aroma of strong coffee burst into the dining room. In the kitchen, the two old women—the household manager and the children's nanny—were dispensing coffee for the *yoshvim* in the synagogue. They took pots out of the blazing sand heaped on the cookstove that sat on one side of the oven, and poured coffee into the cups and glasses the servants were holding.

The aroma of coffee heated since sundown on Friday, together with the Sabbath atmosphere, intoxicated Bat-Zion. She seemed to be in a reverie for hours, waking up fully only when they began the Torah service.

The *ezrat nashim* adjoining the synagogue had been taken over by a crowd of hasidim who had come for the Sabbath of the Song from various towns around Kozienice, so the women gathered for prayer in the dining room. When the cantor reading the Torah began chanting his sinuous trills for the Song at the Sea, the women rose from their benches and in a spirit of exaltation began chanting loudly with him. *"Then Miriam the prophetess, Aaron's sister, took a timbrel in her hand, and all the women went out after her in dance with timbrels!"*[3] A cry of victory swept through the room. Even the old bas-tovim Altah Leah, her face withered from the burdens of child-rearing, was filled with joy.

This congregation of women, wearing headdresses adorned with colored stones, ribbons, and flowers and standing in the densely crowded room, was actually promenading among the seventy palm trees and twelve springs of water,[4] and her mother and grandmother the Rebbetzins, their golden headdresses modestly covered with muslin veils, were striding in front. And here was the manna, whose color was like the color of bdellium.[5] And the quail[6] must certainly have looked like the flock of sparrows that were flying about the courtyard today, thought Bat-Zion.

The spirit of exaltation was intensified by the sunlight, which like a sudden revelation began shining abundantly into the room, its doors open on three sides. The congregation broke out in "Good

Shabbos" greetings, and the women moved to the sides to make way for the Rebbe who had come to greet his mother and family. The older Rebbetzin stepped away from the crowd of women leaving by a side door in order to greet her son the Rebbe, who was standing with his sons and some of his devoted hasidim, sharing Torah thoughts. Bat-Zion, who was standing between her sisters and her mother ready to greet her father with the Good Sabbath blessing, listened with rapt attentiveness.

Her father's captivating voice broke the room's thick silence. "At the time of the Exodus, the Israelites sang as one person, with one voice, as Scripture says, *"I will sing unto the Lord,"*[7] using the first person singular to signify that their hearts were as one. When we will be able to sing in unison as well, then the world and its fullness will sing along with us." Face beaming, he addressed the children and said, "Today is the day to put out kasha for the birds, God's singing creatures. A Jewish custom has the force of Scripture."[8]

The Sabbath dinner lasted a long time. The sound of table melodies carried from the synagogue to the women's dining room nearby, filled with the aromas of Sabbath foods. The Rebbetzins, busy organizing the meal, joined the table melodies excitedly, as did the women seated at the table singing between the courses. When the old household manager brought out the p'tchah and the brown kasha bubbling with oil, Bat-Zion began thinking about the birds with great delight. The diners left some of the kasha in the decorated china plates on the table, and the young servant gathered the leftovers in a tray. The old bas-tovim also gave him her leftovers, saying "take some of my portion for the birds, too" in a tearful tone; her lean face, framed by a white headdress of thin fabric drawn tightly around her head, expressed something akin to pleasure.

As the manager brought out the five types of kugel, the ewe trudged along after her. With her two forelegs she jumped onto the arm of the young servant and bleated to demand her portion. The servant pulled on his tiny beard to suppress his laughter.

"Why, Scripture compares the Children of Israel to sheep," said the older Rebbetzin. She got up and put a piece of challah before the ewe, after which she divided the kugel in equal portions for the seated company. Besides her own portion, Bat-Zion absentmindedly ate from two other kugels, the almond and the apple, which were so delicious. Then her entire being was drawn outside for what was about to happen.

The Sabbath holiness imparted a pure feeling to the outer court-yard. The cold blue air, glistening with rainbow colors reflected off snowy rooftops and trees, captured the voices of the little children and the Sabbath table songs. The vibrations joined with the sounds of the birds, strung together like links in a golden chain.

Flocks of sparrows flew about in the blue air. Open-beaked individual birds glided past the small group, consisting of a young boy and girl, their older sister Bat-Zion, and the Rebbe's personal attendant. They stood between the garden in front of the women's rooms and the Maggid's room, which jutted out from the wooden synagogue. The children threw dark kasha playfully on the snow while Bat-Zion remained standing silently, leaning on the lantern pole near the garden. Something intrigued her about the birds picking out seeds, spreading their wings, and taking off, cutting away toward Heaven in flocks.

She was startled by the arrival of her mother, who was accompanying the old bas-tovim, laden with her troubles, to the Maggid's room. The Rebbetzin paused a few moments, turned to the children and said, "On the first Sabbath in the desert after the Exodus, the Israelites ate manna together with the birds, and when they inherited the Land of the Patriarchs they partook of the pleasures of the good fruit that *Eretz Yisra'el* produces." She buttoned her youngest child's velvet cloak, pulled his gold-embroidered hat down over his frozen ears, and entered the room's outer vestibule. The sun peered through the window, some of whose panes were transparent. One could see the women standing before the canopy bed of the Maggid, the holy ancestor. The sanctity of that bed had been kept exactly as it was one hundred years before.

There's no comparison between sadness on Sabbath and sadness of a weekday, even though we're in the midst of the Shovavim[9] period, during which the Children of Israel were wandering in the wilderness, not having yet reached repose in our Land, thought Bat-Zion, feeling a bittersweet pleasure. She was reminded of how the previous Monday had become a day of wrath when her grandmother discovered that her son was fasting and she admonished him in the harshest terms.

The sad, silent holiness visible in the Maggid's window seemed to blend in with the lament of a bird selecting seeds. The bird, of many colored feathers and crest, flew to the top of a birch and disappeared into its nest, from which little heads stuck out.

"A fine and flaky substance, as fine as frost," [10] rang out the voice of the servant who poured out the leftover kasha from the platter. A flood of chirping filled the frozen air, like the sounds of the ancient Song.

The ewe rubbed its horns on the lantern pole. She jumped and bleated, while an exultant song rang out from the children, "then the world and its fullness will sing along with us."

"Sing to the Lord, for He has triumphed gloriously." [11]

CHAPTER

Fruits of the Fifteenth[1]

It seemed as if the entire expanse of the earth was turning into streaming flakes of snow. It gathered in heaps in the streets of the town of Kozienice on the banks of the Vistula. Waves of it rose to the level of the frost-covered windows of the wood and stone houses that lined the streets. The houses seemed to be set in a foundation of snow, as if they had been torn away prematurely from the craftsman's workshop by a stormy gust of wind, missing doors and bereft of plaster. The old chestnut trees that lined the streets stretched backward under the snow's weight till they were almost supine. It seemed as if they were struggling to shake off the annoying burden from their bald heads.

An unusual stillness pervaded the Rebbe's courtyards. The old wooden houses of the Maggid facing the street were encased in stubborn silence. Then the wind picked up and sheared the snow from hidden repositories, turning all of space to the farthest reaches of Heaven into chaos and void. The slanted roofs seemed just to have buckled, their shingles cracking under the weight of snow heaped over them. The trills of the Torah-study chant rang out frequently from one of the buildings; they roamed about and disappeared, wandering and disintegrating. A tall tree reached over and struck the lamp on top of the pole, breaking it into pieces.

Who can understand the spirit of youth? Just now, in the middle of a snowstorm, the young woman of the Rebbe's house was overtaken by a desire to leave the upper story of the children's residence. Was it perhaps to greet the letter carrier, since the fruits of *Eretz Yisra'el* were due to arrive around this time?

"I wouldn't even let a cat out now," said the old nanny. "There's an unladylike wayward spirit in you, Bat-Zion. Don't you know that soon you're going to be betrothed!"

The young woman paid no attention to the old one. She didn't put on her velvet coat and didn't even wrap herself with a warm shawl. She ran outside with all her strength, wearing only her brocaded winter dress. She covered her face with the curls of her hair for protection from the damp, penetrating cold and the blinding snow. As she ran the length of the courtyards, she stumbled over a low wooden pole at the end of the open courtyard near the kitchens. A long ladder was fastened to the top of the pole, and it led to the roof of the stockroom in the attic. This ladder provoked her to thinking, and she stayed a number of moments at its side. She once got much pleasure from taking a big jump in order to grab on to rungs of the ladder and then swing in the air. Now she had grown taller and just by standing on her tiptoes she could grab hold and swing, but the activity no longer seemed appropriate for a young woman her age. She was already twelve years old. She recalled the old woman's words about her betrothal and sensed that her face had become red with embarrassment. She was happy that no one was looking at her.

Bat-Zion continued on her way. Leaving the pole, she went by the footpath to the open portico. From here on she certainly had no permission to walk alone, into the outside world. Suddenly a feeling of melancholy overcame her and she diverted her mind from childish thoughts. On the other side of the street through the snowflakes swirling about in circles, she could see the large unfinished brick building, its windows boarded up.

Years had gone by and their new house was still not completed. They had begun rebuilding it many years after the fire that had engulfed it, along with the synagogue and a large part of the town. Her father the Rebbe had delayed rebuilding his house, feeling that it was a religiously dubious activity to build homes outside the Holy Land. Instead, he directed the building contributions that came in toward the repair of the large synagogue of the Maggid.

Sadness overtook her as she was seized by the memory of the old house that had gone up in flames, the house with its turrets jutting out on either side, with squirrels jumping on the flowerpots in the corners of the turret just outside the drawing room where the Rebbetzins held teas.

Just as Bat-Zion decided to go back, the tall letter carrier, covered in snow, burst into the portico. The copper buttons on his coat were covered with frost and did not glisten as usual. He had a parcel in one hand and with the other hand he removed his hat, saying hello in Russian. The shiny visor of his cap was also frost covered. Bat-Zion immediately recognized the parcel they had been expecting. It was square, bound in linen cloth, and had red seals prominently visible on all sides.

Yes indeed, these were the fruits of *Eretz Yisra'el*, the fruits over which they would recite the *Shehecheyanu* blessing on the fifteenth of Shevat. It was for these fruits that they had dispatched their letters; in particular, the Rebbe's personal assistant and secretary had been hard at work writing letters and sending the requisite monies. Day after day messengers were sent to the post office. And the conversations about the fruits of *Eretz Yisra'el* flew about during the gray days of fall, blowing a refreshing breeze into the damp, melancholy air.

The morning of the fifteenth of Shevat arrived. The sky was a deep hard blue. The white clouds floated leisurely from east to west. The cold was bitter, the white roofs contracting and trembling from the frost. It was a fine day for a morning walk, a mandatory activity for the entire household. But who was interested in a morning constitutional when the ritual of distributing the fruits beckoned?

The old nanny rushed the girls to put on their velvet coats and silk scarves. On the field between the closed inner courtyard and the open outer courtyard, schoolchildren who had just run out of nearby *heder* schools were shouting as they fashioned a giant snowman from the snow piled up near the horse stables. Little girls, scarves tied around their backs, sang and threw snowballs.

The coachman of the Rebbe's household, tall cap on his head and long whip in his hand, appeared at the horse stables. The children were frightened of him and ran away, some to their teachers' rooms and some to their parents' houses near the field.

Walking with heavy steps and struggling with the piled snow, the coachman slowly opened the big iron stable door. As he entered the stable, the two horses raised their heads from the feeding trough and neighed to him. The coachman patted the back of the gray horse, then whistled and grasped his halter. Then he took out the brown horse and harnessed him on the other side of the wagon shaft.

The Rebbe's personal attendant, wearing a black fur hat, came running. "The Rebbetzin is worried about the cows, you didn't feed them on time," he addressed the coachman. "You've gotten lazy, Frank. It is very cold today"—he said rubbing his hands together—"it's ver-r-ry cold, but you must do your work properly."

The older Rebbetzin hurried to the stable, wearing a velour coat. Her finger was holding her place in the prayer book she was carrying in her right hand. She had interrupted her recitation of psalms out of concern for this important matter.

"How did you forget the cows, Frank?" she scolded the coachman in Polish.

"I've been harnessing the horses to the sleigh, Rebbetzin. It's time for the young ladies to take their outing," said the coachman obsequiously, head facing the ground, pulling on his hair to deflect attention from his lapse.

"You feed the cows, Yashkar-Ber, the animals are suffering,"[2] said the Rebbetzin to the attendant, "Frank has no time right now."

Bat-Zion forgot about the outing, which seemed a chore now. She slipped away from the sleigh and went to the closed courtyard.

After a number of moments, two servants came into the closed courtyard carrying a large tub filled with hot liquid. Columns of reddish steam rose up from the brew, made from leftovers and potato peels. The stall door opened and warm vinegary vapors spread into the courtyard, diffusing an odor of decayed fodder. The mooing of the cows broke out from the feeding trough.

"Why haven't you gone out yet for your outing?" the Rebbetzin asked the girls. "Soon it will be time to come back home. In another hour we'll be distributing the fruits of *Eretz Yisra'el*."

Bat-Zion sat on the upholstered cushion in the sleigh with her sisters, and a spirit of gaiety began to buoy her. In a little while the fruits would be distributed. The parcel was already open in her father's residence. There was even a large coconut. The Rebbe himself had broken the shell with a small saw and opened it with reverence and love since it had been sanctified by the air of *Eretz Yisra'el*.

The coconut shell was put to use on the stove in the Passover kitchen for frying some of the fruits, dipped in the rose honey they had also received. The work was all done by most worthy individuals, everything made ready for the set time of noon on this day, the New Year for Trees.

The sleigh left the field in back of the courtyards, and its galloping horses drew it over the snow through the town's alleys and wide streets, glistening white. Columns of smoke rose from the chimneys jutting out from the white rooftops, signaling life in those shuttered houses. The pump at the end of Magitowa Street, wrapped in snow, was surrounded by men and women carrying an assortment of vessels. They pushed toward the well's mouth, which had icicles hanging all around and a stream of water flowing from it. The doors of the houses on the sides of the streets opened, people gazed at the sleigh, and the doors closed again.

Just as the sleigh reached the wooden houses spread out between pine trees at the edge of the city, their frozen windowpanes peering over their garden fences, a water carrier crossed into the middle of the street carrying full buckets on a pole over his shoulders. The coachman brought the horses to a halt and vented his anger on the water carrier for blocking the road.

Two female figures emerged from different directions. From across the woods came the Crown Rebbetzin and from one of the lanes of the houses came the elderly widow of the Rabbi Reb Pinhas, in her headdress of wide colored ribbons. As usual, her hands were busy knitting, this time a white stocking. Even the Crown Rebbetzin, a short woman, seemed taller in her old velvet hat, which she wore over her wig's bun. She was returning to her house in the town's gentile neighborhood after a morning walk in the forest. "What a nice day for an outing," she said politely as she came up to the sleigh. "In the Russian monthly journal, the tsarina's personal physician has a long discussion on frost and its health benefits."

"And I'm chasing my worries, but I don't want to sin by complaining," said the widow of the rabbi, putting her hand over her mouth and covering the smile on her wise, drawn face.

"We'll come join you to eat the fruits of the fifteenth," the Crown Rebbetzin called out to the sleigh as it moved on.

The sleigh traveled down the road, the snow groaning underneath. Then it passed a forest of tall pine trees bristling with frozen needles, rigid and snow laden, as if a squall of primordial ice had blown through and terrified them. A flock of ravens covered the boughs, shrieking *"caw, caw."* Perhaps they were attempting to rouse the trees from their icy state. A frozen pond appeared through a break in the forest, completely solid, with fallen oak leaves and decaying vegetation in its bosom. It seemed as if the plants had been maliciously trapped by the angry pond and its retinue of frozen puddles.

Thinking of those fruits from *Eretz Yisra'el*, Bat-Zion exclaimed, "I can almost smell the buds on the trees!"

She was getting no pleasure from the outing and was becoming restless. Perhaps her mood had changed because she could see monuments in the cemetery on the hilltop between the trees. And the cuckoo bird, hiding somewhere behind the pond and calling "*cuckoo*" incessantly, made her feel sad.

Snow began falling slowly and stabbed at her frozen cheeks. As she brought the velvet collar of her coat close to her face, she remembered the black woolen coat that the Crown Rebbetzin wore. Woolen clothes are very nice, but the Rebbe's family was not permitted to wear them.[3]

When the sleigh reached the edge of the forest, the sky was partly blue, partly covered with cumulus clouds. From a distance, she heard the crack of a whip, the screeching of wheels, and the sounds of a boisterous conversation coming closer.

"It's undoubtedly a stagecoach from the district capital Radom," said the Rebbe's attendant, "perhaps Jews from the village Yalna?"

Straw-roofed cottages began to appear at a distance from the road. A bucket attached to a wooden pole rose and fell over a well. Neighing horses approached the well, followed by peasants wearing sheepskin coats.

"It's time to go back, Frank," said the Rebbe's attendant to the coachman who pulled on the reins and turned the horses around to the other side of the woods.

A wagon filled with hasidim emerged from the dense forest known as Sabbath Hill, entered the road, and drew near. The stillness of the cold air, basking in gently falling snow, was now broken with sounds of joyous exultation. White meadows, as if grasped by tongs of pine forest, receded behind the wagons. The clouds wrestled with each other, and the sun kept breaking out and hiding.

The *shochet*, seated among the passengers in the approaching wagon, called to the attendant in the sleigh, "Shlomo! The cold must have made you drowsy. We're coming to receive fruits from our Rebbe. This is a time of trouble for the Jewish people, may Heaven have mercy."

The villagers sat all bundled up in the wagon. Some of them were smiling because of the raucous conversation, snatches of which brought a cheerful expression even to the attendant's frozen face. The coachman cracked his whip in the air and the horses began galloping, leaving the slower villagers' wagon behind. The *shochet's* conversation still echoed through the frozen trees.

Bat-Zion was spending her time in thought, pondering the past and the present. She felt a strange jumble of emotions in her soul, echoes of all kinds of conversations. She sensed a longing for something, like those wondrous fruits. . . .

The sleigh sliding quickly over the snow brought her back, as did the streets of the town, which seemed to be waking up from slumber. Even the merchandise hanging from stores' doorposts in the wide marketplace—strings of coral, colored scarves, wool and cotton fabric—seemed to stir the frozen air to life. In the shops, men and women were busily conversing, trading with peasant girls who wore flowing, colored woolen dresses.

The village carts were spread out along the sides of the street, their harnessed horses eating fodder from bags at the end of their yokes. The passers-by looked invigorated, seeming to get pleasure from the steamy vapors rising from the dung under the carts.

On Magitowa Street conversations drifted through the air. Groups of people surrounded the synagogue, with its narrow windows looking outward.[4]

The sky was clearing. A lazy sun shone in a haze of pallid gold. When the sleigh returned home, children could still be heard shouting as they threw snowballs in the field behind the courtyards.

Hasidim streamed from the open courtyard to the closed inner courtyard by way of the small gate. The Rebbe's assistants and household members came from the upper and lower rooms of the wooden buildings at the end of the courtyard to the Rebbe's chambers by the footpath near the garden. The young birch trees in the garden in the corner of the courtyard stood bare and frozen between the ice-covered rows of fallen leaves. The reflection of the bronze sundial at the courtyard's center sparkled on its small white marble stand.

The Rebbe's room—dimly lit, filled from end to end—was bathed in silence. The beams of the low ceiling seemed to be listening mutely, and the double windowpanes watched with frozen, amazed eyes. The hasidim stood and listened. Bat-Zion glided on tiptoes behind the crowd, coming to the lit stove near the door of her mother the Rebbetzin's room. She saw her father the Rebbe sitting on his upholstered chair at the head of the table. His face, captured in thought, beamed steadily, his pure high forehead standing out under his sable *shtreimel*. Speaking the praises of *Eretz Yisra'el*, he drew endless inspiration as he gazed at the rectangular parcel filled with fruit, sparkling in its white wrapping on the polished black table.

His enchanting clear voice, ringing with spiritual rapture, broke the warm silence: "Every grain of *Eretz Yisra'el* is holy in many ways. And surely the fruit it produces is holy. The taste and fragrance of the fruit are hidden within, until the time comes for them to be revealed.[5] Every spiritually aware person can sense this even now."

The hasidim stood huddled together, trembling, listening with deepest concentration. Small fruits began pouring out of the parcel onto the table. The sound of the hard shells tumbling on tabletop resonated in the silent room.

"Now here's a count of fourteen, Da'i.[6] May God say *DAI*, Enough troubles! And here's a count of seventeen, *TOV*, Good!" The Rebbe's voice rang out again as he placed some of the fruits into his holy chest girded with brass bands, used to store sacred writings.

Bat-Zion stood in back of the crowd, beyond the lit stove, the Rebbe's holy chest staring at her. Its green sides, shielded by those brass bands, appeared to her as a wondrous plant kept in some interior chamber. The attendant entered quietly, tunneled through the crowd and placed on the table half a coconut containing seeds fried in rose honey. An air of serenity swept through the warm, dark room. The mood reminded her of twilight at the entry of Sabbath, when one could hear verses from The Song of Songs floating about: *"Your limbs are an orchard of pomegranates. . . . Nard and saffron, fragrant reed and cinnamon, with all aromatic woods . . ."*[7]

Bat-Zion was called to the table by her father, whose face, though smiling, bespoke pain. He said to her, "We once had saintly women: matriarchs, prophetesses, wise women. If you so desire, you can be like them."

He gave her almonds and some seeds. Bat-Zion kissed her father's hand, her fist squeezing the hard seeds. When she came to the threshold of the next room to kiss her mother's hand she detected concern on the Rebbetzin's gracious, radiant face. Her mother the Rebbetzin leaned down to her and said quietly, "Put some of them away, my daughter, for safekeeping."

CHAPTER

The Guests

The canary's sweet song poured into the bedroom, which was bathed in the morning's dim light. Doctor Hayyim had returned the bird to the girls' loft after having nursed it for weeks. Now restored to good health, she once again sounded her pure notes, which had become subdued with the onset of winter. The bird's song injected tangled feelings into young Bat-Zion's heart, pleasure and pain whirling in confusion.

Bat-Zion's eyelids were sleepy, her heart still caught up in the previous night's dreams. But though she closed her eyes, Bat-Zion didn't fall back asleep. For a long while she listened to those pure trills breaking through the room's hazy air, saturated in purple and green. She imagined them to be a song of praise to the Creator or perhaps a distressed soul's outpouring of prayer, yearning for deliverance. . . . In any event, the pulsations penetrated to the depths of her heart. Had she been the type of person who shed tears easily she would have wept profusely; but as it was, her emotions were sealed within her with no way to release them.

She had learned something about herself this year, now that she was twelve years old. A great change had taken place in her soul. Her wild mischievousness had dissipated; she was now more diligent in preparing her homework. She would even steal into her brothers' rooms and listen to their studying. But . . . she felt weighed down by the admonition of her mother the Rebbetzin and her father the Rebbe that, as a grown-up, she must pay attention to the way she conducts herself. And a hidden voice welled up continually from a place deep within her: "Now I've got to accomplish."[1] In dismay, she felt an urge to *do* something. She got off the bed and opened the shutters on the two double windows. A piercing cold penetrated her body. She began to dress quickly in warm clothing, enjoying the fresh smell of a new flannel blouse she was putting on.

She stood in front of the silver-framed mirror a number of moments, taking pleasure in the view of the room and its furniture whose reflection looked like a enchanted rose-colored dream. She listened to the breathing of her sleeping sisters wrapped in their warm cotton blankets, and she imagined that she was participating in their dream scenes. Even the pictures on the headboards of their iron beds—pictures of children playing on a riverbank—seemed to be whispering to her.

The cold wind bursting through the open shutters shook the leaves of the potted lemon tree. At that moment, even the wax fruits in the wicker basket on the mirror table seemed to be alive. While she felt guilty about having allowed the cold winter air to enter the bedroom, she nevertheless felt that she had accomplished something important by opening the shutters. It seemed as if a spirit of life were blowing into everything. After all, she had actually begun working on real projects this year, participating along with her older sisters in casting these wax fruits and other handicrafts. But still . . .

She began shaking the cage in order to wake up the bird whose song had suddenly gone silent, but just then old Nanny Sarah appeared at the threshold, wearing a red winter housecoat lined with cotton.

The nanny whispered a reprimand to her that she was likely to wake up her sisters, who had gone to bed late the night before. They had been sitting in their grandmother's room with her dear guests, Aunt Leahnu the Rebbetzin of Parchev and Aunt Feigenu

Rebbetzin of Grodzisk.[2] Both had arrived yesterday, having made the difficult trip from the Garbatka train station to the town of Kozienice.

Bat-Zion did not respond to Nanny Sarah. She remained standing some distance from the open window, watching the patches of clear blue breaking through the clouds as well as the rays of sun bursting forth from the eastern horizon and climbing up the top of the frost-drenched bare birch tree in the courtyard. It seemed to her that something was becoming clear to her as the semidarkness of early morning dispersed.

She was always happy when those dear guests came, from the family of her father the Rebbe and from the family of her mother the Rebbetzin, since the whole house would be filled with a festive air. But this time something was troubling her. She was speaking and acting with reserve around her aunt Rebbetzin Feigenu because her son, who was about Bat-Zion's age, was her intended, designated to be her groom. . . . On the surface, her aunt was paying no attention to her at all on this visit. The entire reason for the visit of her dear aunts to their brother the Rebbe Rabbi Yerahmiel Moshele was to influence him to pay attention to his health, which was being drained by his extreme, self-sacrificing commitment to every minor as well as major religious practice. Nevertheless . . .

For a long time Bat-Zion was not able to shake off her disturbing thoughts, even when she joined the house girls in dusting the rugs and her sisters in arranging the *objets d'art* and the embroidered wall hangings in honor of the guests. How much she longed to return to her childhood, to sit closed up in her play corner and to dream dreams about magic gardens in some distant future!

But the truth was that she was really growing up; and what was worse was that the dignified demeanor she was supposed to adopt still eluded her. She looked for a solution everywhere, in every glance of the eyes, but . . . How disturbing were those looks from other people! Recently, she noticed that men had begun to stare at her[3]—just for spite it seemed—and embarrassment overwhelmed her to the point of fainting.

That morning she prayed with a worried heart. Along with supplications for deliverance from all troubles, she added her own special prayer that Heaven might bestow upon her "something of the
wisdom of King Solomon and the grace of Queen Esther." She had
already been offering this prayer for several years, when she would
go with her mother the Rebbetzin and with the entire family to the
room of the Maggid their ancestor, whose holy presence still hovered there, even after a hundred years.

Against her will, tears fell on the pages of the small prayer book
she held in her hand, bound in a green velvet binding with carved
silver flowers. She had received this prayer book as a gift from her
aunt Rebbetzin Feigenu and her uncle Rabbi Yisraelnu, the Rebbe
of Grodzisk.[4]

As the nanny passed in front of her with logs in her arms for the
bedroom stove, she hid her head in the books of the small bookcase
so that the old woman would not notice her tears. When she disappeared, Bat-Zion resumed pouring out her soul in prayer. The
vapor emerging from her mouth seemed to form the shape of the
words of her supplication, "Please, God, grant me wisdom and
grace."[5] But then she had second thoughts, sensing a voice shouting from deep inside, *"How? How? Perhaps by a miracle? You are
praying for something impossible.[6] Your time is passing with nothing to
show for it, and you're being swept into adulthood."* As much as she
tried to remove profane thoughts from her heart, nevertheless she
was assailed by worrisome, alarming notions. Around this time,
she had begun to examine the source of those feelings with a sense
of curiosity bordering on the rebellious.

Her distress grew to the point that she started thinking about
death, about the time when the angels of destruction attack the
person on the obstacle path she must traverse when the soul leaves
the body. She found the verses after the *Shemoneh Esrei* prayer.[7]
With intense concentration, she recited the verses whose initial letter correspond to the first letter of each name respectively, and
whose last letter corresponds to the last letter of each name. When

she concluded the verse corresponding to the name Bat-Zion, *"Blessed is the Lord, God of Israel from eternity to eternity. Amen and Amen,"* [8] she was startled by the coarse voice of instructor Weiner.

"Taking so long to say your prayers?" called the instructor, their teacher for secular subjects. He was a native of Podolia who had wound up in this Polish town on the banks of the Vistula as a soldier in the tsar's army, and he still retained his distinctive regional pronunciation. He stopped talking immediately so as not to distract her from her prayers, tiptoed over to the large bookcase, took out a book and began examining it. After she had concluded her prayers, instructor Weiner turned to her and asked with suppressed laughter, "Where are Mademoiselle's notebooks? Mademoiselle's homework has started to improve."

Bat-Zion stood silently, without letting go of her small prayer book. The way he addressed her so respectfully wounded her deeply. This was an affected seriousness. He was mocking her, since she had only begun preparing lessons recently. But on the other hand, perhaps she was mistaken? This is a person without guile. Furthermore, his deferential manner toward her was nothing new: Since the beginning of studies this winter, he had begun addressing her with a title of respect, "Mademoiselle."[9] Had she really grown up that much?

But she didn't have much time to think about him, since her sister Hayyah Miriam'l had already sat down at the table and had begun presenting, in Russian, an oral summary of a story. Her heart pounded louder as she realized that her turn was coming, and she had not prepared her lessons well. One mustn't rely constantly on miracles, especially since she had given up this year on the hope that an angel would come in a dream and convey all branches of knowledge to her, as happened to righteous Joseph of the Bible.[10]

The instructor's bemused face brought her out of her consternation. His square chin shook as he chuckled, and his thick lips widened to his protruding jaws. He was always a bit cross-eyed, but now his eyes closed nearly shut. He got such pleasure out of listening that his hand slapped the brass buttons on his coat, with its red epaulettes. How good-hearted was this coarse-faced person!

Just as he took pleasure in his students' knowledge, in equal measure he pretended not to notice their errors. He would surely try not to cause her embarrassment.

She hoped that she wouldn't stumble; but as she read the Russian-language history book, she became so agitated that the letters got blurry, her hands trembled, and the voice that rang in her ears seemed that of a stranger.

Once she saw that instructor Weiner was sitting in silent attention without making any remarks, her confidence about the familiar story increased. This was the tale of the two children abandoned in a forest and suckled by a she-wolf, the founders of Rome. Now she remembered the story quite clearly, but then her heart got agitated again when her thoughts turned to the destruction of the Temple in Jerusalem by the Romans, an event that was mourned every year in the middle of the bright days of summer. Bat-Zion got stuck in her sad thoughts, sitting silently until her sister whispered in her ear, "Go on, for shame!" Smiling broadly, the teacher said, "What thoughts overtook my pupil? Please, I pray you, share them with us." Bat-Zion blushed and with an embarrassed stammer she conveyed the story, but it seemed to her that she got the details confused.

Nanny Sarah saved her from her embarrassment by carrying in a fragrant cup of coffee and fresh cakes, which she placed before the teacher, taking his mind off the lesson for a few moments. He hugged the steaming cup in his large hand, took frequent sips and looked at an arithmetic book that lay before him. Bat-Zion's mind had quieted down a bit, but the book in the teacher's hands instilled a kind of fear in her since she hated arithmetic exercises and had a hard time with them. She glanced impatiently at her sister who was completely focused on her arithmetic notebook, her head and her black braids bent over, hardly moving at all.

The logs that the nanny had added to the stove in the nearby bedroom caught fire, and warmth spread through the entire area. The rooms were gripped in a tense silence, until finally the door opened and the Rebbe entered, accompanied by the girls' melammed, Reb Aharon.

The warm silence in the room, with its four frost-covered windows, took on a life of its own, as if the room were listening to a cryptic voice carried aloft by the sound of books and tablets being leafed through and examined by the Rebbe.

The two young women stood at attention, not moving a hand or foot, waiting for the verdict. They were fearful that their father the Rebbe might find something inappropriate in their studies. Just one look of his shining eyes would be enough to cause deep pain, making one's heart tremble to its innermost parts.

Instructor Weiner strode cautiously toward the Rebbe and said with his distinctive pronunciation, standing straight at attention, "Honorable Rabbi, please forgive me, may I please explain, the book that his honorable daughters are studying from is only a history book and contains no trace of atheistic views."

"The Torah permits us to study the history of the world, as Scripture states, *'Remember the days of old, consider the years of ages past,'*[11] the Rebbe responded to the instructor warmly. After pausing a few moments, during which time his wide forehead was furrowed in thought, he continued, "the verse uses the word 'CONSIDER' (BINU') quite advisedly. For BINAH (discernment) is the foundation of our knowledge and the beginning of our efforts to understand the ways of God and to follow His path.[12] Just as He is compassionate to every people, every person, every creature, so must we be compassionate.[13] And with respect to the story you've read, my daughters"—he pointed to the Russian book—"your melammed Aharon surely taught you the rabbinic *aggadah* about when the city of Rome was built. You learn from this that when an Israelite sets himself apart, even if he is a king and wiser than any man, the result is destruction."

The face of Aharon the melammed, which had seemed frozen, now came to life with a smile of satisfaction. He said, "Yes, our Rebbe, I do believe I've read the rabbinic *aggadah* with them. When Solomon married Pharaoh's daughter, the angel Gabriel thrust a reed into the sea and from that, the great city of Rome was built.

My pupils surely remember." The two young women lowered their heads in embarrassment and their eyes, with a look both smiling and troubled, met at an angle. They had never learned the *aggadah* and the words of the melammed bewildered them. Aharon the melammed was absolutely not a liar, but his poverty was making him lose his bearings. Perhaps infirmity had affected his memory.

The melammed realized his error immediately and changed the subject by saying, "If we are permitted to learn the history of peoples, we may certainly learn natural history and the sciences. An essay was just published on Maimonides' *Laws of the Sanctification of the New Moon* in *He-Asif* by the scholar Slonimski."[14]

The Rebbe responded to Reb Aharon, "Regarding the scholar Slonimski, we've endeavored to have a discussion with Reb Noson the rabbi of Turov. He was my melammed when I was a child, and currently he is a rabbi in the holy city of Tiberias.[15] In our opinion, Slonimski is incorrect on the issue of establishing residency for seafarers. Furthermore, he made a serious error on the subject of calculation of distances from the equator."

"Nevertheless perhaps our Rebbe will permit one of my pupils to copy the essay, which I will then bring him. I would like to know his holiness's opinion of this essay."

After the Rebbe gave his consent, the melammed turned to Bat-Zion and said, "So you copy the essay, since you have beautiful penmanship."

Bat-Zion turned red from ear to ear. It seemed to her as if the room had turned completely dark. She would have hardly noticed her father's departure had something important not happened to rouse her.

Aunt Rebbetzin Feigenu entered the room after spending a short time in the outer room with Bat-Zion's mother—Feigenu's dear sister-in-law Brachanu—and with Feigenu's sister Rebbetzin Leahnu. As usual, they had been pouring out their hearts to each other. The Rebbe, who was already standing on the threshold of the half-open door, went back inside in joyous haste. He had abundant love for every human being, but his sisters received a double measure. Feige was his half-sister by the same mother. Feige's father, who had died around the time of her birth, was the Rebbe's step-father the tzaddik Rabbi Asher of Stolin, to whom the Rebbe had been deeply attached. So it was her esteemed brother who raised her, and she related to him as a daughter to a father.

When she kissed his hand in good-morning salutation, he responded with deep affection. In the course of a short conversation he gave her loving admonition,[16] making observations about the education of her firstborn son, who was designated to be his son-in-law:

"My wise brother-in-law[17] displayed his astuteness, now as always, by obtaining the services of Gedalyah as melammed for the household. Gedalyah has a clear, straightforward intellect and knows how to explain talmudic discussions in accordance with their plain sense, in contrast to Yerahmiel, the melammed who preceded him, who had a penchant for the dialectic casuistries of *pilpul*. Excessive *pilpul* is likely to weaken a child's tender mind; your child is blessed with great abilities and his development needs to be carefully nurtured. So my sister Feigenu, please don't insist on an overly severe education for your child. Don't push him to excessive diligence at his studies. His energies have already been sapped."

The cautionary words that her brother the Rebbe addressed to her were just the cue Rebbetzin Feigenu needed to address the painful issue that had prompted her visit in the first place.

"Please forgive me, dear brother, when it comes to pushing too hard no one comes close to you. Your sons spend day and night in the field of talmudic studies[18] and, with the exception of a short constitutional walk, they never get a breath of fresh air." Rebbetzin Feigenu had begun speaking with head lowered and a meek tone. But then she pulled herself up vigorously. Leaning on the back of the chair in front of her she continued in a voice filled with anguish, a tinge of redness covering her gaunt cheeks, "Now, my brother, may I be bold enough to comment on something that causes pain to all of us. I'm referring to your strictness with regard to yourself, which has already taken a severe toll on your health. How can you survive the way you drive yourself incessantly and your ascetic denial of life's necessities? It's incomprehensible."

She stopped talking and a deep silence filled the room. The ice melted on the two windowpanes facing east and sunlight burst in. It seemed as if the hidden anguish that had just emerged was penetrating everything in the room. Aharon the melammed felt a sting in his bluish face and instructor Weiner, whose back hid the bookcase, groaned involuntarily.

How sad things look in this room now, thought Bat-Zion, her heart heavy. *Even the longings of the leaves of the potted plants shining in the sun are anguished longings.*

After moments of deep silence, the Rebbe spoke in a hushed tone; his face, very pale, radiated an extra measure of splendor: "The human intellect would not exist but for the fact that there is something beyond it. As our ancestor the Maggid, his soul in Eden, interpreted the verse '*It is beyond my knowledge; it is a mystery; I cannot fathom it.*'[19]

"The fact that some humans allow their awareness to detach itself from God is incomprehensible to me. We know that there is no place void of the divine presence. Therefore, '*All this I tested with wisdom. I thought I could fathom it, but it eludes me*'[20]—that is, I don't understand how it is possible to leave the state of *devekut*, ecstatic communion with God, since common sense requires that we remain in communion with Him forever."[21]

When he finished his words he left the room quickly without looking at anyone, followed by the melammed and the instructor.

Rebbetzin Brachanu, who had been following the conversation from behind the door to learn what would come of it, entered the room, wiping her tears with the end of the muslin kerchief on her head so that no one would notice that she had been weeping. And her sister-in-law Rebbetzin Leahnu turned pale when she entered. She had been gathering her courage, preparing to speak strong words about her esteemed brother's neglect of his health, but now he had simply left.

The three sisters-in-law stood with their heads down in front of the table covered with a plush cloth, overcome by pain. For a short time they made no sound at all. The frozen tableau accentuated the graciousness of the three women.

Moments of quiet sadness always add a tender graciousness to Mother's radiant face when she furrows her brow in worry, Bat-Zion thought. *And then the dimple on her right cheek stands out even more prominently.*

And Aunt Leahnu, too: her mother would always admire her beauty, for Leahnu was not only her sister-in-law[22]—since Bat-Zion's mother was thirteen, when she married the Rebbe—but her friend as well, and her soul felt an intense love for her. Even now, her pale face looked so appealing with its dreamy blue dove eyes. And the hairpiece with its curled silk strands that she wore in place of the golden hair of her youth, suited her so well. What a pity those yellow spots caused by a blood deficiency detract from the beauty of her face. Bat-Zion's grandmother, the older Rebbetzin, said that the blood deficiency comes from her excessive piety, which causes her to disregard the advice of her doctors out of concern that she won't be able to fulfill the essential mitzvah that married woman must fulfill properly.[23] But this is kept a secret from unmarried girls.

And Aunt Rebbetzin Feigenu, who was not exceptionally beautiful, with an overly prominent aquiline nose, had fiery green eyes that bespoke intelligence and dynamism. She did not fear any man when standing up for principle, and she directed her house with exceptional strictness, in accord with family traditions, as her brother the Rebbe taught her, zealously insisting that every religious practice be observed meticulously.

Bat-Zion felt a shiver in her body as she thought about these things. She was happy that no one was paying attention to her as she leafed through the Russian history book she had been studying a short while ago.

The Rebbetzins sat down at the round table covered with a thick plush tablecloth, sighing but not saying a word. They couldn't bring themselves to talk about that most painful topic: the infirmity of the beloved Rebbe—brother and husband—because there was nothing they could do. Asceticism was in his blood, it was a family legacy. There had already been an argument yesterday behind closed doors when the expert physician from the district capital Radom had come, but they had made no headway.

The Rebbe had asked the doctor, a gentile, a general in the Russian army and a friend of the family from way back, if he thought of his health when he stayed up late going to theater or playing cards. "Why is it," he asked, "that people are only concerned about health when it comes to spiritual activities?"

After some minutes of stifled silence, Rebbetzin Leanu's voice was heard in the warm room, as if out of a dream: "What power do we have to influence him, if our dear mother fought with him in vain even when he was a still a little child? I remember how it was in the Kolodny estate—"

Before she was able to complete her sentence, the three of them were stirred, like a cool wind after a heat wave, by the mention of the Kolodny estate in Polesia, which the older Rebbetzin had purchased from an heir to the Polish throne. The young age of the three Rebbetzins was even more noticeable as their faces filled with a childlike joy. A lively and heated discussion ensued among them, as Nanny Sarah came in with a tray of apples from the nearby Strykowice estate.

"It's too bad we can't treat you, dear sisters-in-law, to apples like those produced by the soil of Kolodny," said Rebbetzin Brachanu, "but even these apples are not usually found in Poland. They come from trees whose saplings were brought by my mother-in-law, your dear mother, from Italy. But even these apples are no comparison to the ones in Kolodny."

She spoke her words with emotion as she peeled the apple's thin reddish yellow peel. The old nanny, who was taking in the apple's pleasing smell with each breath, blurted out, "And what could be better than this?"

"It's not just with respect to the fruits that Kolodny was superior to Strykowice, but also in its beauty and the joy that prevailed there. And it's no wonder. We were there as children," said Rebbetzin Feigenu. "Do you remember, my sister and sister-in-law, how you tried to chase after the doe that jumped from the woods and ran into the field behind the courtyard? I was dying to run after you, and if not for Zlotke the teacher who restrained me, I would have kept running thoughtlessly because I was very young, and I might have wound up with the wild beasts in the forest."

Her words rang with a pure, childlike laughter. Getting up from the upholstered chair, she hugged the shoulder of her sister-in-law and said, "Do you remember, Brachanu? Weren't you . . . ? At that time I think you were . . ."

"Don't hold back, Feigenu," said Rebbetzin Brachanu. "Indeed, I was nine months pregnant then. Movement is good at that stage of pregnancy. I was very young and I ran almost as fleetly as a doe. It seems to me that you, Leahnu, didn't catch up with me, even though you were younger than I. But you must have deliberately held yourself back for a reason."

"I'm amazed that you forgot, sister-in-law, the reason why I held myself back. The esteemed noblewoman Lady Strykowice, friend of our dear mother, suddenly appeared in her coach. You came back immediately as well, and the two of us welcomed her in front of the marble pillars of the girls' wing. She had come to invite us to the wedding of her son the prince, a young man of exceptional culture and refinement."

"You're right, Leahnu, I've had memory lapses recently. We were preparing to hold a soiree that day in their honor. And my mother-in-law, long may she live, put much thought and energy into planning the event since Lady Strykowice and her entire household were *hasidei umot ha-olam*, saintly gentiles."[24] She was silent for a number of moments, and after that she added, "Since we're on this topic, it's important to note that with all the grandeur and regal elegance that characterized my dear mother-in-law's house, she also instilled a spirit of profound piety that is rare for this generation."

Rebbetzin Brachanu moved her eyes to her daughters— who were sitting on the sofa and listening spellbound to the conversation—to caution them that worldly splendor and beauty were not the main things in life.

"And it's good that our dear mother brought Zlotke the teacher from Hungary. She was very devout," said Rebbetzin Feigenu, "even though she often read to us books in German by Schiller, like *Die Rauber* and *Die Jungfrau von Orleans*. Thanks are due our mother that she also employed a melammed for the girls' religious studies, so that we were not exclusively immersed in the literature of the nations."

She spoke very emotionally, and her sister-in-law Rebbetzin Brachanu discreetly added, "It's a good thing I was so young when I got married so that I could study together with you. As our rabbis put it, 'Studying Torah in one's youth is like writing with ink on fresh paper.'[25] And you, Feigenu, you were still a child, and you had the chance to learn much more, at the teacher's insistence. You were even required to know the Book of Daniel—of all books!—by heart; and good for you my sister-in-law, for as your honored brother has pointed out a number of times, women as well as men are rewarded for study of Torah."[26]

"Study of Torah always protects a person," Rebbetzin Leahnu joined the conversation, "while a mitzvah, a good deed, confers protection only at the time the person is engaged in its performance. Our rabbis mention this in the context of their discussion of mitzvot that women are obligated to perform.[27] The talmudic passage cites a parable: 'To what may this be compared . . .' "

She paused a moment, her dreamy eyes looking far away, as if she wanted to recall the continuation of the passage. Just then the Rebbe's third sister, Havvahnu, entered. She too had a reputation for scholarship but her manner was different from the others. She would go to bed late and get up late and took little part in daily events. Even though she was still wearing her long dressing gown with its long wide sleeves, her short physique—a characteristic she shared with her sisters—was clearly evident.

With all three sisters now standing, they rose just a bit higher than their sister-in-law the Rebbetzin Brachanu who had deliberately remained seated so as not to emphasize her tallness, lest they be chagrined by the contrast. Despite their differences in height these esteemed women blended well together because the sisterly spirit that prevailed among them imparted charm to them all. And in their velvet and silk clothing, which the guests were wearing in honor of their visit and which Rebbetzin Brachanu wore in honor of her guests, they appeared especially aristocratic, like on festival days. The only thing that made the picture less than perfect was sister Havvahnu's coiffure: The hairs of her wig were not yet combed properly.

"I see, Leahnu, that you've forgotten the words of our rabbis in the Talmud," Havvanu began in her distinctive accent. She was a Litvak, having been born to her mother, the older Rebbetzin, in Stolin of Polesia, and she maintained her pronunciation zealously. She was all set to continue the rabbinic parable that her sister had begun, but her sister-in-law gave her a peeled apple.

At that moment they remembered the apples, which had not yet been eaten. As they all bit in, the room was filled with a pleasing aroma.

This reminds me of Rosh Hashanah, when the blessing Shehecheyanu is recited over fruit, Bat-Zion thought as she sat snuggled up on the sofa. She took pleasure in the room's variety: the decorative items on the black varnished table in the corner, the potted trees on the tripod, and the apple peels on the table. But what lifted her spirits more than anything was the intensely festive expressions on the faces of the Rebbetzins. She was so taken by the mood that she forgot about her uneasiness associated with her aunt Feigenu. . . . Then her aunt Havvahnu returned to her sister's topic; and before she finished swallowing what was left of the juicy apple, she began quoting the rabbinic *aggadah*.

"Come, let's both recall the rabbinic parable," she said as she grasped the right hand of her sister the Rebbetzin, playing with the small fruit knife:

Rabbi Menahem son of Rabbi Jose expounded: *"For the commandment is a lamp, the teaching is a light."*[28] The verse identifies the commandment with a lamp and Torah with light. The commandment with a

lamp to tell you that as a lamp protects only temporarily, so the fulfillment of a commandment protects only temporarily; and Torah
with light to tell you that as light protects permanently, so Torah protects permanently. And it states, *"When you walk it will lead you; when
you lie down it will watch over you; and when you are awake, it will talk
with you."*[29] *"When you walk it will lead you"*: in this world; *"when you
lie down, it will watch over you"* : in death; *"and when you are awake, it
will talk with you"*: in the hereafter. A parable!

This may be compared to a man who is walking in the middle of
the night and darkness and is afraid of thorns, pits, thistles, wild
beasts, and robbers and also does not know which road he's traveling. If a lighted torch is prepared for him, he is saved from thorns,
pits, and thistles; but he is still afraid of wild beasts and robbers and
does not know which road he's traveling. When dawn breaks, he is
saved from wild beasts and robbers, but still does not know which
road he's traveling. When, however, he reaches the crossroads, he is
saved from everything.

Another point: A transgression cancels the merit of a commandment, but not the merit of study of Torah; as it is said, *"Many waters
cannot quench love, nor can the floods drown it; if a man would give all the
substance of his house for love, he would be utterly scorned."*[30]

Chanting the rabbinic *aggadah* to the end in the Talmud-study
chant, Havvahnu stood on tiptoes, as if stretching her exceptional
memory. At that moment Aharon the melammed entered, the thick
journal *He-asif* under his arm.

Silently he approached Bat-Zion who was sitting behind her two
older sisters on the couch, a small wool shawl draped on her
shoulders. She was surprised and terrified by the figure who had
emerged from the darkness and who now whispered in her ear to
follow him into the next room.

Bat-Zion placed her writing implements between the small wicker
baskets, with their lifelike wax fruit, and the other decorative items
on the mirror table and sat down to copy the journal article onto

Reb Aharon the melammed's long writing tablet, the kind he would use to write requests to the Russian authorities on behalf of the townspeople.

He leafed through the *He-asif* and pointed to the page she was to copy. "Here it is," said Reb Aharon. "Here is where the scholar Slonimski begins his essay on Maimonides, interpreting Maimonides in light of his own views."

She understood very little of what she was writing, but the canary's sprightly chirping in the green cage made the copying a more pleasant task. She had secret hopes that at this time the subject would come to her without studying; didn't she pray for realms of knowledge to be revealed to her miraculously?

Maimonides writes:

> All that we have said concerning the fixation of New Moon Days on the basis of observation of the new crescent, and concerning intercalation of the year because of the season or because of other reason of necessity, applies only to the Sanhedrin in *Eretz Yisra'el* or to a court ordained in *Eretz Yisra'el*, to whom the Sanhedrin had granted the authority to do so. . . . In times, however, when no Sanhedrin exists in *Eretz Yisra'el*, fixation of New Moon Days and intercalation of years are effected only by such methods of calculation as we use today. . . .[31]

Maimonides continues in the next chapter:

> The court would ascertain by calculation, and with great precision, according to the methods of the astronomers, the exact time of the (true) conjunction of the moon with the sun in order to find out whether the moon could be visible (on the night of the thirtieth day) or not. The first step in this calculation is the operation . . .[32]

Enchanted figures overwhelmed Bat-Zion's imagination. She saw the crescent moon in conjunction, there by the pond in the pine forest or there, far away in *Eretz Yisra'el* between the mountains where the Sanhedrin sat. She wrote diligently until she encountered numbers and calculations, which she despised. She began to feel dizzy; and as much as she attempted to be careful about her penmanship, the letters did not come out rounded as always. And

in particular, when she reached Slonimski's commentary she nearly twisted the words around.

As Aharon the melammed began examining the manuscript, a
dark cloud seemed to sweep over his bluish face. He pulled impatiently on his scraggly beard, speaking in bitterness, as if to himself,
"This is not what I expected! I had a different opinion of you! You
can't say this is bad handwriting but when writing matters of the
greatest importance, you should have been very careful. Good
handwriting is, after all, fundamental. You ought to understand,
my pupil, that these are the words of the 'Great Eagle,'
Maimonides; and the contemporary scholar Slonimski is also not
an ignoramus. Even though he is one of the *maskilim*, he should not
be dismissed with a stroke of the hand—"

Before he had a chance to finish his emotional remarks, her
mother the Rebbetzin came in to the room, accompanied by her
sisters-in-law.

"Reb Aharon is right. It's your responsibility, my daughter, to be
precise in your writing, especially since we're bringing it to your
honored father, long may he live," her mother the Rebbetzin said
as she took the tablet and showed it to her sisters-in-law.

Rebbetzin Leahnu approached Bat-Zion, who stood before the
melammed like an accused in the dock, tears gathering in her eyes.
Her aunt gave her cheek, already red, a light pinch. Wanting to let
her off the hook, she said in a consoling tone: "There's nothing to
be ashamed of, sweetheart, the handwriting is absolutely fine."

"You're right, sister," responded Rebbetzin Feigenu as she
peered at the tablet. "The writing isn't bad at all. It's not as precise
as Bat-Zion's hand when she wove my name and the name of my
husband—your honored uncle, long may he live—into verses
accompanying her Purim gift; but this is nice too."

While she spoke, her aunt the Rebbetzin did not look at the girl's
face, which was covered with embarrassment. Only after the
melammed left the room with the tablet and the journal in his hand
did she turn to her and say with feeling, "Look, Bat-Zion, I've
brought you a small gift. Please excuse me for forgetting to give it
to you until now."

She slipped a leather bag from the pocket of her velvet dress and took out a small gold pin inlaid with diamonds.

"You know the glitter of diamonds is superficial. We hope that the inner glow of good character will shine within your soul, young lady," she said with emotion and gave the pin to Bat-Zion, the daughter of her brother the Rebbe, pledged to her son from birth, with the actual betrothal ceremony to take place after the groom became bar mitzvah.

Bat-Zion kissed her aunt's hand, who was so moved that her pale cheeks flushed, giving her a youthful attractiveness. Her aunt was only thirty-two years old but her habits were those of a much older person.

When everyone had left the girls' residence and Bat-Zion was alone, her mind went over everything that had transpired in the course of the day, and her heart was filled to bursting. She paced between the strewn chairs and breathed in the mixture of aromas that had collected in the air. Along with the smell of fruit leftovers, of writing tablets and books, of tobacco and the cigar butt that her father the Rebbe had left,[33] one could still hear reverberations of the recent conversations, conversations laden with suffering, virtue, and abiding joy.

The glitter of the little diamonds in the small golden pin refracted in the silver-framed mirror as she passed nearby. She stood a while as if in a stupor. "Glitter is superficial; but an inner glow must shine in your soul," her aunt Feigenu had said. Indeed, everything here was nurturing her insides until there was no more room. Yet . . . she was drawn to the reflection gazing at her from the mirror. She stared at herself and her surroundings. In that image, everything was properly formed. She was getting more and more mature. Tears choked her throat, and she returned to the bedroom. She flung herself on the bed, as tangled emotions of fear and confidence coursed through her soul.

CHAPTER

Grandmother's Tale

Translator's Note: This chapter highlights the role of the older Rebbetzin, Sarah Devorah Shapiro (Bat-Zion's grandmother) as the true head of the family. She is the force behind the project to rebuild the family mansion lost in a fire around 1900. She is deeply concerned about her son's health; and in line with the medical thinking of the day, she is worried that the low ceilings and consequent poor ventilation in her son's current residence are damaging his health. (Her concern gains poignancy when we note that in actual fact, her son died in 1909, a few years after the time in which this story is set. Sarah Devorah survived her son for over a decade; she lived through World War I and died in 1921.)

But her interest in the family house has a symbolic element as well. Sarah Devorah is the family member most concerned with the continuity and preservation of the Hapstein and Shapiro lineage, the hasidic house of Kozienice. She is the guardian of family memories and transmitter of sacred traditions. This chapter highlights these roles, as she tells a story that spans several generations and returns to her own childhood.

As we go back in time, we are also presented with several concatenations of story within story. The narrator begins in Kozienice around 1905, with a scene that includes Sarah Devorah, her son the Rebbe Rabbi Yerahmiel Moshe, and a group of hasidic intimates. Then Sarah Devorah begins telling her story, which takes us back to an incident from her early childhood (c. 1848–1849, when she was four or five years old). She recounts a tale she heard about a journey from Kozienice to Mogielnica, an encounter with Elijah the prophet, and a message that was transmitted to her grandfather Rabbi Hayyim Meir Yehiel Shapiro of Mogielnica. At a later point, the message is transferred to her father, Rabbi Elimelekh Shapiro of Grodzisk, and finally to Sarah Devorah herself.

Periodically, the narrator moves forward, returning to 1905 and the scene of Sarah Devorah telling her story to her son and the assembled hasidim. To help the reader follow the various time periods and story levels, I have indented the story within story and then return to full lines whenever the text reverts to the "narrative present"—1905. As mentioned, most of the story within story takes place in 1848 or 1849; the last part, which moves from the era of Sarah Devorah's grandfather to that of her father, takes place in 1860.

In the evening, a delegation of staunch friends of the family entered the private rooms of the inner courtyard to persuade the Rebbe Rabbi Yerahmiel Moshe, may his light shine, to support the hasidim in their efforts to rebuild his house, a project that had dragged on for many years and had made no progress at all. The delegation was composed of veteran hasidim as well as wealthy visitors who had come by sleigh to Kozienice and had spent some time at the court. Ordinary householders on the building committee, such as Reb Heshel, did not go in; it was assumed that the Rebbe would undoubtedly reject their advice, since "the sensibility of householders is the opposite of Torah sensibility."[1]

A sacred silence prevailed in that room, illumined by two candles in silver candlesticks resting on the table. The candles sputtered softly, hinting at secrets held in the tall bookcases, which reached to the ceiling beams. There was a knowing smile on the Rebbe's face , as if he had anticipated their arguments and was set to refute them all. Only old Reb Moshe the ben-tovim and the old Rabbi Reb Hirsheleh were seated at the table. The wealthy hasidim stood hunched over, listening intently.

"Even our Rebbe is obligated to fulfill the verse '*For your own sake, therefore, be most careful,*' "[2] began Reb Moshe, his white-bearded face reddening. "These low ceilings are harmful to health. The wealthy hasidim (no Evil Eye!) have already made their contributions. This is truly a worthy charitable cause. The Rebbe must give the word. Instead of—" He stopped in embarrassment, not daring to continue his thought that the Rebbe must give the word for the monies to be directed toward building his house, for that was the intention of the donors, and he should not disburse them for other charities.

The Rebbe put a small booklet inside the book he was perusing while Reb Moshe spoke, closed the book, and said emphatically, "When it comes to this mitzvah of preserving our physical well-being, we overdo it. Didn't my step-grandfather, the author of *Bet Aharon*, give a hasidic interpretation of Maimonides' second principle of faith: 'The Creator . . . is not affected by physical phenomena.' Rabbi Aharon taught that whoever grasps physicality cannot grasp the Blessed Holy One."[3]

"Our Rebbe is the light of our eyes and the breath of our nostrils. We beg him to please have mercy and attend to his health and vitality, which is our own vitality!" The entreaty erupted from the old Rabbi of Apta, tears choking his throat.

The Rebbe gently responded, "Vitality comes to a person from his desire to realize the will of his Maker, for that is the source whence our lives come. So the individual must suffice with the minutest amount to sustain his physical existence, if Heaven has not blessed him with more."

"If Heaven has not blessed him with more, our Rebbe says," Velvele, the fund-raising emissary for *Eretz Yisra'el* now joined in, jumping forward from the standing hasidim. "Here's Reb Bunem." He pointed to a tall, wealthy man who stood leaning on the shoulder of Reb Hayyim Wolf, a textile factory owner. He was wearing an ermine fur coat but was nevertheless shivering as if from a feverish chill, and his face seemed weighed down with burdens. "They'll contribute thousands more to improve our Rebbe's health."

"That goes for all of us," Reb Noah the flour mill owner stammered quietly. "All of us will dig into our pockets and the house will rise. All of us, young and old."

"Scripture says 'young and old, they were smitten with blindness,'"[4] the Rebbe addressed the group with a smile. "This verse can be interpreted to refer not only to wicked sinners, God forbid, but to people in general. There are partitions in front of people's eyes that mask the truth. There is much repair work to be done before we consider building new houses. The time is short, very short."

The Rebbe concluded his words with a sigh, and his mother, Rebbetzin Sarah Devorahleh, who was standing on the threshold of the door near the bedroom following the course of the conversation to see if anything productive would come of it, hurried impatiently to her son the Rebbe's armchair as those standing made way for her.

"My son," she said bitterly, "man was created with a body and it is impossible to live on sacred intentions alone. After all is said and done, you must preserve your health in order for you to survive until such time as—It's within your power, son, to bring us to that time—to the final redemption. Even your holy ancestors testified to this."

The Rebbetzin stopped talking and sat down on the chair that her son the Rebbe had brought her. Her thick eyebrows met in her wrinkled forehead; on her chiseled face were inscribed bitterness and pain. Once again she rose and pressed her short fingers on the table, whose polished surface reflected the candle flames. The shadows of the twelve standing and seated individuals made the dimly lit room appear to be filled with people.

Her robust voice, filled with anguish, broke the heavy silence.

"Listen, my son, let me tell you what I saw with my own eyes and heard with my ears," the Rebbetzin began telling her story.

In those days, the hasidim were accustomed to go by foot[5] to visit the great tzaddikim of the generation. A group of hasidim left Kozienice, in order to reach Mogielnica[6] in time for the Sabbath of *Selichot*. Their journey was blessed with providential guidance, for the group lost its way in the forest; and in those days, the forests were home for beasts of prey as well as robbers who hid and lay in wait for passersby. The forests were thick; this was before the time that lumber merchants had begun intensive harvesting of trees in order to send timber downriver by raft. When the members of this group reached the court of my holy grandfather, they were bundled up against the cold, their clothes were rain soaked, and they were tired and weary, but their spirits were upbeat. In a buoyant mood, they told about their adventures and, in particular, about the time when one of the group disappeared, a hasid known simply as Reb Bereleh. Now he was back with his friends, but did not utter a word.

Between the afternoon and evening services, when the Mogielnica court was filled with the hazy, weepy atmosphere of the days of repentance and mercy, the foot-traveling hasidim sat on a long bench in the back of a large wooden shed that had been set up for the High Holiday crowd and told their stories to the hasidim in their *tallitot*, preparing for the *Selichot* service. The wind whistled, lightning clapped, and raindrops fell from the clouds making their way in haste, as was appropriate for nights of divine service. The stars had already appeared quietly between patches of red clouds, like the eyes of an accused being brought to the dock. One hasid began telling the story, his voice instilling a spirit of faith in the hearts of his listeners:

"We left the town of Kozienice,[7] nestled in the midst of the forests, by the highway. Kozienice was where our holy Rebbe was born,[8] and in Kozienice stood the cradle of his mother the tzaddeket, the Maggid's daughter.[9] We rejoiced in the feeling that we were emissaries on a sacred mission. We were brave pilgrims walking in reverence to greet our Sovereign. We knew the forest trails well; their rustling trees sent us their aromatic resins and their birds sang hymns that united with our prayers. Even the armed forest guards greeted us warmly and no brazen dogs barked. The woods came and went, separated by huts and fruit trees, with empty meadows casting a benign eye upon us. Peasants drawing water from wells gave us their blessing, which we took to be a favorable portent. The words of the blessing were no doubt put in their mouths from Heaven. Surely a year of blessing is in store for us.

"We continued our way in a joyous mood, receiving with love the blessed rain as well as the blazing rays of the late summer sun. We reached that dense forest that our wealthy brothers in the city purchased from Polish magnates.[10] Perhaps this was the forest belonging to the distinguished Madame Temerel,[11] since there were business clerks dressed in small *tallitot*—their tzitzit hanging down to their knees—holding discussions with Germans, while Germans and Poles loaded logs onto wagons. The sky had already turned cloudy. Wrapped in a steely gauze, the sun set in the west; the loggers attacked the oaks with saws, chopping away with their axes. About twelve sweating, bareheaded men were cutting branches from a tall ancient linden tree and removing its roots. While this was going on, we were busy with thoughts of our sacred mission, gazing at the wonders of God's creation, at the edenic variety of multicolored birds and the granaries of ants accumulating their provisions in the summer, hidden in mounds of tree roots.

"Not knowing the clerks who were busy arranging the transport of the timber, we waited in silence until they would finish their mundane activities and begin praying, at which time we intended to join their service. But suddenly calamity struck! Robbers attacked us, with arrows and bullets flying about. The loggers ceased working and grabbed their axes as weapons, while the guards shot their guns at the approaching gang of armed robbers.

"Terrified, we began running away from the battle together with the hasidim. Arm in arm we ran until the road became more and more difficult to follow. Eventually, we found ourselves in a thick forest with no idea how to get out. As the sun slipped into its sheath of twilight and the oak and linden treetops caressing the sky took on a red cast, we offered the afternoon prayer with distraught, broken hearts. The prayer leader was reciting the *Kaddish* when a voice roared out from afar. Hidden somewhere behind us, it boomed the congregational response, '*Amen Yehe Shemey Rabah*,' 'Amen, may His great Name . . .'

"Could it be that in that forest, with its primeval trees that rose to the very Heavens, we'd reached the ancient kingdom of David and Solomon? Or perhaps after the destruction of the Holy Temple in Jerusalem, the Jews wandered until they reached those forests, finally settling there in the Kingdom of Poland, and it was the voices of those Jews that we heard?

"Those were the kinds of ideas going through our minds. And even though we were terrified by the sound of beasts growling, getting louder and closer, we strove to keep our focus on the pilgrimage. So as we walked cautiously along, seeking a safe haven for the night, we jousted each other with halakhic arguments and discussed hasidic teachings, trusting that the Blessed Holy One would save us from wild beasts and robbers. We studied Mishnah by heart and offered the evening prayer as deep darkness settled over us. Brief incandescent flashes glowed and disappeared, probably the gleam in the eyes of wolves that were common in those forests. Or perhaps the stars' twinkling had penetrated the thick branches. Or maybe something Not Good was sent by the devil himself to frighten us, for we heard a humanlike voice and powerful wild laughter that rang like a thunderclap.

"With all this, we put our faith firmly in Heaven. We came to the hollow trunk of a large tree, big enough to hold a number of people. The nimble among us climbed up the tangled branches in order to hide from the beasts of prey.

"Now a storm hit, a fierce wind blew, the forest roared and raged. Our tree trunk, with its many branches, was on the verge of overturning and we were at the edge of catastrophe. Thunder shook the whole world, and bolts of lightning struck the trees. The Heavenly chambers opened and a deluge of water surged earthward.

"Suddenly out of the thunderstorm and the flood of water, melodies from *Selichot* rang out, a choir like the choirs of our Rebbe the Seraph of Mogielnica. We broke out in weeping and began to join with the choir, our voices emerging willy-nilly: '*The soul is Yours, and the body too, have compassion upon Your work. . . .*' Then all of a sudden we heard the sounds of instruments, sweet notes as if from a virtuoso violin, and, along with them, what sounded like a voice quietly calling the name 'Bereleh.' We looked around and a silvery, radiant light blinded our eyes. The forest, trees, and branches all lit up; streams of water swept down from a tall mountain, as if the fabled River of Light[12] was flooding its banks. Then the light faded, and we noticed that the moon had come up. It was hanging between the clouds spread over the mountains, beyond the streams of water. We gathered together again, counted our men and discovered that our Bereleh was missing. We were quite astounded, but—"

The storyteller stopped to take a breath, and all the members of the group joined in jokingly, "But our Bereleh had gone to see Elijah the Prophet."

The Rebbetzin adjusted the muslin veil covering her embroidered hairpiece, pulled hairs from her eyebrows that ran into each other, and turned to her audience listening in attentive silence. "I am telling this to you so that the truth of these miraculous events associated with my ancestors, the tzaddikim of their generation—that I saw with my own eyes—will be passed down from generation to generation."

I was a little girl then, just five years old. I was standing in the corridor at the entrance to the wooden shed, which was lit with oil lamps. As I listened to the story, I watched Bereleh, a shriveled fellow who was sitting next to the narrator, his head resting on his knees as if he were fast asleep, not hearing a word. He didn't even respond to the jokes. Just then a door to one of the inner rooms opened in the corridor and my holy grandfather appeared at the threshold and called out, "Bereleh." The members of the group rose hastily, respectfully moving toward the open door, stretching out their hands to greet my holy grandfather. But only Bereleh was ushered inside.

I slipped in along with this fellow, who had just arrived from a journey filled with wonderful adventures. I entered the inner sanctum, the room I loved so much. That simple room, with its lone armchair, its canopy bed, and its many books—its mysteries attracted me. I saw the souls of our holy ancestors hiding in that room. I hid myself behind the armchair and, filled with trembling, listened in on the conversation. Trying not to attract attention, I didn't move from that spot even though the tone of my grandfather's hushed voice, his face shining like an angel of God, struck terror in me.

"Nu, what message did they give you," my grandfather addressed the shriveled, frail hasid who was simply called Bereleh, standing before him bent over, speaking quietly as if in confession.

"What can I say? This humble hasid heard a voice calling me by name. My comrades disappeared, and I was carried as if on the wings of the wind, finding myself standing at the edge of a burning river rocked by waves of fire. And I saw a human figure wrapped in a mantle, rising from the reeds of the stream up the slope of the tall mountain, where the moon was shining anew in full splendor. 'Pay attention, Bereleh, and I will tell you when.' A sweet and pleasant voice emerged, spreading through all my limbs until I shook uncontrollably and lost my breath. 'Pay attention so that you may deliver the message to your Rebbe, while there is yet time. . . .

"And Israel is destined to be renewed. . . ."[13]

The Rebbetzin stopped speaking and sat down in the armchair, exhausted. Then she rose again, looking at her son the Rebbe's face that had turned very white. The candles had burned low and were sputtering softly. The hasidim stood in silence, sighing, their bearded faces on edge. The only one to rise was Reb Moshe, speaking excitedly. "Rebbetzin, I knew Bereleh, the upright man who had a vision of Elijah." He stopped talking immediately, and the Rebbetzin continued with her story.

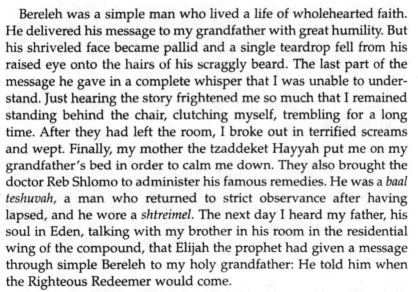

Bereleh was a simple man who lived a life of wholehearted faith. He delivered his message to my grandfather with great humility. But his shriveled face became pallid and a single teardrop fell from his raised eye onto the hairs of his scraggly beard. The last part of the message he gave in a complete whisper that I was unable to understand. Just hearing the story frightened me so much that I remained standing behind the chair, clutching myself, trembling for a long time. After they had left the room, I broke out in terrified screams and wept. Finally, my mother the tzaddeket Hayyah put me on my grandfather's bed in order to calm me down. They also brought the doctor Reb Shlomo to administer his famous remedies. He was a *baal teshuvah*, a man who returned to strict observance after having lapsed, and he wore a *shtreimel*. The next day I heard my father, his soul in Eden, talking with my brother in his room in the residential wing of the compound, that Elijah the prophet had given a message through simple Bereleh to my holy grandfather: He told him when the Righteous Redeemer would come.

The news also traveled to the hasidim encamped in the courtyards, who were offering their petitionary prayers in this period of repentance and mercy. Now the pilgrims stopped joking about the disappearance of their shy comrade. Instead they spoke in anguished tones about how they found him lifeless on the bank of the river that had become calm at dawn, its waters flowing placidly.

The religious awakening was so great then in the holy courtyards that along with the windswept rustling of the solitary oak tree's leaves by the gate, people's hearts were shaking as well. Everyone's eyes looked expectantly above and below, across the road, where the peasants' hay wagons passed by, ponies running ahead of them. Maybe he would come as a humble man riding on an ass.[14] Or perhaps he would come out of the gray clouds colliding above, sending their thunder and lightning; a pillar of cloud would suddenly descend, and our righteous Messiah would emerge from it.

But within the Inner Sanctum, divine service went on as before, and the tones of my grandfather's voice leading the prayers and supplications continued to ascend from the synagogue, piercing the heavens. At that time, I hid myself in the pumpkin patch beyond my parents' residence; and, without permission, I ran with my girlfriends to predawn services. The air was cold and an annoying rain poured down, but we children were not deterred; we wanted to see the Messiah. We ran breathless till we were caught by the kitchen staff, who had also left their work when they heard the sound of the shofar emerging from the synagogue; but they brought us back to our parents' house. After many years, I came to find out that a bit of that conversation was revealed to my father of blessed memory, and that he was keeping track of the year predicted for the End.

The older Rebbetzin stopped talking, and the silence in the room intensified. Stepping on tiptoes, the attendant brought in lit candles and placed them in the melted tallow, reviving the flame in the silver candlesticks. Those present watched the Rebbe, who took a white hair that had fallen out of his pure beard, opened a book of the Zohar, looked for a number of moments at a passage that spoke of the mystery of the final redemption, placed the hair in the book, and closed it.[15] He continued sitting in silence, his tall forehead knotted in anguish and his penetrating eyes gazing ahead into the dreamy air filled with vapor emerging from the gaping mouths of the listeners.

The Rebbetzin rose again and addressed the group's elders, "Do you perhaps remember what once happened on *Parashat Bo'*?"[16]

"I believe it was on *Parashat Bo'* that the Rebbetzin's father, the tzaddik Reb Elimelekh—may his merit protect us!—would generally come to Kozienice from his home in Grodzisk, after he had been appointed head of the rabbinic court of the town. He presided in Kozienice after the passing of his father, the Seraph of Mogielnica,"[17] said the attendant Yashkar-Ber, a native of Grodzisk, who was about to leave the room.

"That is indeed when it took place."

Wednesday night, my father, his righteous memory a blessing, reached the town at a late hour with his entourage. Snow had covered the roads, and the wagons dragged off-road through the forests until late at night. The frozen hasidim hurried to the lit stove in the *beit midrash*, little icicles hanging from their beards, asking for something hot to drink; but my father, his soul in Eden, stood on the threshold of the *beit midrash*, wrapped in a fur coat, with the cane of my ancestor the Rebbe Reb Elimelekh of Lyzhansk in his hand, and asked the people who had come to greet him, "Nu, how is Bereleh?"

He would ask this question every year when he would come to Kozienice during the week of *Parashat Bo'*. But this time he received the answer that Bereleh was lying on his sickbed. My father ordered that Bereleh be brought to him on his bed, and messengers left in haste to Bereleh's house.

The messengers arrived at the sick man's house and carried him in his bed to the door of the *beit midrash*. Quickly, my father brought him to the Maggid's room, and he was closed up with him there for a long time. After they brought Bereleh back to his house, my father went to the suite that had been prepared for him. His face was radiant but he was silent and did not respond to questions from his intimates.

The next day, Bereleh passed away. Crowds came to his funeral, as if he had been one of the great figures of his time. And since my father and the hasidim accompanied the bier to the cemetery, the entire town turned out for the procession, and all the houses closed their shutters. People even said that Bereleh, that upstanding man, must have been one of the thirty-six righteous of the generation,[18] for the sky became overcast with heavy clouds during the procession, darkening the face of the earth. And the sound of weeping rose up from all corners of the town, and no one knew the source of the weeping. But my father said nothing more about Bereleh, and no one dared to question him on the topic.

Then came the year 5620 [1860], whose Hebrew letters can be rearranged to spell *KETER*, "crown." Many great rabbis of the day thought that the year would be the time of the messianic advent, and wherever Jews lived, there was an awakening to prepare for the coming redemption.[19] And people even felt that all the signs pointing to the coming of the Messiah had been fulfilled, for there was a popular tradition to the effect that "if the coachman of the king of Turkey should come to Mogielnica in Poland and would tie the reins of his horse to the well-post in town, then you may expect the Messiah."

Now that year, the Russian army of the tyrant Nicholas brought Turkish prisoners to Poland after the battle of Sevastopol, and the streets of Mogielnica were filled with them. Despite the fact that the prisoners came bedraggled, barefoot, and hungry—not riding on horses—people's hearts nevertheless pulsed in hope that this was indeed the sign. The distinguished Madame Temerel was still alive at that time and even she, a devoted hasidah of the house of Mogielnica, sent couriers to my father with various questions, one of which was whether she should continue sending timber shipments by barge up the Vistula to Danzig. And factory owners turned to him with questions about their businesses, all of which he answered by saying that the year would be a year like all others, with no difference.

Only then did I gather my courage and dare to plead with my holy father to reveal to me the truth about the talk in the community: that his closed-door conversation in the Maggid's room with Bereleh before the latter's death had been fruitful and that my father indeed knew the time of redemption.

After a long silence, he turned to me and said: "You've hit upon the truth, my daughter. According to the little I heard of that conversation from the next room, Bereleh was obliged to transmit the things revealed to him to one of my holy father's children before he died. That's why I looked forward to my annual visit to Kozienice, thinking each year that it might be the auspicious time. When I heard that Bereleh was ill, I hurried to speak with him. So now I tell you that this year is not the year of redemption. Perhaps in the time of your grandchildren. And that's why I am trying to dispel this belief from the heart of every Jew, so that no one might come, God forbid, to lose their faith in the aftermath of disappointment."

"Really, Father!" I cried out bitterly.

And he answered me: "We are referring, of course, to the scheduled date for the messianic advent. Now is not the time preordained for the End of Days. But the Talmud also allows for the possibility of a hastened redemption.[20] In view of that possibility, every day is a redemptive moment if the generation be worthy, due to the tzaddikim in its midst. And God has graced you with a precious possession—this son, who has the power to bring the redemption closer."

"And so, Moshenu, you have the responsibility to guard your health with great care, so that you may persevere and bring our redemption closer. A spacious residence is a necessity for you, according to what the Russian physician told me," said the Rebbetzin summarily, in a critical voice.

Rising from his leather armchair, a bitter smile on his pale face, her son the Rebbe replied, "What Mother wants me to do is self-contradictory: to aim for physical comfort and to bring the redemption closer. The way to redemption is filled with obstacles. Redemption is rooted in self-sacrifice; there is good reason why our sages had so much to say about the birth pangs of the Messiah.[21] The supernal root of redemption is present in all our material activities such as eating, drinking, and sleeping; so when we are engaged in these material activities we must dig deep to find that root, and this involves suffering."

He paused with a sigh, turned to the wealthy hasidim standing around his armchair and said, "If every one of us would understand this, if we would perform the necessary mundane activities of our lives with faithfulness and integrity, and—even more essential—we would show the same integrity in our business transactions, then the way before us would be clear. We would then make a shortcut in the forests of the exile that are filled with wild beasts and brigands and would arrive redeemed at our holy mountain." The Rebbe fell silent, standing deep in thought; and his mother the Rebbetzin was also silent, the furrows of her forehead deepening.

113

The silence was so profound that only the whistling of the wind outside filled the room's dark space. The stove radiated more warmth. Finally the Rebbetzin got up to leave, fastening the button of her velvet coat. Standing in front of the open door, she turned her head, covered with a muslin veil, to her son the Rebbe who was escorting her and said, "You're right, Moshenu, in what you said that we'll make a shortcut in the forests of the exile. That reminds me of the story I was told by an old hasid who knew the Maggid: A band of thieves that was terrorizing travelers once appeared before our ancestor the Maggid, his soul in Eden. They said they knew a path by way of caves and tunnels leading from Kozienice to *Eretz Yisra'el*, and that the journey would take only twelve hours. They offered to show him the way in the hope that this would atone for their deeds, but the Maggid didn't listen to them because they were thieves."

For a number of moments, the cold wind rushed into the room, and the hasidim who had crowded close to the door in order to listen forgot about their mission for the evening. They straightened out their coats and tied their warm scarves around their necks, as if they were all set to make their way to *Eretz Yisra'el*.

Preparing for Passover

Bat-Zion had followed the conversation with intense anxiety as she sat behind the curtain in her mother's darkened bedroom. She enjoyed her grandmother the Rebbetzin's story, but in the end when the discussions about building the house had concluded in disappointment she was overcome by feelings of despair and rebelliousness. She went out the back door without anyone noticing and ran around for a long time in the dark courtyard without a coat until her teeth chattered from the cold of the night. She came to the outer rooms, where a spirit of exasperation prevailed, since hopes for the quick completion of the new building had come to naught. It was painful to look at her mother the Rebbetzin's face, with dejection written on the furrows between her brown eyebrows and on her pointed chin that had widened a bit as she pressed her lips tightly together.

As for her grandmother, she dared not approach her at all, for in her irritation any small thing was likely to set her off. Her grandmother's small lithe figure ran about hurriedly from her own room to the dining room and from there to the kitchens and back, again and again, all the while giving various orders that had no relation to what was really bothering her. Her charitableness came out at this time more than ever. There was the fine material that had been set aside for summer dresses for the girls, which she now sent to the girls of bnei-tovim families in town. And when the greengrocer came to collect money for the beets and potatoes that had been stored in the ground since the previous summer for Passover, she sent him to her daughter-in-law the younger Rebbetzin Brachaleh, despite the fact that the latter had surrendered all authority over household affairs to her mother-in-law, out of filial respect. The only thing that dispelled the tension a bit was the jovial voice of the Rebbe's personal assistant, who had remained in the courtyard after the members of the delegation had returned to their lodging at a private home or the *beit midrash:* "God has many worlds both here and in the afterlife, worlds of rage and of joy."

Bat-Zion went by herself to her father's residence to say good night, despite the rule prohibiting the children from going out alone at night. For a short while she stood, lips pursed and silent, by the lit stove. Even though her esteem for her father the Rebbe was beyond description, she was now irate and a blazing teardrop fell upon her palm. This was a tear of anger laced with stinging pain, for her dreams of witnessing the grandeur of the new house and to experience again the pleasures of that old cherished house that had gone up in flames were coming to naught. As that horrible event receded into the past, the sweetness of her memories filled her soul more intensely. In order to get her mind off her anguish, which bordered on physical pain, she began thinking about the amazing tale that grandmother had told a while ago. Soon she was absorbed in trekking through that forest where Elijah had revealed himself.

Her father the Rebbe was leaning over the table immersed in a sacred book, in his usual practice of studying while standing. It seemed to Bat-Zion that he had not noticed her at all, and she was delighted that she could be alone with her thoughts. She had a boundless love for Elijah the prophet, whom she had seen in her childhood imagination in various guises. It was he who was the hidden visitor at the Passover Seder. He appeared to the poor and unfortunate in bustling marketplaces, helping them out in their moment of distress. And the time was coming soon when the sound of his great shofar would fill the entire world with the tidings of the Messiah. A number of times she had seen Elijah the prophet in a dream, wrapped in his cloak, standing on scaffolding and building the house of the "pious man" from the traditional melody sung in honor of the departing Sabbath.[1] In the course of Saturday night, the house rose to completion.

The stove continued radiating heat. Her entire body was covered with sweat, and it became hard for her to remain standing; but she was afraid to move from her spot. She now realized that her father was deliberately averting his eyes from her. Undoubtedly, he must have sensed her grumblings or perhaps he had found some other fault in her.

She stood anxiously and listened to the silence weighing upon the darkened room filled with secrets. Suddenly she was startled by the voice of her father the Rebbe, "Where did you get the idea that you had permission to go out alone at night?" Amazed that her father discovered that she had come without an escort, she stood there in deep embarrassment, not able to utter a word. After a number of moments she began walking with head bent to the other side of the table, watching her long shadow move on the polished wood floor. "Scripture states *'Let your camp be holy'*[2] and in order not to cause a breach of propriety, an individual must always be on guard. Promise that you will be careful from now on not to go out alone."

As always, the deep warm tone of his words evoked in her respect and awe, but this time there was also a feeling of rebelliousness emerging from a place of bitterness in the recesses of her soul.

She knew that her face was red and covered with tears but she raised her head high and burst out in a trembling voice: "May Father forgive me, but had the new house—with all rooms adjacent—been finished, there would be no need to grope in the dark through the courtyards from one residence to another." Startled by her own voice and by the fact that her father the Rebbe's face had turned white, she once again bent her head and stood motionless. The silence intensified, as if demanding a response to her father's request. Finally she said emphatically, "I cannot give my word to my honored father, because I will not be able to keep it."

117

"It's good that you're saying the truth, my daughter. Someone who accustoms himself to lie, God forbid, severs the bond between himself and his Father in Heaven, and his path in life begins to fall into disarray." He said these words in an encouraging tone as he extended his hand for the good-night salutation. As Bat-Zion kissed the hand of her father the Rebbe, her heart was filled with regret that she had disobeyed and caused him distress. The encouraging tone along with the smile on his radiant face penetrated deep into her soul, and when she returned to the girls' loft, accompanied by Nanny Sarah, she felt a heaviness of heart such as she had never experienced before. Immersed in her worries, she didn't notice the mound of snow piled up near the temporary cow shed, and she stumbled and fell. The nanny recoiled in fright but before she was able to bend down to help her, Bat-Zion jumped up from the pile of snow with a laugh, making the nanny furious. "I thought you were a person of intelligence, but now I see you're just a she-goat jumping around with no sense," said Nanny Sarah.

The nanny's words banished Bat-Zion's playful mood. She had always been a fearful child; this year, the year she became mature, she had resolved to conquer her vain fears. But at that moment she was very tired from the events of the day, and her heart was pained by her dashed hopes and by her own self-flagellation; so she surrendered to her fearful thoughts. Along with the mooing of the cow that had burst out from the stall, she also heard the sound of the bleating goats that were running around wildly inside. After a short while—as she listened to the echoes of the recitation of *Shema*[3] coming from within—they disappeared as if they never were.

That night she slept fitfully. A family was prostrating itself at the holy sepulcher of her grandfather the Maggid behind the woods nearby; and in her sleep, the sound of their weeping merged with the day's discussions about building the new house. During the night, she dreamed about her departed aunts and grandmothers, whose honored resting place was in a sepulcher adjoining that of the Maggid. According to stories she had heard, their lives were burdened with hardship but sanctified with good deeds, and they arrived at the World of Truth free of any sin. She dreamed that these women came to extinguish the great fire. She saw the smoke rising and the flames spreading across Magitowa Street, and there they were with their shining countenances and white burial shrouds, bringing water in buckets. Suddenly, the brick kiln located on their country estate burst through the smoke, its smokestacks billowing. And with the help of that brick kiln, the new building rose up in all its grandeur and magnificence.

The arrival of spring also ushered in a flood. The great snows of that year melted, the ice turned liquid, and the rivers, which in the winter had become one mass of ice, now tempestuously broke out of their bounds. The water streamed over the riverbank, covering towns and villages. The great Vistula flooded unchecked, eventually reaching towns twenty-five miles away. The washed-out roads posed a barrier for travelers, for merchants going to market in the large cities, for the poor who had set out for various destinations in order to knock on the doors of the wealthy, for fathers wandering to find matches for their sons and daughters, and for those making pilgrimages to the graves of their holy ancestors. Even the railroads were interrupted for a long time. In addition to the flood, they had to contend with strikes in the aftermath of the revolution that had spread to all parts of Russia.[4] The tsarist regime reneged on its promise to set up a democratic government, and even the establishment in Petersburg in 1904[5] of a national elected body, known as the Duma, was not successful in stopping the wave of imprisonments.

Police would follow a young person's every step, meting out corporal punishment in response to the slightest word against the government, and Cossacks would frequently leave their barracks and go out on a rampage, killing civilians. Despite the regime's severe measures, strikes increased. The strikers would assemble in public places to demonstrate, and every half-baked ideologue would get up and speak, vilifying the government bureaucracy and the tsarist regime. Children rose against parents and workers against their bosses. Even children of the Russian nobility and of officials rebelled, traveling to all parts of the empire to open the eyes of the people. And they eventually arrived in Congress Poland, preaching revolution against the bloody regime, urging people to break the iron fetters and to usher in an era of freedom.

These events caused everyone's work to come to a standstill and delayed all seasonal preparations. The return of the Rebbe and his entourage was also held up. Coming back from visiting the graves of her grandfather the Grodzisker Rebbe[6] and his father the Seraph of Mogielnica,[7] they were forced to travel in a roundabout manner. Instead of traveling by railroad to the Garbatka station, which was about five miles away from the town, they plodded along by horse-drawn wagons, by steamship and fishing boats for several days from Warsaw the capital until they reached the town of Kozienice—in normal times, a trip that would have taken but a few hours. In the towns and villages through which the Rebbe and his entourage passed, these were days of rejoicing and spiritual exaltation. The hasidim greeted the Rebbe, the tzaddik of his generation, with lit torches, song, and music.

Especially so in the city Mishiev on the banks of the Vistula: There the joy was unimaginable. The family Kosman, owners of the liquor factory, set up gates of honor and welcomed them with lavish feasts. For it was in the merit of the prayers of his holy ancestors that all this wealth had come to them. Everyone knew of the miracle; its memory was transmitted from father to son and from son to grandson. Once before, when the Vistula rose and was about to flood all their property with its stormy waves at the end of the winter, the elders of the family hastened to invite to their town the tzaddik, the Rebbe Rabbi Elazar, his soul in Eden, the grandfather of the present tzaddik, the Rebbe Rabbi Yerahmiel Moshe, may his light shine. After standing in ecstatic prayer near the water, he said, "It's amazing! Isn't it possible for the raging waves to move to one side?" Immediately, the waters of the Vistula moved away and their entire property was saved.

With the return home of the Rebbe and his entourage, the holy courtyards came back to life. The harbingers of Passover were already peeping through the latticework and from the moss on the shingles of the old roofs laid bare of snow. Light clouds hovered in the blue sky. The sun began to warm up slowly and the members of the household ran around busily, their hands full of work.

Zundeleh the miller had already come to the old *beit midrash* where bags were hanging since last summer, filled with *shemurah* wheat, "safeguarded from the time of harvest."[8] With his deep bass voice—with which he would sing *"Ha-aderet ve-ha-emunah"*[9] at the Rebbe's table during the third Sabbath meal at dusk—he instructed his energetic children to bring the new upper millstone for mounting on the Passover wheat grindstone. And the Rebbe also broke away briefly from his studies to devote time to Passover preparations. Before anything else, he made sure to arrange for distribution of supplies to the poor; and then, with the help of his sons, he took charge of the preparations for grinding the *shemurah* flour.

Along with the continual dripping of runoff from the roofs and the water streaming from gutter pipes at the corners of the houses, one could hear the echoes of the massive Passover preparations in the sweet air of spring's advent. These courtyards—both the outer, open one and the inner, closed one—that normally were filled with hasidim coming with their wives and children from towns in the region were now transformed into work space for various implements. Even Yashkar the chief carpenter of the Rebbe's court and his sons, who were busy with the woodwork for the new building under construction (its windows, doors, sills, and shutters), had already brought their tools. They had set up their work stands in the open courtyard, taken out the boards for matzah baking from the storerooms, and had begun smoothening them with their planes. The Rebbetzins were walking busily to and fro, coming and going from one building to another, emptying their bureau drawers and then shaking them out to remove any possible crumb of bread. They handled even the smallest items respectfully, since most of them were part of the legacy of the family's holy matriarchs, their headdresses, vests,[10] silver prayer-book covers, and flasks of perfume. They instructed the household apprentices, their daughters, and the workers to be especially meticulous in their Passover preparations. In particular, they were to distribute charity to bnei-tovim and the poor in general, who were already gathering at the entrances of the courtyards to have their pots filled with pickled borscht from barrels, which the women of the household had begun preparing after Purim, and with goose fat, which the younger Rebbetzin Brachaleh and the household manager Malkah had prepared over Hanukkah.

The Rebbetzins also went to the inner sanctum to discuss the laws of Passover. They were joined by the old rabbi of Apta, the town's young rabbinic judge, as well as some of the veteran hasidim and the assistants in order to hear from the Rebbe the essential laws and supererogatory rules and stringencies that the family's holy patriarchs had instituted on the basis of hasidic and mystical traditions.

The young Rebbetzin Brachaleh assigned Passover jobs to most of the women of the household. Some were working on the Passover utensils stored away in the attic, bringing them to the closed room to put them through kosher-for-Passover processing once again. Some were supervising the gentile workers in their tasks. These workers, who had been brought from the estate specifically for Passover preparations, were scrubbing the table boards and benches with sand, scraping with knives and brushes, rinsing with cold water and plunging the cleaned utensils into hot water.

The older Rebbetzin Sarah Devorahleh, who was always managing many projects at once, was particularly busy directing activities now at the start of spring. She had finally renewed contacts with the brick-kiln owners in town, and the construction of the house was set to resume soon.

In the open courtyard, gentile construction workers were walking about with their foreman. They were all wearing their holiday garments and new caps with lacquered visors. Tipsy on liquor, they were fighting among themselves about raises, flinging insults at the foreman with his thick mustache. At noon, the noise quieted down with the arrival of the older Rebbetzin, who was still holding a prayer book in her hand. The workers removed their hats and bowed low, greeting her with "Good morning, Lady Rebbetzin." The foreman thought this would be a good time to discuss with the

Rebbetzin the quantity of building materials he needed and to bring up the matter of raises. He also took the opportunity to explain to the workers the dangers of the moment: The police were prohibiting strikes and were delighted to find any excuse to put workers in jail. The authorities were already eyeing their crew with suspicion because of complaints lodged by some property owners, and the foreman explained that this job could serve to protect them since the Russians too had great respect for the Maggid.

In Polish that was fluent but for an occasional slip, the Rebbetzin listed the building materials she had procured, and she emphasized their obligation to remember all the benefits the Poles had received from her holy ancestors for a period of over one hundred years and to do their work conscientiously. Toward the end of the discussion, the conversation was joined by the gentile brick-making expert from the Strykowice estate. He had arrived together with the women workers from the estate in order to report on the status of the brick kiln located on the estate's peat bogs. In an obsequious tone he echoed the Rebbetzin's words and urged them to listen to everything that the "Lady Rebbetzin" had to say. The workers left the courtyard quietly and respectfully, having achieved agreement on an eight-hour day and procuring a slight raise in pay. After they left, the master brick maker began joking in Yiddish, which he spoke fluently. He strutted among the workers, some of whom were planing boards on sawhorses and others who were scrubbing utensils. Dressed in his hunter's outfit and wearing a green velvet cap with a feather, he poked around with the stick in his hand into a puddle of water that reflected his image, humming a Christian religious melody.

"The waters of the holy Vistula reached to here—right here. And so, my friends, beware of the extreme sanctity," he said. The Rebbetzin admonished him sharply: This was not the time for jokes, and the workers must be punctilious and earnest in their work, which affects the sacred rites of Passover, the festival of redemption for body and spirit. His sly look evaporated and he put on a serious expression. He began poring over the report on the brick kiln: As a result of the strikes, they were not successful in producing the quota of bricks that had been ordered by property owners in town whom the Rebbetzin had contacted. And not only that, more funds were needed to cover the rise in wages. The Rebbetzin once again responded to the brick maker's complaint with an admonition that he must take his job more seriously and not absent himself from the brick kiln during the morning hours. She turned away sharply, irate that he had distracted her from sacred matters. At that moment what she wanted was to forget her burdens and devote herself fully to the sacred activities of the season. These mitzvot were anchored deep in her soul. All other undertakings were ancillary, only of value insofar as they prepared the way to perform mitzvot more fully, thereby hastening the redemption.

With the severe gaze of the older Rebbetzin Sarah Devorahleh, the courtyard fell silent and the clanging of work tools could be heard with greater intensity, along with the chirping of the birds. Once again, a feeling of elation permeated the fresh air of the open courtyard, preparing itself for Passover.

CHAPTER

The Flood

That elation did not pass Bat-Zion by. She had a particular love for this season because now she was excused from homework and she had the opportunity to follow everything that was happening. It seemed that even the sounds of scrubbing and rinsing blended with the music of spring that filled her soul. Arriving buoyant and cheerful from the courtyards to the girls' loft, she had the desire to act mischievously, to perform pranks as she once did as a child. But she restrained herself in the spirit of solemnity that began to inhabit her in this twelfth year of her life. She channeled her excess energy into various projects, reserved for this age, that were already occupying her sisters; their rooms were filled with joy and exultation as the work went on. The rain on the windowpanes washed away the frost flowers that had adorned them a short while ago, and the sun's rays flooded the rooms with abundant light. The potted lemon and fig trees and other plants appeared to have risen to new life with a lush array of fresh leaves.

One could hear the whirring of the sewing machine in the middle room where her sisters were dashing off tablecloths, towels, sheets, and cotton housedresses. The girls loosened the completed gold-embroidered festive yarmulkes from their wooden frames, covered them with thin paper to prevent the gold from turning green (although this was unlikely since the gold was pure) and hid them in one of the bureau drawers. The three sisters also worked together on other embroidered items, decorative wall hangings, and pillowcases. The oldest, Hannah Goldeleh, was engaged in cutting fabric to size for dresses, a skill she had learned from the noblewoman in the gentile quarter, while Hayyah Miriam'l and Bat-Zion took turns using the sewing machine. And the fourth sister, little Havvaleh, walked about among the workers, her dark eyes beaming. The apprentice girls entered frequently with bolts of cloth. At the same time they brought news from town, breaking out in peals of laughter.

"That young man whom the townspeople call a simpleton came from Warsaw dressed in a new suit and pressed collar, his shaved chin held up high. It was he who stood at the head of every political circle, promising freedom to them all. And what do you think about the fowl merchant's daughters who went to their mother's coops, loosened the leg bands of the chickens and geese, announcing that freedom had come to the world and that even birds should not be chained, since Nicholas's reign in Russia was coming to an end?"

Tucked between the bolts of cloth were propaganda pamphlets that the girls had obtained. Bat-Zion stood on a chair and read in a mock-serious tone from the pamphlet *Workers of the World Unite*, and they all responded with loud applause. Only Hannah Goldale did not join in. She was looking through the books on the small bureau, and found German monthlies that ridiculed the tsar and revealed secrets about the royal court. Here was a caricature of the princesses, the tsar's daughters, riding with Rasputin, the peasant priest who captured the women of the court in his net under the mask of religion. And here was a full-length drawing of the tsar with his pointy beard, pouring out the rights of man from a cornucopia to his faithful subjects, but their hands remained empty.

The girls' good spirits intensified until the apprentices returned and told about sensational events in town. The priest and nuns had gone out with icons to the flooded fields in order to stop the Vistula. Reminded of the flood, a melancholy spirit passed through the room. Immediately, they began thinking about leaving to assist the victims and along with that to see the marvel of the Vistula's waves raging onto fields near town. The girls first destroyed the pamphlets and pictures denigrating the Russian royal court by burning them, and then Bat-Zion went down to get permission for a trip to the outskirts of town.

At first her mother the Rebbetzin and her grandmother—who were busy discussing various plans—scolded her, saying that there was so much work to do and this was not a good time for a trip. But they immediately reconsidered, seeing that the girls might be able to be of assistance. Her mother the Rebbetzin came with her to the open courtyard to direct Frank to hitch the buggy for a journey. She even suggested to Bat-Zion that she should ask Hayyim'l the master of the apprentices, who was now in the attic storage rooms, to accompany them.

The cutting rooms above the kitchens served as a safe place to keep all kinds of utensils needed for Passover. They were also used for storage of *hametz* utensils during the holiday. Between the roof beam support columns stood the cutting machine for preparing animal fodder. At that moment the old horse, taught by the clever stable boy to climb the steps, was harnessed to the machine. He circled about, his eyes covered with a kerchief and his head lowered, his scraggly mane falling on his neck, looking like an elderly servant shouldering the burden of a sacred task. The cut straw poured out of the machine into fodder sacks, emitting a pleasant smell of hay.

Bat-Zion took great pleasure in the whole scene. Mischievously, she breathed in deeply and sneezed loudly. Her dear Hayyim'l had experienced troubles in his dealings with the Vistula fishermen, but he joked as usual as he went down the steps with the stable boy carrying a sack of fodder. Soon after, preparations began in the courtyard for departing to help the victims of the flood. The touring horses were hitched to the buggy, which held the girls, the house managers, and the Rebbe's personal assistant. They galloped past the gardens of Mr. Garski[1] near the normally quiet river[2] running through the town, which at that time had spilled over its banks in mighty waves.

With the melting of the ice, the fields surrounding the southeast corner of the town were also flooded by the waters of the Vistula, normally about twelve miles from the town as the crow flies, and by highway a distance of sixteen miles. Most of Mr. Garski's orchards and gardens by the turreted palace, as well as the rows of pine trees trimmed like a wall, were sunk in waves of flooding water, looking like enchanted islands.

Crowds streamed to the hill overlooking the fields near the nobleman's properties. Some of them gazed out of sheer curiosity, and others came to see the wonders of the Creator who sets boundaries for the seas, at it says in the Book of Psalms, *"You set bounds they must not pass so that they never again cover the earth."*[3] Now, however, the barriers had been set loose; and the waters of the deep had broken out, flooding other domains without limit.

The turbid waters of the Vistula raged into the fields surrounding the town, mercilessly pillaging the fruits of human labor from town and village. Everything that happened to be in their way—doors and their bolts; wooden roof shingles; household items such as tubs, barrels, and straw mattresses; and so on—was all carried along in the stream. Small fishing boats passed by hurriedly, laden with weeping women, peasant and Jewish, screaming infants in their arms. Boats with military men also passed by, taking pleasure cruises in the flooded fields. On the one hand, there was the weeping of the women and children and, on the other, the merriment of the Russian army officers, their wives made up with eye shadow and rouge, ostrich feathers on their hats.

The voices of the rescuers mingled with the other voices. They came with wagons carrying clay, sand, stones, and bricks, with chains and poles, in order to pour an embankment. Some of them came by foot, carrying loaves of bread and bottles of beverages in their knapsacks. From all parts of the town, from all directions, crowds streamed through the square bordering the nobleman's gardens and the church garden, toward the southeast corner of town. The square was flooded with a variegated crowd of people, like on Thursday market days. The peasants who had escaped the flood, wrapped up in their sheepskins, were in wagons along with their wives and children, together with snorting piglets. The horses hitched to the wagons neighed, and the tied-up cows mooed in chorus. Priests and nuns wearing black meandered among the wagons. Jewish women peddled baskets of bagels and sweets, their headdresses festooned with ribbons. The noise and tumult got louder and louder.

People kept coming to the hill from town, gathering on the balconies of small houses encompassed by gardens and in front of straw-roofed huts. In one of the huts lived an aged gentile man, one hundred years old, who still remembered the Maggid.[4] When he heard that the Rebbe's daughters—descendants of the holy Maggid who had blessed him with long life—were coming to assist the victims, he hurried out to greet them. He presented them with fresh water in an earthenware jug, drawn from the well by his sons in their honor.

The old man told the girls, who had brought food and clothing for the survivors, that there had also been a flood in the days of the Maggid. The man had saved Jews from drowning and had received a blessing from their holy ancestor; that was why he had reached such an extraordinary old age. As he told his story, tears fell from his dim eyes onto his clean-shaven face, which looked like a worn-out rag. Meanwhile the Rebbetzins and their escorts arrived in a covered buggy, and the swinging of the whip of the coachman Morshchin, dressed in a white leather suit with brass buttons, rang through the air. The girls resumed caring for women and children arriving in boats in tattered clothes. They refreshed them with various foods—crackers, eggs, jam—as well as clean, dry clothes.

The aged gentile turned to greet the older Rebbetzin as she arrived. After conversing with her about those old days—days of piety and faith in holy persons, a time when princes and dukes came from all parts of Poland in order to seek miraculous intervention from the holy Maggid—he requested from the holy Rebbetzin his descendant an added blessing: that the thread of his life not break for many more years to come.

"If my ancestor the holy Maggid, his soul in Eden, who was like an angel of God, gave his blessing, what could I possibly add? But we will offer a prayer that the Righteous Redeemer, the Messiah, come quickly in our days, and that the honorable sir be there to see him."

The old man crossed himself as he said, "Amen," and strode vigorously like a youngster back to his cottage. Just then dear friend Hayyim'l hastily approached the Rebbetzin before she began helping the victims. "And what about your own, Rebbetzin?" he said emphatically. "I also need a blessing. This year I joined a group of wealthy farmers in leasing Mister Garski's orchards over there. I paid one hundred rubles—borrowed money. May it be God's will that the fruit not rot after such a flood, and that I get my money back after all that labor, and some profit besides."

"So may it be God's will," the Rebbetzin responded with a quiet sigh. "God makes miracles happen all the time, just like the miracle of the splitting of the Sea of Reeds, which is fast approaching."[5] But her two bushy eyebrows came together on her creased forehead and she continued with a touch of temper. "It was foolish on your part to have sunk a small sum of money into an investment of wealthy lessees worth thousands of rubles. Even if the trees produce good fruit, you would only receive a small percentage, especially this year, with the concern that the fruit may be wormy, and all you'd get would be your watchman's pay. But I don't want to open my mouth to Satan.[6] Worst of all, it may come to pass as the rabbis say, that wealthy people are typically tightfisted. Who knows if they'll pay you for all your labor and trouble. You were consumed by fatigue from sleeping in a tent at night and by the blazing sun in the hot days of summer harvest. *'The Lord protects the simple,'*[7] and your folly may actually bring you success. It may just be that this year the fruit will be good quality and that small sum you invested will bring you a big profit. *'Is anything too wonderous for the Lord?'*[8] May you have good days to compensate for your days of suffering."

The Rebbetzin concluded her words with a deep sigh. She turned away from him; and, holding onto the train of her dress, she hurried to approach the exhausted women and men, who with their last strength had climbed the hill to high ground.

"Holy Rebbetzin, what is God doing to us? We've been left without a roof over our heads. All our belongings are sunk," rang out the bitter lament accompanying the weeping of the injured. The Rebbetzin stood mute momentarily, then sighed and said, "It is forbidden to question God's ways. Surely whatever He did is for our benefit."

"Indeed, whatever God does, He does for the good, but the blow is harsh and it's hard to bear it," answered some of the men, while the women's weeping grew louder.

Bat-Zion had been in control of her emotions, standing firmly for quite a while, but now she was so moved that her body began to shudder. In order that no one notice her tears, she turned away from the victims. She found a secluded corner behind a hut that overlooked the fields and leaned against a shaky picket fence. While her heart tightened to see the survivors of the devastation swept along in the flood, she nevertheless deeply breathed in the fresh, clear air. The picture of the waves glistening in the sun and advancing in such a wide sweep thrilled her eyes. After a few moments she returned to join the others assisting the victims.

CHAPTER

Welcoming Passover

The days of winter had come to an end, and the sun peeked out with a gentle eye from patches of blue between the parting steel gray clouds. The trees had shed their snow, and the chirping of the birds returning from warmer lands mingled with the shouts of children returning from *heder* and of people's conversations on current events. The disastrous flooding of the rivers from melting snow was almost completely forgotten, and all hearts were filled with the joy of the festival of freedom peering through the lattices cleansed of leaven,[1] despite the work that still lay ahead. It seemed as though God's world had risen for resurrection; and the cryptic utterance that had come from the Rebbe's mouth in those frosty days on Shabbat Shirah—" *'I will sing to the Lord.'* The singular subject suggests: with one heart; then the world and all its fullness will sing together,"[2]—that utterance seemed to be a bit more comprehensible in these days approaching Passover.

At the same time, however, both personal and communal worries weighed upon the courts of the Rebbe, who was occupying the seat of his great-great-grandfather the Maggid of Kozienice, his soul in Eden. Those courtyards were already filled with the bustle of Passover preparations along with the usual sounds of Torah, prayer and sacred song. But there were pauses when one could hear conversations on political developments and their impact upon the household. In the open courtyard between the tall birches, near the pole rising over the roof of the synagogue, hasidim from towns in the district as well as local residents stood around in a circle, deep in conversation.

"The rebels will come up empty-handed in their insurrection against Tsar Nicholas. After having shot the wicked interior minister Stolypin,[3] another villain is likely to take his place," said Zalman Baruch, a town resident who was well informed on politics, as he took a deep puff of tobacco from his long pipe. "And upon whose head will the authorities pour out their anger? Upon the Jews of course."

"And who are the carriers of the red flags? Mostly our own people who throw off the yoke of Heaven, the yoke of Torah and the Commandments, as they cry 'Freedom, freedom,'" said the veteran hasid Reb Elijah Hayyim of Lublin. "We really need God's help."

The Rebbe's personal assistant, who had just returned from Warsaw with a cargo of raisins for making Passover wine, got involved in the conversation. "In the capital city Warsaw, the Cossacks ran through the demonstrators like reapers in a grain field. It's outrageous and appalling. To what end are our fellow Jews giving up their lives?" He spoke with irate passion, as he hastened toward the large cellar with the iron door, where barrels were already in place, wines draining of their lees.

The participants in the discussion, including Reb Heschel, one of the householders from town, as well as Shammai the lessee, were startled when the older Rebbetzin, the Rebbe's mother, left her residence's garden and began listening in on their conversation.

"Instead of chattering on about this, that, and the other, you ought to pour your hearts out to our Father in Heaven to send the Righteous Redeemer speedily in our time. These events are the birth pangs of the Messiah,"[4] the Rebbetzin said emphatically.

And the participants all responded in unison, "The Rebbetzin's words are correct; these events are indeed the birth pangs of the

Messiah. In our day we have even seen the prophecy of 'the child shall behave himself proudly against the elder'[5] fulfilled. May we also merit the coming of the Messiah speedily in our time."

While they were speaking, the court's carpenter approached, a plane in his hand. The carpenter, who was also the foreman in charge of constructing the new house ever since the fire, complained bitterly, "Yes, the prophecy has been fulfilled, and we are indeed living in times of the Messiah's birth pangs. Servants break away from their masters and children from their parents. And that's why my holy work is going so slowly."

The Rebbetzin furrowed her high forehead, which protruded from the muslin veil covering her embroidered headdress. She pulled at her thick eyebrows with one hand, as she typically did when she felt morose, and added to her earlier words, "And until the Righteous Redeemer comes, you had best be concerned to improve the health of the Rebbe, my son, long may he live, who expends his energies on your behalf."

When she concluded her words her heart filled with distress, for she knew that the real reason for such a great delay in building the house was not neglect on the part of the carpenter, nor was it the insolence of the workers. Rather it was the ascetic piety of her son the Rebbe, long may he live, who was depriving himself of life's necessities.

With an air of tense silence, the Rebbetzin turned toward the room of the family's grandfather,[6] the holy Maggid, his soul in Eden— that sanctified room brooding its age-old musings, with its double roof in back of the old synagogue. There at the entrance stood the old rabbi Reb Hersheleh, deep in thought, half listening to the conversation. "You're our faithful friend, please find a way to influence the Rebbe, my son, long may he live, to cooperate in the project of completing his house," said the Rebbetzin, sighing quietly. "Even the Russian army physician Doctor Orzhechovsky, who is a great authority as well as a friend of our family, considers his weakness to be a serious matter and warns us about the potential danger, God forbid, from the low-ceilinged residence."

"Our Rebbe builds edifices in the world of Torah and service of God, the eternal world, which is entirely good. If only he might be granted many more happy years, until the time of the redemption, which he is helping to advance," answered the rabbi quietly, as if speaking to himself.

And the Rebbetzin responded, "Amen, so may it be God's will that your words will be fulfilled."

As the Rebbetzin turned to go, Reb Hersheleh bestirred himself, and his agitated voice rang through the courtyard saturated with fresh aromas, "It is indeed our responsibility to come up with strategies for completing the building. After all, who should live in a nice house if not you, especially since our Rebbe, long may he live, needs pure air for his health?"

The Rebbetzin did not respond to these last words, which were spoken as he joined the group in the courtyard. She let out a deep sigh from her heart and withdrew into her personal thoughts, which shook her entire being. It was not the way of the Rebbetzin, the Rebbe's mother, to give up. The power of faith was strong in her heart, and all the winds in the world could not move her from her place. Most of all, she knew that the merit of her holy ancestors would help her and that she would bring her vision to fulfillment.

Her plans would also benefit the unfortunate and needy people who find shelter in their court and knock on the Rebbe's door daily. And that would please even her son, who labored indefatigably in his sacred work to bring divine assistance to Israel. One could put faith in the words of the rabbi, who was an old and dear friend: "Heaven will give him strength, until the time of the redemption, which he is advancing. And who is more likely to bring the redemption to Israel if not your holy son Moshenu who lives a life of self-sacrifice? From the time you weaned him, you saw that he was blessed; an otherworldly light shone from his face. His whole way of life is marked by holiness and purity. He grasps everything not only with his brilliant mind but with the apperception of the holy spirit—the tzaddikim of the generation have testified to this."

Unconsciously, the Rebbetzin touched the pouch tied around her neck. Looking for a safe spot secure from the commotion of the upcoming festival, she had placed there the holy letters she had received from tzaddikim, including appreciations of her son the wonder child, a shoot from the stock of the Holy Maggid.

At this time, her pouch held more than sacred epistles. It contained plans for the Kolodny estate, which she had once maintained in Polesia, but which the authorities of the Russian tsar had taken from her as a result of the edict prohibiting Jews from owning land on Russian soil. The edict did not yet apply to Poland, so the estate she had purchased there was still in her hands for now. The Rebbetzin was holding on to the Kolodny plans for the future era, for the time when the property stolen from her would be returned, along with all the other thefts by the gentiles, which one day would be restored by Heavenly decree. A number of years ago, she had used the pouch to carry her jewelry during her travels, as well as the pearls of her Galician *binda*[7] headdress, which she sometimes wore in order to please her mother-in-law the Kozienicer Rebbetzin Tzipporah,[8] a scion of the Rebbe Rabbi Naftali of Ropczyce in Galicia. But now she had hardly any jewelry, having sold most of it to pay for expenses related to real estate, as well as for charitable donations.

Trusting in Heavenly aid, the Rebbetzin strode confidently, and she traversed the open courtyard, which was alive with ferment. From the courtyard, the voice of the Rebbe's personal attendant burst out with bitter, sarcastic words. "It's cold in this world, cold," he announced, his teeth nearly chattering. "There are no real friends, there's no real devotion. I'm forbidden to reveal how weak our Rebbe really is, but I know. He ordered me to be silent, so that no one would interfere with his path of self-sacrifice, but I can't hold myself back from speaking. Hasidic factory owners contributed thousands for the rebuilding project, but the Rebbe, long may he live, applied the funds to the restoration of the Holy

Maggid's communal synagogue. And none of the Rebbe's dear friends have said anything."

The attendant's words, whose bitterness reflected true devotion, roused those present. Mr. Heschel, a householder who was a member of the building committee, got very incensed, yet he restrained his anger, because one may not mar the sacred with personal emotions. After a period of silence, he turned cautiously to the Rebbetzin, who was approaching, and said in his coarse voice, "Doesn't the Rebbetzin own a brick kiln on the peat bogs in your Strykowice estate? Why not direct the plant manager Mordecai to send over several thousand of the bricks manufactured in the factory, and then we'll be able to resume putting up the house's inner walls. We must hurry before the problem of insurgent strikes spreads to our town."

Mr. Heschel's words provoked an angry response from Shammai the lessee from the village of Policzna near the estate. "With all due respect for the Rebbetzin, it is unseemly for the Rebbetzin to listen to the advice of people who are unfamiliar with her business. In my view, the honored Rebbetzin ought to pay more attention to the estate's affairs, so that the income would cover expenses, and the honored Rebbetzin might succeed in emerging from the thicket of debts."

"Things are not so bad as all that, Reb Shammai," said the Rebbetzin as she pulled herself up and furrowed her protruding brow to defend the estate's business. "In spite of everything, we can afford to allocate some bricks for building the house until the negotiations with the brick-kiln owners in town are concluded and you arrive at an agreement with them."

Reb Eliyahu Hayyim, a hasid and dear friend, added, "But the main thing is that our honored Rebbe, long may he live, agree to help us, seeing as how he disperses his money to those who flock daily to his door seeking his assistance. In addition, our holy Rebbe is not pleased with the idea of erecting buildings outside the Land."

After lengthy deliberations it was decided that Shammai was right, and that it would be better not to mix the entangled affairs of the estate with the building of the Rebbe's house, which was urgent.

It was necessary to begin the work immediately, before the workers' strike spread, despite the fact that preparations for the fast-approaching Passover holiday had everyone fully engaged in body and spirit. The whole discussion ended with a decision to bring the matter before the Rebbe, with a request that he support those engaged in building his house for the sake of his health and the glory of his Court, since so many years had already gone by from the time their magnificent house had gone up in flames. At least he should not discourage them when they come before him with a delegation of hasidim, wealthy industrialists who had traveled to the Rebbe at this season from the great cities of Congress Poland.

The elderly Rabbi Reb Hersheleh buttressed this plan with the following point. "It's true that our Rebbe does not wish to erect edifices outside of the Holy Land, but the homes of tzaddikim are classified as synagogues, which one day will all be transported to the Holy Land along with the Children of Israel in the messianic era."[9]

Reb Eliyahu Hayyim agreed, emphasizing, "That thought will enable us to attain our goal, since the heart and soul of our Rebbe, long may he live, are always in the Holy Land. Furthermore, at this time of year when the Festival of Freedom is fast approaching, this project will be an aspect of *athalta di-ge'ulah*, the dawning of redemption."

As the older Rebbetzin Sarah Devoraleh broke away from the conversation, she was overcome with a feeling of weakness. She remembered that she had not tasted any food yet that day. She also recalled that she had to prostrate herself at the holy sepulchre of grandfather the Maggid, his soul in Eden, together with her son the Rebbe, after their trip to the holy Hillula[10] of her father the tzaddik of Grodzisk, on the first of Nisan.[11] It had been quite a while since her son the Rebbe, long may he live, had left for the sepulchre with his sons and the hasidim. There he was communing with his holy ancestors, occupied with eternal life, while she was still involved in transitory matters.

On the other side of the birch grove in front of her room's window, she met her daughter-in-law the younger Rebbetzin Brachaleh, accompanied by the devoted household manager. Rebbetzin Brachaleh was already dressed in her fine silk dress and velvet coat, the customary garb for the Rebbetzins' visits to the graves of their holy ancestors.

"You're being excessively courteous, Brachaleh my daughter-in-law. Don't you know that you don't have to wait for me?" the older Rebbetzin said in a critical tone. "You should have gone ahead to the sepulchre without me, the girls are waiting for you for breakfast. They must be feeling weak by now."

As always, out of courtesy and sensitivity for her feelings, the younger Rebbetzin did not reply to her mother-in-law's reprimand. The horses were already standing and neighing outside the stable, and she hurriedly ordered the coachman to harness them to the carriage. She continued on her way to the other side of the closed courtyard, whose buildings were already spotlessly clean for Passover. In the servants' rooms were stoves that were kept from contact with leaven all year long. Women peddlers were waiting there with sacks of potatoes that had been stored in pits since the previous summer in gentiles' fields, for use by the Rebbe's household.

The beets dug from pits after Purim had already been put up in barrels that were standing covered in the room, and the beet juice dispersed a fresh vinegary smell to the courtyard, *"like the smell of the fields that the Lord has blessed."*[12] The Rebbetzin gave instructions to the household manager, who was dressed all in white, to distribute beet juice to the needy individuals who would soon be coming with their containers, and also to settle accounts with the peddlers. Accompanied by her mother-in-law the older Rebbetzin and benot-tovim, she turned toward the buggy harnessed to two horses that awaited them in front of the open portico.

The Rebbetzins spent a long time in the holy sepulchre, following the outpourings of the Rebbe's heart. Dressed in a sable *shtreimel,*

the Rebbe stood totally absorbed in intimate communion with the spirits of his ancestors. His pale noble face shone in the light of hundreds of candles, in that sepulchre of grandfather the Maggid and his holy successors, in the graveyard among the pine trees behind the great synagogue.

As psalms burst forth in stormy passion from the Rebbe's children and the hasidim, the Rebbetzins' group joined them also, pouring out their hearts in petition to God for personal and collective salvation, for deliverance from the harsh exile, for the coming of the Messiah and the resurrection of the dead.

When they returned, the Rebbetzins ate a light lunch just before the afternoon service. Since it was Monday, the meal was dairy; on Mondays and Thursdays the Rebbetzins ate no meat. As usual, the meal was eaten in silence.[13] The only sound to be heard in that warm dining room with the low ceiling was the clinking of spoons and forks, along with deep sighs. These were sighs of contentment and inner spaciousness. They reflected deep faith in the imminence of redemption and resurrection that awaited behind the wall, peering through the lattice[14]—the crevices of the rooms that had been made pure for the Passover holiday.

Although the delicate eyes of the younger Rebbetzin Brachaleh were swollen from weeping, her bright face beamed with serenity and great warmth. The sculpted face of the older Rebbetzin showed no sign of weeping, but it too was saturated with repose, a repose borne of faith and trust. All personal matters, including those of greatest urgency, seemed to be forgotten at this time. Even the young girls did not speak to each other. They were flooded with a buoyant feeling of hope that emerged from some hidden recess.

It seemed as if the atmosphere of the room, with its decorated wallpaper, double cupboard, and polished windowpanes, were becoming clearer and fresher, like the air after a spring snowstorm. "The cheese blintzes are so tasty; it seems they never tasted this good," the girls whispered among themselves as they shook off crumbs of *hametz* from their dresses and hurried to recite the Grace after Meals with their mother and grandmother, in order to be ready to help with holiday tasks.

The kitchen areas and their grandmother's room were already cleaned for Passover. When their doors were opened, the light of the setting sun streamed in by way of the open windows, and the gleam of polished copper and silver utensils flashed all through the rooms, with their sawdust-covered floors. In the pile of silver items on a special table one could see Elijah's cup. Catching golden rays from Heavenly horizons, it scattered sparks everywhere, as if broadcasting the light of redemption's harbinger.

At that moment one could hear the hasidim returning with the Rebbe from the cemetery, singing sacred Passover melodies. The notes danced and sparkled, spreading far and wide, along with the rays of redemption of the Festival of Freedom.

CHAPTER 13

Drawing Water to Lodge Overnight[1]

Click-clack, click-clack, this is where the holy work is happening, announced the millstones in the Maggid's old synagogue. New stones had been set up in the kasha mill that was now being used for grinding *shemurah* wheat, carefully safeguarded from the time of harvest from any contact with water,[2] to be used in baking matzahs.

The wheat had been harvested by the Rebbe Rabbi Yerahmiel Moshele and his sons, who had prepared themselves with sacred acts of purification. The harvesting, witnessed by a festive crowd of hasidim and communal leaders, took place in a field near Kozienice that had been leased from gentiles after the previous Passover.

The large wheel geared to the mill turned round and round, clattering loudly. Clouds of dust billowed up in the hall of the synagogue, with its whitewashed walls and ceiling. Those engaged in the holy work observed silence. They listened to the quick steps of the Rebbe coming from the study nearby, where the tall bookcase's doors were open wide.

A young man read aloud from a slip of paper attached to an earthenware jug: "Threshed on the day after harvest; each grain chosen individually for our Rebbe." He gave the jug to the Rebbe, who was immersed in silent contemplation. The Rebbe poured the wheat from the jug into the mill's funnel and turned the wheel until drops of sweat glistened on his high forehead. The flour spilled into the white linen bag. Zundeleh the miller tied the bag with new linen strings and gave the full bag to the *yoshev*, who handed it to a young man, who hung it from a roof beam.

Once again the man looked at the paper and proclaimed, "Twenty times sixty."[3] He handed jugs of grain to each of the Rebbe's sons: the oldest, Rabbi Aharon Yehiel; the middle, Reb Asher Elimelekh; and the youngest, Yisrael Elozor'l, who hugged the neck of the jug with his two hands, assisted by the melammed. The Rebbe waited while his sons poured the jugs into the mill and turned the wheel. His clear, penetrating eyes watched the hasidim tying the bags of wheat and hanging them on the ceiling, exclaiming frequently, "Nu, nu, keep concentrating on what is in your hands."

"We know, we know. We have our Rebbe's *shemurah*—safeguarded—flour in our hands," called out the old *yoshev* Yehoshualeh with fervor.

"The Hebrew word '*hittah*'—wheat—has the numerical value of twenty-two. This corresponds to the twenty-two letters of the Hebrew alphabet with which the Torah, the life of the Jewish people, is written. And our people have been 'safeguarded' since the time we left Egypt by our vigilant self-sacrificing devotion," responded the Rebbe pointedly, as he headed toward the study.[4]

The clatter of the millstones drew Bat-Zion to the main hall of the synagogue. She opened the door quietly, stood in amazement and listened. Her middle brother, Asher Elimelekh'l approached her and whispered playfully, "Turn it over and over again, for everything is in it."[5] She followed him to the mill and began turning the wheel with intense pleasure and with such speed that she lost her breath.

The clouds of dust basked in the rays of sunlight. The wheat berries jumped glistening into the hopper while the noise of the mill swallowed the sound of her father the Rebbe's light steps, walking from the nearby study to the main hall and back again. It seemed as if he were stretching an invisible line from here to there and back again. The letters in the book that lay open before him and the sanctified grains were one and the same. She recalled hearing about a grain of wheat upon which had been written a section of the Torah.

The clattering of the millstones resounded for some days. Shifts rotated day and night so that there would be no pause in the sacred work. A large quantity of flour was prepared in order to supply all the members of the Rebbe's household, his assistants, and the *yoshvim* as well as the veteran hasidim. The sound of the millstones drifted through the courtyards, and the air was heavy with the fragrance of spring blossoming. The sound mingled with the tumult of Passover preparations, with the knocking of the blacksmith's hammer, with the scraping of the carpenter's plane, and with the painstaking cleaning and scouring by the servants.

During those days, Bat-Zion was in an intensely joyful mood, excited by the events around her. As she walked through the open courtyard, she looked at the small puddles of water that had collected near the old cellar, whose iron door was open wide. In this cellar, which one hundred years before had served as a refuge for the Jews hiding from the Cossacks and the insurrectionist Poles, the steward had begun making wine from choice grapes months ago. The fragrance from the wine burst into the courtyard and mingled with the smell of trees in the garden, already sprouting greenish buds.

"Safeguarded wine, safeguarded wine,"[6] the steward's playful voice rang out, as he rolled empty barrels that needed repairing up the steps of the cellar. He brought them to the courtyard where the gentile blacksmith tested them with his heavy hammer. He banged on their iron bands and mended their cracks.

The older Rebbetzin Sarah Devorahleh entered, wearing simple, clean cotton clothing, as befitted the pre-Passover season. Her hands were holding rings of keys, which had turned black after being heated in fire to the point of glowing.[7] She conversed with the elderly rabbi of Apta about obtaining food for the cows and horses that would be completely free of any trace of *hametz*. The collector of charity funds for the Holy Land interrupted her with a jest.

"Not to worry. The animals will get by with food of affliction here in the Diaspora, and when we all get to *Eretz Yisra'el*, we'll feed them carob."

The Rebbetzin paid no attention to his words and turned quickly toward the open stable, where the horses were neighing. Bat-Zion stood between the boards spread over sawhorses and played with the yellow shavings that snaked around like curls of hair.

"Young lady, what are you doing standing idle," her grandmother the older Rebbetzin upbraided her. She had just returned from the gate of the closed courtyard, near the cow shed. "Tonight we'll be drawing water for the matzahs, and all preparations in the other courtyard need to be completed."

Bat-Zion stood still in embarrassment. She had indeed been wasting time. Until now it had seemed to her that she was busy along with everyone else, but in reality she was just watching the others go about their work. She began walking quickly while looking wistfully at the flock of ravens cutting through the clear air, cawing.

The tumult of the workers, the chirping of the birds, and the rustling of the trees broadcast the arrival of spring and of freedom in the open courtyard: All these sounds were focused in the inner courtyard, condensing into a mantle woven entirely of holiness. From that sublime ethereal mantle, Passover burst forth on all sides.

The closed courtyard was filled with books airing out, spread over long benches. Utensils of all kinds, which had not yet been returned to their rooms after their pre-Passover cleaning, were piled up all over.

In the small birch grove between the servants' room and the woodshed stood the household manager. She was taking items reserved for Passover use and putting them through kosher-for-Passover processing, out of concern that they might have accidentally become unfit at some point during the year.[8] Planed boards for tables, planed benches, basins, stands, poles: All of these passed through her hands. She had been engaged in kosher-for-Passover processing since after Purim, all the while whispering frequently "In honor of holy Passover." Her young son Shlomo assisted her, passing red-hot stones over the utensils and plunging them in boiling water. The rising steam obscured the young trees in the grove.

The windows on both floors of the building were wide open, and on the sparkling windowpanes one could see the reflection of blue sky and floating clouds. It seemed as if the Heavens were settling in on the courtyard as it was purified for the Festival of Freedom.

The courtyard began filling up with hasidim because the time was approaching for the drawing of water that would rest overnight for baking matzahs. The process of drawing was very involved and demanded intense spiritual concentration. Young and old hurried to complete the airing out of the books. They got ready to don their black *gartls*[9] made of interlaced mesh, to be worn when they would return the books to the Rebbe's residence.

A musty antique smell rose from the books that Bat-Zion handled, arousing in her the curiosity to examine those very books that lay closed before her. She was furious when she saw that she understood absolutely nothing in them. Just then her middle brother, Asher Elimelekh'l, came along carrying some heavy volumes, and his handsome face looked at her with a kindhearted smile. Immediately her anger dissipated. She kissed him on his soft curly *peyos* and brushed off the dust from his blue silk jacket.

As she continued working, her curiosity unabated, she began reading the titles of the books aloud: "*Pri Etz Hayim. Brit Menuhah.*"[10] Suddenly, she started in fear; her father the Rebbe was approaching.

He took one of the books from her hands and said with a warm smile, "The reading of letters that were written with the holy spirit is a meritorious act. Even if one doesn't comprehend them, one's soul still senses the wellspring of holiness that has been opened."

The Rebbe pored over the book for a short while. He then sat down on a bench, removed a parchment scroll from the pile of books, unrolled it and said, "This scroll is The Holy Tree, a chart of all the Worlds[11] that our ancestor the Maggid, his soul in Eden, sketched with his own hand."

Her heart pounding, Bat-Zion approached cautiously and listened.

Her father the Rebbe conversed briefly with a group of hasidim. His face beamed with an inner light and his powerful, captivating gaze seemed to embrace the entire universe around him, holding it under his spell. It seemed to her that all the winds in the world could not shake his concentration. He spoke about the orbit of the sun; the constellations; and the first point of Aries, which the Egyptians had made into a god. His words rang out in the cool, clear air like the notes of a mystical melody:

"Nowadays humans desire to explain everything in a natural way. But even the hosts of Heaven are nothing other than emissaries of their Creator. Were they to diverge from the line of motion marked out for them, the entire world would return to primordial chaos. It was by virtue of faith that the Children of Israel were redeemed from Egypt and arrived at the spot chosen for God's holy House; everything we do now is with the holiness we acquired then."

Finally, the Rebbe exclaimed, "Nu, we must rush to get ready for drawing the water for seder matzahs." He entered his residence and gave the Tree to his oldest son, Reb Aharon Yehiel. Bat-Zion hurried over to him and began reading the words inscribed on the branches of the Tree: "The World of Making. The World of Formation. The World of Creation. The World of Emanation."[12]

A gentle, cool wind carried the conversation of the group standing outside by the sundial. "Our Rebbe wishes to elevate the disciplines of astronomy and mathematics to their source, just as Samuel the moon reckoner[13] did long ago, and to draw salvation to Israel from the supernal wellspring," the old rabbi of Apta whispered into the ear of Reb Hayyim, who had been the Rebbe's melammed when he was a child; the hairs of his *peyos* and white beard looked like bristles. "I spent time in the Inner Sanctum, I've seen the light, I'm not able to let the words leave my lips."

"He conceals himself from us, he's exhausting all his energies," answered Reb Hayyim son of Reb Meir, his voice trembling from age, "I knew him when he was just a child of three, when I transmitted to him the first letters of the holy Torah. Already one could perceive his quick mind, his clear eyes and his holy endowments; all this even before his father passed away in self-surrender to God."[14]

Bat-Zion was enjoying the conversation; and as she listened, she recalled earlier discussions on an exchange of letters between her father the Rebbe and his teacher during his youth, the learned Reb Noson, now serving as rabbi in Tiberias.[15] Those letters were full of mathematical allusions. The disagreement between Reb Noson and the scholar Hayyim Selig Slonimski regarding Sabbath observance on sea voyages had prompted her father to discuss Slonimski's essay on sanctification of the new moon, published that year.

"Afternoon prayers, followed by drawing water for matzah," the voice of the attendant Yashkar-Ber rang out, interrupting Bat-Zion's thoughts.

Between the river Staw,[16] whose overflowing banks were held back with sluice gates and embankments, and the narrow brook winding its way in the ravine through the fields, one could hear the prayers of those engaged in drawing "mitzvah water."

The sun was swallowed by the horizon, disappearing in a flaming kiss of Heaven and earth. Purple clouds bearing the surviving embers of the expiring day's light jostled each other at the sky's edge. Fiery ribbons were cast into the seedbeds of the fields, the expansive meadows, and the oaks in the grove on the hill, as if offering holy fires to seal a covenant between humans and Heaven. Even the raging waves of the river Staw responded in a firestorm to the hushed prayer of the Rebbe and the crowd of hasidim. From the buildings of the copper foundry beyond the nearby hedges came the pounding of metal and the groaning of giant furnaces all fired up. Dull echoes traveled far in the fading light of sunset as if they were spitting out the day's secrets into the silence of the night. It seemed as if this knocking, together with the raging of the river storming over its banks, were a trumpet accompaniment to the sacred work. The crescent moon was already roving about, hiding and revealing itself among the gold-crested floating clouds; and the preparations for drawing the water were not yet completed. The crowd of hasidim, swaying to and fro in the red-and-silver-hued dim light, swelled ever larger. They joined forces with the trees shaking in the woods and with the shrubs strewn along the riverbed. And the brook that emerged from the belly of the river Staw crept along slowly, winding and twisting till it reached the rows of fir trees in that palatial garden[17] at the edge of the still-flaming horizon.

"The crowd is larger today than in the past," Bat-Zion said as she washed sheets in the narrow brook along with the old household manager and the young apprentice girls.

"Perhaps they're souls, holy souls that came for the occasion," said the old woman with a sigh, after which she fell silent. Then the sound of the women rinsing the linens, hidden among the willows at the side of the brook, could once again be heard.

Bat-Zion stood and looked across the stormy river. Among the crowd standing in reverence, she recognized her father performing his sacred work. With brisk movements, restraining his trembling, he drew water from the brook with an earthenware vessel, pouring it into a basin held by the hasidim. He drew and poured, he drew and poured, in a sequence corresponding to a numerical pattern of divine Name combinations.

Out of the sound of murmured prayers, her ears caught the words "water of mitzvah." The word "mitzvah" seemed to hover in the air. Her father the Rebbe uttered that word with extra emphasis, since the Hebrew letter "*vav*"—the "v" of mitzvah—represents the divine attribute that unites Heaven and earth.[18] And it is that connective *vav* which, inserted into "matzah," completes it and makes it a mitzvah. It seemed as if the myriad little stars twinkling in the Milky Way had intentionally formed the elongated shape of a *vav*. She was reminded of the words of the old rabbi back in the closed courtyard, "Our Rebbe wants to attract the power of salvation for Israel from the Root of all Roots, from the supernal wellspring."

Just then a song broke out from the banks of the river Staw. The hasidim, who were carrying the full basin covered with a linen cloth on a pole, strode after the Rebbe and his sons, who were holding small pitchers of water wrapped in cloth. The crowd of hasidim streamed after them, singing thunderously.

The stars had shifted in the sky. Radiant worlds were being destroyed and created simultaneously. The last bit of purple in the horizon was departing with a silent trumpet blast. The sacred march melody got louder and louder, penetrating and cleaving the silvery air. It enveloped the fields and meadows, the river and the woods, finally disappearing into endless myriads beyond the Heavenly firmament. The procession passed between garden lanes bordering the buildings of the copper foundry. The hasidic owners joined in, lighting torches at their gates. From the bridge over the brook, the chanting hasidim carrying the sanctified water strode toward the main street, which ran the length of the entire town.

The town's Russian mayor left his reception room with his bodyguards, bareheaded and formally attired with swords. They watched the procession of "the Rabbi Maggid" and listened respectfully to the majestic march that blanketed the entire area. The crowd kept getting larger, the townspeople following the hasidim with lit candles in their hands. There were also candle flames in the windows, kindled in honor of the Rebbe's mitzvah preparations associated with the water for matzah making that would rest overnight.

Bat-Zion walked excitedly arm in arm with the apprentice girls Esther Reizel and Alteh Tzipporah, along with old Malkah. They climbed a pathway up the channel, made a shortcut through narrow alleys, passed by the wooden houses bordered by trees and gardens, and listened to the sounds of the march. It seemed as if a hidden spirit had burst forth from the deep chambers of the night. The slumbering town had come to life. The roofs of the houses in hills and valleys, with their smoking chimneys, and the double-vaulted roof of the great synagogue of the Maggid visible above their heads took in that soul-song. The song hovered in the air with the crescent of the moon and with the bedecked clouds; it was the song that made the water rise up out of *that* brook[19] for the baking of the bread of affliction, the order of the day before Passover—baking mitzvah matzah.

Bat-Zion was silent as they walked through the alleyways, trekking through the mud and puddles that had collected during the day from people washing their pots and pans for Passover. The sacred march melody seemed to stream into her blood. She gave her hand to Esther at her side so that the girl could feel her racing pulse. Esther laughed at her, but Bat-Zion once again surrendered to the melody. She felt a exaltation of spirit, just like the times when she would listen to her father play his consecrated violin or flute to accompany a sacred service. Exhausted, she returned to the girls' loft.

The air in the loft was entirely pure; the wooden floor was sprinkled with sawdust. The windowsills and railings, against which the wide open doors were banging, still had pillows and cushions spread over them. The shining cherry-colored round and square tables were scattered about in no particular order. The polished nickel kerosene lamps were not lit, and the moonlight spilled into the darkness of the newly freshened rooms. The shadows of the tall trees in the courtyard played on the sawdust and on the potted plants like figures whispering in a garden. Her sisters were busy doing various tasks by the moonlight, preparing tablecloths, towels, and decorative objects. They asked Bat-Zion questions, but she was so tired she did not answer. When echoes of the singing began drifting through the courtyard, her sisters left their work and went to the open windows. Bat-Zion, only half-awake, put her head

down on the freshly fluffed pillows resting on the window.
Thoughts of the water-drawing floated through her mind in a jumble, along with memories of the airing of the books before sunset.
"In those gardens and in those rivers, a young woman has no right
of entry." She remembered with sadness the words she heard her
brother say when she was gazing at the Tree of Mysteries, the Tree
of the Worlds, sketched by her father the Rebbe.[20]

"And there, in Egypt, where did the Children of Israel draw
water for matzahs?" asked Malkah the old household manager.

Bat Zion's oldest sister, Hannah Goldeleh, who had been standing, pensively listening, answered cautiously, "The Nile River runs
there and it waters the entire land of Egypt."

"In Egypt the river was smitten with plagues, with blood and
frogs, but here the rivers have been long been sanctified by your
holy ancestors," said Malkah.

Bat-Zion looked at Hannah Goldeleh's face, as the girl resumed
speaking softly, "Indeed our ancestors are holy, but not necessarily
the rivers in Poland." Her gentle face seemed anxious in the
moon's pale light, and her brown silk wig lent it a deep sadness.

All that night Bat-Zion dreamed strange dreams. The stars fell
from Heaven into the river at the time of the water drawing, and the
blades of the mill changed into giant birds, the kind she had once
seen in her grandmother's estate. They settled on the frame of the
new building, which was still under construction all those years
since the fire. And they filled the courtyard at a barren spot where a
well was being drilled, but water had not yet been found. Suddenly,
the Tree sketched by the Maggid blossomed. Its branches reached
toward the sky, scintillating with shooting stars, and a wonderful
fragrance of pure aromatic balm arose and covered them.

Bat-Zion woke several times. She inhaled the fresh smell of the
just-cleaned bedroom and once again fell into a sweet slumber.

CHAPTER

Songs of Redemption in the Rebbe's Court

Translator's Note: At this point the author makes two notable changes in her writing: The narrator's voice moves from third person to first person and the temporal location shifts from the narrative present to the retrospective recall of past events. Instead of writing of "her (Bat-Zion's) father the Rebbe, may his light shine" as in previous chapters, Shapiro now writes "my father, his righteous memory a blessing." Shapiro does not signal to the reader her intention to make these changes or provide an explanation for them. The discussion of Passover preparations is simply picked up where it left off, now in a different—and retrospective—voice. The shift has the effect of revealing what had not been stated explicitly before: that the young protagonist Bat-Zion is the author herself, as a child. The shift also brings into view for the first time the author's knowledge of the eventual fate of the Kozienice Jewish community, imparting a new weightiness of tone. It is here that the autobiographical and elegiac nature of the work emerges unmistakably. —N.P

That old hidden melody that constantly wells up in response to sparks of sacred service burst forth from my father's house on the day before holidays. Hidden from view, holy hands strummed on stringed instruments and ancient melodies broke out in a powerful storm on foreign soil, yearning for redemption—the redemption of Israel that stands just behind the wall.[1]

At the first rays of dawn from the clear sky's horizon, a crowd murmuring words of Torah poured into the grain fields, watching in reverent anticipation for the cutting of wheat for the *shemurah* matzah. And there were the holy reapers: My father, his righteous memory a blessing, accompanied by his sons, his sons-in-law,[2] and a group of hasidim waved the sickle in motions of rapture that united physical action with sacred intention.[3] Gentiles bowed deferentially at the gates of their gardens and cottages, like those sheaves of grain, which quickly fell to the feet of the reapers in satin caftans, intoning an angelic chant as the sickle waived.

The entire universe awoke to this intense song of holy rapture. Bright rays of redemption streamed in abundance from the sun's healing wings.[4] They hugged the treetops, the chimneys of the cottages, and the well spouts, shouting for joy along with the freedom song of the holy reapers.

Was this not the harvest of the Land's produce, the sheaf of first fruit that the priest waved before God and offered in the Sanctuary long ago? Were these not musical notes that have long lain dormant, but now risen for resurrection?

Our picture moves forward, and those grains of wheat that were carefully protected from the time they were harvested in alien fields now swing in earthenware jugs hanging from low beams in the old *beit midrash* built by the Maggid, his soul in Eden. They sing together with the blowing winds, the winds of eternal longing for the ancestral cradle on holy soil.

Those notes from ancient melodies resounded during festive preparations on the eve of the holiday. And from each note, the light of the festival of freedom shimmered: *"When Israel went forth from Egypt."*[5]

Each year on the day before Passover, during the baking of matzah from safeguarded wheat berries ground in holiness, primeval music rose up, notes concealed for eons behind the Heavenly *pargod* screen.[6] The same notes accompanied acts of charity, quiet prayers of the heart, and Torah studied with devotion unto death, during the days of sun and rain in summer as well as the snowy, icy days of winter.

In that ancient *beit midrash*, in air purified of the sourdough's leaven,[7] the nightingale's trills joined those gracious melodies sung to the verses of *Hallel*, floating above the bustle of *shemurah* matzah baking and the patter of feet stepping briskly on leather mats.

The bird awakened in her nest above the sparkling window-panes, now freed of their burden of ice and open wide to the vibrant, verdant world. There were sweet fragrances from the pine trees, and from fresh vegetables, which women swathed in piety had brought from the God-blessed field to my mother, her memory a blessing. She examined those greens, which had been kept hidden in the ground, with a sigh of faith and delight, while listening attentively to the soul-melodies enveloped by the song of the bird.

Even the bird's trills seemed to have been carefully preserved from a much earlier age, hidden in an eternal repository from the time when all the universe stood still and not even a bird chirped,[8] the time when the God of Israel revealed Himself to the tribes of Israel, who had just been cleansed from servitude's forty-nine gates of impurity. Having delivered them from slavery to freedom, He would one day bring them as free human beings, a holy nation, to the Land of their ancestors.

There between the mountains, in the free air of desert expanses and sands parched by the sun, living waters burst forth from the twelve springs of water near seventy palm trees,[9] symbolizing the eternal wellsprings of the tribes of Israel among the seventy nations. Those secret wellsprings disappeared temporarily during dark periods in Israel's wanderings, when our bare feet stumbled on stones[10] along the path through the sands of the nations. But in times between the periods of darkness, those bubbling springs of eternal Israel broke out in force. While no one notices, their current carries the seeds of redemption at the end of days, along with that ancient primeval song.

And in our exilic abode of Poland, in the sanctified city of Kozienice on the banks of the Vistula, those melodies escorted us during that season when the fruit trees blossomed in our family's gardens, and the voice of the turtle was heard along with *"When Israel went forth from Egypt."* At that time, the coals in the oven hissed and crackled while baking the bread of affliction and, to accompany the distribution of baked matzot, the song *"In distress I called on the Lord; the Lord answered me . . ."*[11] burst out on its own accord.

In this manner, breaking waves surged from the wellsprings, and a long-concealed light now came clearly into view. Its multihued splendor pulses with a halting, jumping rhythm on that evening when the sacred festival of Passover was ushered in. The word "Passover" (*Pesah*) can be parsed as *"Peh Sah,"* "mouth speaking"— words of praise and adulation to God, who took us out from slavery to freedom.[12] And the gematria of *"sah"* (speaking) is equivalent to that of *"chayyim"* (life), because life and death are controlled by one's use of language[13]—and we are commanded to *"choose life."*[14]

On Seder night, that hidden light[15] was visible everywhere in the hall. It shone from the pure silver of the antique vessels, hundreds of years old, the legacy of forebears who wandered through the forests of Poland from Germany and Spain after having sanctified God's name in public acts of self-sacrifice. One saw it in the sparkling of the safeguarded wine, brought from overseas, from the Holy Land. There was also choice raisin wine, prepared with the greatest care in the Maggid's cellar chambers, where Jews had once hid from the terror of Cossacks and insurrectionist Poles.

The wine sparkled in four cups corresponding to the four expressions of redemption.[16] The drinking of each cup was preceded by the kabbalistic meditation: "For the sake of the union of the blessed Holy One, and His *Shekhinah*," recited in sacred rapture. And everything was bathed in a blaze of candlelight from silver candlesticks.

The melodies of the Haggadah were so enchanting. They streamed like sparks of that ancient flame: "We were slaves to Pharaoh in Egypt. . . . *'And the Lord brought us forth from Egypt,'* not by means of an angel, and not by means of a seraph, . . . but the

Holy One, blessed be He, in His own glory and in His own person." The melodies longed to expire in that supernal union described in the prayer, "The spirit of every living thing shall bless Thy name."

And behold: A hot tear glowed, having fallen from the luminous eyes of my father, his righteous memory a blessing, upon his pure beard and his shining satin caftan from *Eretz Yisra'el*, as he stood up from his seat, rising tall to his full stature, together with his holy sons, guests from the Holy Land, *yoshvim* and elders who were fixtures in the holy court's *beit midrash*.

The freedom melodies thundered out in majestic dignity, breaking partitions, resounding in words: *"Mountains skipped like rams . . . Tremble, O earth, at the presence of the Lord . . . Who turned the rock into a pool of water, The flinty rock into a fountain."*[17] From an ancient time, surging wellsprings reverberated in song: Those twelve springs of the tribes of Israel in the desert who had just become a free people, joined by the spring of Miriam the prophet's well, that well that accompanied the Jewish people in all their exilic wanderings.[18]

Every Saturday night at Sabbath's end we, too, sipped those well waters, in the form of fresh water that the water man pumped from the well of our ancestor the Maggid, his soul in Eden, in Kozienice on the Vistula. Now we sipped them on Passover's night of majesty. And we young girls, along with our delight at our bright holiday dresses, we too drank deep from that invisible spring as we sipped wine from goblets, ate the delicious matzah, the bitter herbs, the gefilte fish, and the turkey.

In that room, conveying the mood of antiquity, a holy spirit hovered. It surrounded us as we sat together at the table of Mother, peace be upon her, and of Grandmother, her memory a blessing, in her velvet gown with its long train, sighing deeply in anticipation of the speedy advent of the Righteous Redeemer. As we drank the wine in the company of the other women—household managers, daughters of holy individuals, women of *Eretz Yisra'el*—we youngsters shared those feelings of yearning and faith. And we listened to the captivating soft prayer of Mother, her soul in Eden, dressed in brilliant fine silk, moving her lips in communion with God, at

159

that great moment of splendor after the exhausting work that preceded the Festival of Freedom.

A paradisial atmosphere filled and illumined that old hall, which seemed of its own accord to be uttering sacred words and singing soul-melodies along with those of holy humans, some manifest and some invisible. The anticipation mounted for the arrival of Elijah the prophet, harbinger of redemption, who was standing and waiting for the sacred moment when the door would be opened. Now my father, his righteous memory a blessing, his face beaming with the exultant light of redemption, returned from the entrance of the hall, having opened wide that door normally kept tightly shut, in order to greet the harbinger. And yes, the harbinger was already sipping the precious wine from that antique silver cup in unseen rapture.

Now the majestic night of redemption was dancing herself out in a blaze, hiding her afterglow in the flash of morning's first rays, which peered in, awestruck, from the hall's windows, just as the march for "Concluded is the Passover Seder" began to thunder. This march had gone through many incarnations over time since that original song of freedom during the Exodus. No doubt it had once echoed quietly in underground chambers during the Inquisition. It had wandered with shepherds' flutes in the wilderness of the nations, becoming sanctified in the Carpathian mountains, Belorussia, Russia, and Poland. And now at the conclusion of the Seder—the time when the lights of the night of majesty would be hidden away—the march's notes thundered out, accompanied by the steps of invisible legions, holy choirs taking their leave with the words "Concluded is the Passover Seder / According to its law and custom / . . . Speedily lead the offshoots of thy stock / Redeemed, to Zion in joyous song."

The dawn cleaving the air with the *Shekhinah*'s presence broke into song, joining the holy exultation bursting from the hearts of the participants, who stood throbbing with yearning to return "Redeemed, to Zion in joyous song," "Next Year in Jerusalem."

Now came the chanting of The Song of Songs, the song of Solomon—that is, *Shelomo:* the name of God, the King to whom *"Shalom"* most truly applies. Together with the trills of the turtledove, the notes of the chant were carried on hidden wings of the wind to spice mountains in the Land of Life, the Land flowing with milk and honey, the Land of the forefathers.

Alas, those melodies of the house of my father the Rebbe, his soul in Eden, which were heard in Israel's Diaspora in her exilic habitation, are silenced, done in, along with entire households of our holy ancestors from Kozienice, their souls in Eden; Grodzisk, their memory a blessing; and many, many others throughout Poland, Galicia, Russia, Ukraine, together with all the holy communities, our annihilated brothers and sisters, may God requite their blood. The rich brew of exilic life in those lands turned sour, spoiled by the acid[19] of Nazism, may their name be blotted out. Those lands have been polluted with the blood of holy communities crying out from stained soil.

But the wellsprings of eternal Israel still burst forth unceasingly. *"That garden spring, a well of fresh waters, a rill of Lebanon"*[20] continues to nurture the roots of Israel's tree and its shoots wherever they may be, from the dawning of deliverance until the complete redemption.

We can now hear in our Land the "feet of the prince's daughter"[21]—the collective soul of Israel; and along with her, *"the vine shall produce its fruit"*[22] in the vineyards of the King to whom *"Shalom"* most truly applies. *"The king is held captive in the tresses."*[23] As the Maggid of Kozienice interpreted this verse, "God bound himself with an oath that He will cause His *Shekhinah* to dwell in Israel" (*Avodat Yisra'el* for Passover).[24] And as we drink the safeguarded wine linked to the four expressions of redemption from the vineyards of Ein Gedi, Judea, and Sharon, Israel's collective soul will be forever adorned with the voice of the turtledove heard in our Land, and by the Heavenly voice proclaiming: *"How lovely are your feet . . . O daughter of nobles!"*[25]

Foiling a Heavenly Adversary[1]

Translator's Note: This story of the High Holiday season does not follow in direct temporal sequence with the previous chapter. It is a separate vignette that Malkah Shapiro inserted here, one must assume, to augment her portrait of Kozienice. —NP

On that road used by wayfarers near the water mill and the sand dunes, the hasidim took a rest stop. They were going to the town of the Maggid, to his descendant the incumbent Rebbe who occupied his holy ancestor's seat, totally devoted to his teachings and holy ways. On the surface, life seemed to be proceeding as usual. But at second glance, one noticed a profound disorder, as if the very laws of nature had been turned upside down. The aged prayer leader Reb Yekele had a voice as clear as that of a young boy, just as the tzaddik of his generation had blessed him in his youth. But now his belly felt like an empty pit, and his voice seemed to be trapped in his body, refusing to leave his throat. That night was the eve of *Selichot*, the penitential prayers preceding Rosh Hashanah. With the first rays of dawn, he would be called upon to stand before the Holy Ark and lead services in the Rebbe's synagogue.

The birds' silvery trills filled the damp, cool air, saturated with odors of hay and cut grain. The draw horses, harnessed to wagons filled with young and old, drank leisurely from the river, chatting with their reflections in the water. The mill's gears seemed to clatter in time to the melodies of the hasidim, who were resting between the dunes and the river following the conclusion of the afternoon service. The old man stood bewildered after having finished his prayers. His scrawny face turned yellow, his wrinkles multiplied, the white hairs of his long beard bristled. His lips moved but his voice did not obey. The day was coming to an end; Heaven and earth kissed the sun hanging on the horizon. People bathed and performed ritual ablutions in the river's clear waters. Young hasidic members of his choir, wearing knitted *gartls*, would not let go of the old man, sunk in his misery.

"Reb Yekele, just one melody, just one tune," youthful voices rang out. Soon the young people were joined by a group of veteran hasidim from the prayer leader's hometown, the district capital Lublin.

"Wake up, Reb Yekele! To get in the mood for representing the holy congregation before the Day of Judgment in our Rebbe's synagogue, let's hear just one refrain of 'Remember the Covenant with Abraham and the Binding of Isaac' and perhaps a bit of the sacred melody for 'A Crown Is Given to You,' which the holy Maggid overheard from the ministering angels in Heaven!"[2] Trying to rouse him, they began singing the march in chorus.

The old prayer leader opened his mouth wide, tried to sing, but his yellow face contorted into a twisted smile that froze on his dim eyes, and his voice choked in his throat. It seemed as if Heaven and earth weighed upon him, and he fell silent.

The anxiety of the hasidim grew as they lingered a while longer at the water mill. Perhaps the exhausting journey had so weakened his frail body that the power of speech had abandoned him. Or perhaps it was the fault of the gentile hooligans from the village of Ruda, who had stared from the fences of their shanties, hissing and throwing stones. Maybe that's what had instilled fear in his heart? And perhaps . . . perhaps his time had come. After all, Reb Yekele the prayer leader was well into his eighties. It's true he had been blessed with a youthful voice and a long life. But it was quite possible that some minor sin had gotten in the way, and that he had exhausted his blessing.

The sun's orb had already plunged into the depths of the horizon, filling the damp air with shimmering redness. The horses, hitched again to the peasants' wagons, lifted their legs at the flick of the drivers' whips.

The hasidim in the wagons chanted High Holiday melodies, encouraged the prayer leader with song and a drop of whiskey for toasting *l'chaim*. But he just sat there, depressed and shaking. He listened to the melodies he knew only too well, which he used to sing with such fervor, but some inner torment pressed upon him and his silence intensified.

For a long while the wagons dragged on an unpaved road between rows of oaks. As night fell and the stars came out, just when water carriers were running along with filled buckets drawn from the well on Magitowa Street, the wagon wheels clattered into the street. The wagons had arrived with their passengers and their somber chanting. The wide street, planted with chestnut trees in front of wooden and stone houses, swarmed with Jews rushing to synagogue or to their homes. In a mood of festive joy, they all shouted greetings to the wagons: "There's Yekele, our Rebbe's prayer leader with his silver voice, and his choir! No doubt Heaven has already written us up for a good new year!" The voices rang out from all sides. But who could have fathomed the meaning of the old man's silence? His soul churned in agony, pained by the burden of the melodies and chants. He was dumbstruck, unable to utter even a single note.

Wrapped in his heavy coat, the exhausted prayer leader arrived at his guest room in the home of the Rebbe's personal attendant, along with his companions. Most of the guests dispersed to their own lodging, but a few went on an urgent mission to summon the town's lone physician, in the hope that he might have some reme-dy for the strange illness that had struck the old prayer leader. But when they reached the gate of the physician's house, they were dis-tressed to find it locked.

The house was empty but for a gigantic guard dog on a chain. The physician, a bachelor, had been practicing in town but a short time since the old Dr. Zhurzhinsky—who had been a good friend of the town's Jews in general and of the Rebbe's household in par-ticular—had passed on. But since, as the Talmud put it, "physicians have a mandate to heal," it was important to obtain even such a one as this, who lived a life of wantonness. The young men on the mission, joined by the young attendant Shlomo who had come out to welcome them, watched the house in the gentile quarter enclosed by a flower garden, as if laying siege. When they saw the short, obese physician stagger half-drunk toward the gate, they ran after him, crying in great distress, "Someone's very sick, Doctor, please hurry!"

The physician, who was not particularly fond of Jews, roused his shotgun-carrying guard to warn the group to leave immediately and not disturb his rest. The two of them, the physician and his guard, disappeared into the darkness of the garden and made their way into the small brick house through one of the entrances. The garden gates and house doors were locked and the shutters were closed, but the group of hasidim did not leave the house. Building up their courage, they stationed themselves behind the windows near the fence and called out boldly, "The doctor ought to know that the Heavenly Court will have already pronounced sentence on him if he does not come to assist the sick old man who came from far away to the Rebbe the Maggid in honor of the New Year."

Their warning echoed in the winds rumbling through the night's blue darkness and smothered the wolf-dog's murderous barking as the animal ran back and forth in an angry heat, almost breaking the iron chain around his neck, which was anchored to the thatch doghouse.

It didn't take long for the door to open. The physician came out alone to the yard in his nightclothes. As he approached the yard's gate, he found his arms linked to the arms of the young hasidim, and in a few moments he was standing in front of the sick old man, who was sitting head bowed, dejected, a faint cry struggling to break out from deep within.

Persuading the pharmacy to reopen after closing time, they obtained the medicine prescribed by the physician. The old man took a few spoonfuls, to no effect, and refused to take any more. In speech that was difficult to understand, he expressed his desire to turn to the tzaddik, the Rebbe, Rabbi Yerahmiel Moshe. For that was the whole point of his coming, to be in the Rebbe's presence and to stand in his holy house in supplication before the Creator of the universe, that He grant forgiveness to the congregation of Israel and inscribe them in the Book of Life. The old man's request tore the heart of the hasidim and they consented, although they were fearful of causing distress to the Rebbe, who would be beside himself with worry.

In fear and trembling the members of the delegation traversed the courtyards of the Rebbe's home. The sound of the trees' falling leaves blended with the melodies and prayer chants coming from the old *beit midrash*, the legacy of the Maggid. In the closed courtyard buzzing with hushed prayers, noisy talmudic discussions, and the frequent sighs of those engaged in sacred service, the door to the Inner Sanctum opened.

The Rebbe was leaning over a sacred text spread out on the table between two silver candlesticks with lit candles. After hearing the words of the delegation, he straightened up. His noble face turned pale, furrows spread on his high forehead, and it seemed as if his beard had just sprouted gray hairs. "It was enough that they brought the physician and paid his fee. As for the medicine he prescribed, you may pour it out, there is no need of it," he said firmly. After a short pause, his captivating voice rang out again in that low-ceilinged room piled high with books: "Let Yekele the prayer leader's ears hear this: The blessing that our holy ancestors, may their merit protect us, bestowed upon him is fully in force. Any Heavenly adversarial power that may wish to deter him at the time when our holy community gathers to enthrone our Father in Heaven will fail. The voice of Israel will rise in unison and overpower all angelic opposition. By virtue of his strong faith, his voice will be heard during these High Holy Days. If only the Judge of all the earth would acquit us, so that we could shape our own verdict during these days of repentance and mercy: a pure heart, a clear mind without sadness. This was always the wish of our holy ancestors, our teachers. May we be inscribed immediately in the Book of Life."

The Rebbe directed that the old prayer leader be brought before dawn to the cantor's lectern facing the holy ark, to lead the *Selichot* services for the day before Rosh Hashanah. And he ordered his personal attendant, who had ushered in the delegation for their audience, not to allow the old prayer leader to leave the attendant's house where he was staying as a guest until the attendant gave him some of the coffee that he prepared for the Rebbe every morning.

"Everybody knows that my attendant Yashkar-Ber is a great expert at preparing elixirs. He performs his work faithfully, and what he produces will have healing power." He flashed a smile as he said these last words, and the members of the delegation sprang past the outer door to fulfill the Rebbe's behest. Vapors of the pungent coffee spread to the entrance of the attendants' room, and they drew in deep breaths of the aroma.

Dawn broke slowly through patches of cloudy sky. The sun poked out from the tops of the pine trees onto the tall synagogue of the Maggid, his soul in Eden, with its double-vaulted roof. And there was the voice of the old prayer leader Reb Yekele, ringing out like the voice of a young lad. The sound of his prayer rose in trills; it spilled out forcefully from the narrow windows[3] illumined by the synagogue's many lamps, and blended with the clear tones of the Rebbe's ecstatic prayer.

At that moment, a multitude of voices burst forth, joining in prayerful supplication, like the roaring breakers of powerful waters: "Remember the covenant of Abraham and the binding of Isaac. . . . Raise up Your desolate Temple before our eyes, and restore the captivity of the tents of Jacob, and save us for the sake of Thy name."[4]

In the Heavenly realm, as the clouds vanished in the shimmering sunrise, it seemed as if the fading stars were joining the holy congregation in its sacred song and petitions for forgiveness and mercy, which the angelic hosts brought before the throne of justice at that moment leading into Rosh Hashanah, the day of divine sovereignty.

Contending Spirits

Translator's Note: Here Malkah Shapiro continues her narrative in the first person, beginning this chapter in her own present time, probably the 1950s. She indicates that her parents are no longer alive by appending to their names such phrases as "her soul in Eden," and "his righteous memory a blessing."

The theme of the chapter is the clash of cultures between two hasidic lineages that are uniting in marriage. Its centerpiece is a story told by Shapiro's mother, Rebbetzin Brachah Tzipporah Gitl, which takes us back to a family wedding when Brachah was a child. The reader will note the similarity to Chapter Nine, in which the story-teller is Rebbetzin Sarah Devorah, the author's grandmother, who recalls a story from her childhood in the mid-nineteenth century. As in Chapter Nine, this narrative is structured as a story within a story. The outer frame story, set in Kozienice around 1905, depicts the young Malkah Shapiro listening to her mother telling her story. The inner story is from her mother's childhood and takes place in Chernobyl, Ukraine, around the year 1866. The central personality in the inner story is Brachah Twersky's great-grandfather (the author's great-great-grandfather), Rabbi Aharon Twersky of Chernobyl (1787–1872), who was about seventy-nine years old in 1866.

Note that—as in Chapter Nine—it is a family matriarch who preserves the narrative that gives the family its sense of self and spiritual location within the world of Hasidism. As repositories and transmitters of sacred memories, they provide a bridge to the mid-nineteenth century and links to Hasidism's foundational period.

To assist the reader in following the levels of the narrative, Brachah's story is indented.—N.P.

In one of those post-Sabbath moments on a winter Saturday night, I listened to a story that my mother the Rebbetzin, her soul in Eden, used to tell with a sense of wonder and holy awe. She was still wearing her precious dress of fine silk with its long train, which enhanced her stately beauty and made the serene grace of her shining face stand out powerfully.

She adjusted the lace kerchief covering her gold-embroidered headdress (her own handiwork), closed her prayer book, and folded the page at the verses of blessing for the coming week, *"Ve-yiten lekha, may God give you of the dew of heaven . . ."*[1] Her enchanting voice rang out in the warm air of the heated dining room, which was still hovering in that space between holy Sabbath and mundane weekday.

"When the Sabbath takes leave, the demonic forces have no power in our habitations, God forbid. Nevertheless, it's appropriate to reveal how our holy ancestors of blessed memory struggled with them and overcame them."

She was quiet for a few moments, and silence prevailed among the group of old-time close friends of the household who had come to wish the blessing of a good week to my mother the Rebbetzin.

The candle flames in the silver candlesticks on the table sputtered secrets, as if giving voice to the quiet patter of the Sabbath Queen's departing steps. The light from the oil lamp, which had just been brought in, seemed to reveal a hint of the hidden presence of Elijah the harbinger of redemption. Strains of *"Eliyahu ha-Navi,"* the song in honor of Elijah, were coming from the sacred room of our holy ancestor, the Maggid of Kozienice. In the Maggid's room were my father the Rebbe, his righteous memory a blessing, his sons, and a group of hasidim, singing melodies of redemption in holy ecstasy, in concert with the violin's sublime song.

Sighing quietly, my mother resumed her story:

Yes, our ancestors struggled and overcame them. It happened when I was a little child trailing my mother's skirts.[2] My great-grandfather the tzaddik Rabbi Aharon was celebrating the marriage of his modest granddaughter, Batya Nehamaleh, to her mate the great Rabbi Yashkar Bereleh of Belz.[3] The wedding festivities rocked the foundations of my holy ancestor's court, especially since they had just made a sudden decision to celebrate the wedding of another granddaughter, my dear aunt Malkaleh, at the same time.[4]

Only light winds were blowing on that autumn day. Fallen leaves drifted about in the orchard, and patches of azure sky appeared through the clouds in the holy courtyards. The male and female servants went back and forth carrying utensils from one wing of the compound to another, from the children's residence, from the kitchens. The conversations of the hasidim were laden with worry, injecting a sour note into the band's music and the melodies drifting through the courtyards. "Their holy ways are different from ours; who knows what might happen," the learned elders said to each other. They tiptoed past the shutters of the Inner Sanctum, straining their ears to catch a wisp of the conversation behind closed doors.

Wedding revelers dressed like Cossacks and Hussars went out together with the assembled hasidim, all shouting in joyous exultation to greet the fine groom and his saintly relatives at the banks of the Dnieper. When the Rebbe's assistants came into the Inner Sanctum to tell him that the ship had already anchored at the riverside and in a short while the party would arrive in town, our holy great-grandfather let out a sigh that could break a man's body. He rose shakily from his bed where he had taken a short rest and, leaning on the arm of my dear father, he walked slowly into a room filled with the smell of books and tobacco. My father had been raised by his grandfather, after his own father, Rabbi Nahum, the oldest son of my great-grandfather, his righteous memory a blessing, had died an untimely death. Drawing back the curtains from the window, he gazed at the horizon, where a black cloud the size of a man's hand[5] was rising. With the full force of his voice, eyebrows raised, he said, "Our path is the path of calmness and serenity.[6] It is not our way to confront the demonic forces of the Other Side head on. But they, our relatives-by-marriage from Belz, long may they live, have taken it upon themselves to declare a holy war against them. They even forcibly banish spirits by exorcism. But that only incites the demons to go after us. It looks as if a storm is building up."

Furrowing her prominent forehead, my mother the Rebbetzin, her soul in Eden, continued her story.

And indeed the storm did come. The cloud that arose from the western horizon continued to expand until the entire sky became overcast. Thick thunderclouds greeted the descending sun. They were filled with rage, they were blood soaked, and they billowed smoke.

Along with the thunderous singing of the hasidim and the marches of the klezmer band that accompanied the groom and his tzaddikim relatives as they approached town, a windstorm with thunder and lightning was gathering force, the likes of which no one had ever seen. And these sounds were accompanied by the wailing of people stricken with illnesses, God spare us, who were possessed by *dybbukim*, wandering spirits. They had been drawn to the holy wedding, hoping to be healed by the groom's father, the tzaddik who forcibly expels *dybbukim* by exorcism.

Even though the sound of the wailing was masked by the music and the singing, it nevertheless struck terror in the celebrating crowd. They avoided the vestibule of the synagogue, where the *dybbuk*-stricken people had encamped.

Here was a woman banging her head against the wall and crying out with a man's voice, "My wife, my wife, were we partners in treating people unfairly? Did we not do business honestly? But I barely had a chance to live, and the Cossacks came and killed me. I'm a wanderer through the worlds with no rest."

And here was a maiden seated on the synagogue's doorstep, head bent over, with a boy's voice moaning in her throat, "We made a solemn agreement, sealing it with a handshake when we were children, in the orchard that my father had leased from the nobleman. I broke my vow, and my life was cut short at the time of the plague; now I wander through the universe without rest. Please go to the court to release me from my vow and forgive me."

So there was wailing on one hand and on the other, storm winds beating on the windows and doors, howling and shrieking strangely, like cries of despair from the legions of the unseen.

And in the *ezrat nashim*, the bridesmaids in their velvet and silk dresses were waltzing to the rhythms of the klezmer band, their radiant faces turned toward the bride Batya Nehamaleh. She was the very epitome of the talmudic "beautiful and pious bride,"[7] resting on her silk upholstered armchair, between tables with candles burning in silver candlesticks; her face, touched by a gracious halo, beamed at the dancers.

The young women danced the scissors dance, while older women with their pearl-studded velvet headbands shining under silk kerchiefs jumped the kazatzke.

The celebration and festivities grew louder and stronger. But, in spite of that, the terror that had cast a pall over the hall's appearance, its music and its singing, did not abate.

The young bride was seated at the center of the *beit midrash's* main hall. The women were loosening her braids, sobbing prayers and supplications that the bride rouse divine mercy for them and their children; that diphtheria and other diseases not infect their babies; that their children should survive and grow up in the path of God and His Torah; and many more requests for divine assistance relating to problems of childrearing, economic distress, and harsh governmental edicts.

The renowned *badchen*[8] was in the midst of his routine, including the part where in plaintive tones he chastises the bride to repentance at that time of divine mercy. The bride was sobbing and entreating God to forgive her sins, to bless her and her distinguished mate with good fortune, and to bestow upon the Children of Israel their hearts' desires for good.

She had already soaked her handkerchief with tears; but now the assemblage of hasidim was approaching with the groom, Rebbe Yashkar Bereleh, who cut a resplendent figure as he strode arm in arm with his holy groomsmen. Wearing sable *shtreimels*, holy awe on their visages graced with pure beards, they stood facing the dear bride.

For just one moment the groom raised his downcast eyes and gazed at the bride, her eyes red from weeping; for the bridesmaids had removed the kerchief from her eyes so that the groom would not transgress the talmudic prohibition that "a man must not betroth a woman before he sees her."[9]

The groom covered the bride's head and face with an embroidered veil. Waves of tightly jammed hasidim streamed after the groom and his attendants and the bride and her attendants. They were all carried along from the pillars of the spacious *beit midrash* to the large courtyard for the marriage ceremony. But still, supernatural forces intervened to disrupt events; demonic powers were given free reign to turn everything upside down.

Black clouds gathered in larger and larger formations, storming through the night air, dazed by thunder and lightning. Insolent winds blew, uprooting trees, knocking over lamp stands, which became elongated tongues of fire, and pulling at the poles of the wedding canopy.

Terror intensified. The guests were already emotional and apprehensive as they waited for the ceremony to begin. They all knew that at that moment the souls of the departed ancestors of the groom and bride would be present. Moreover, people were fearful of the rage of the gentiles, who begrudged the Jews their moment of celebration. Ever since the Cossack massacres, Amalek's[10] venom still seethed. Now the souls of Jews martyred in pogroms, who had possessed stricken individuals, wailed incessantly in consort with the capricious, terrifying storm.

Dawn burst forth from the expanse of clouds as if from the River of Fire,[11] and the wedding blessings rang out in melodious chant, "May there soon be heard in the cities of Judea and the streets of Jerusalem, the sound of delight, the sound of joy, . . . the sound of grooms' jubilation from their canopies . . ." The bride and groom were carried above the heads of the crowd to the *yichud* room[12] and then back to the halls, accompanied by the music of the band, which gladdened the heart and gradually stilled the anxieties of the guests. And finally my holy grandfather left for his room, followed by his new kinsman, the tzaddik Rabbi Yehoshualeh of Belz.

Outside it stormed, while inside singing and dancing prevailed. But in the Inner Sanctum, in that holy room, the relatives of the new couple were discussing matters of cosmic importance.[13] Pale and weak, my great-grandfather the tzaddik Rabbi Aharon pulled on his holy beard with his closed fist and said, "Please, my dear kinsman, your way does not seem appropriate to me. Our generation is a humble one. If, because of untoward events, there are wandering souls that have no rest, our task is to raise ourselves up with the splendor of our good deeds. We will then be able to influence this generation to know the God of our fathers, to bond intimately with Him and follow His path. Then the demonic powers that came into existence because of those events and have seized a purchase on the powers of holiness will go away of their own accord. They will vanish, and the wayward souls will find their rightful place of rest. It is not up to us to go out and openly do battle with the forces of the Left Side,[14] thereby giving them the power to respond in kind."

His relative-by-marriage the tzaddik of Belz rose, smoothing the hairs of his *peyos* and wiping his wrinkled forehead. Barely restraining his anger, his voice boomed, "With might, our right arms will bring salvation.[15] The wicked will get the punishment they deserve; we shall indeed battle fiercely with demonic forces wherever they may be. Wandering spirits will come to us, and we will forcibly deliver them from the hold of the forces of darkness."

My great-grandfather Reb Aharon, his righteous memory a blessing, held fast to his view. "But the blessed God always joins the attribute of mercy to the attribute of judgment, to enable the world to survive.[16] We must walk in God's path and not bestir the attribute of judgment, which would lead only to an increase in the numbers of those afflicted by a *dybbuk,* and further calamities for the Jewish people, God forbid. And if you don't agree with us, then let's celebrate two weddings together, with God's help. Since your son his excellency Yashkar Bereleh, long may he live, just married my granddaughter the tzaddeket Batya Nehamaleh, long may she live, according to the law of Moses and Israel, let's now set up a second marriage canopy with God's help for the other couple pledged to each other. Your dear son Leibishl, long may he live, will marry his dear bride, my granddaughter Malkaleh, long may she live. Afterward you will go home in peace, and you'll be able to continue on your path, with your attribute of rigor."

"That's fine, he is indeed thirteen years old, ready for marriage," answered his kinsman the tzaddik of Belz, sighing deeply. "But I am deeply pained that you don't want me to come back here, to have the pleasure of being with you."

"What can I do?" exclaimed my holy great-grandfather Rabbi Aharon of Chernobyl, his righteous memory a blessing, pulling a hair from his thick eyebrows. "What can I do if your way is the way of forcefulness and ours is the way of *tiferet*, compassionate grace.[17]

177

I don't want demonic forces to be stirred up in my abode. Look at that storm raging!"

He got up from his seat and, leaning on the shoulder of my dear father, he looked out the window to the dark courtyard that was packed with people. Above their heads broken lanterns flickered, tree branches swayed, and the sheet metal of the tin roofs flapped.

My mother, her soul in Eden, wrapped herself in the small woolen shawl that her devoted household manager had placed on her shoulders, since the embers in the stove had grown dim and the temperature in the room had fallen a bit. She leafed through the prayer book before her and, in concert with the mysteries sputtering from the flickering candles, her voice rose again in holy awe.

I was very young at the time, and I couldn't really comprehend the meaning of those discussions on cosmic matters, nor did they interest my tender mind. But along with my happiness that my aunt Malkaleh would soon be a bride, I was seized for some reason by a great fear, and I hid my head in the satin sleeve that draped my dear father's arm. I closed my eyes to avoid gazing at that room filled with secrets, furnished with only a small bookstand, a table that held burning candles and many books, and leather chairs for the saintly relatives to sit on.

After a number of moments of deep silence, the doors flung open, seemingly of their own accord, or perhaps from the wind, and a delegation of hasidic elders entered the Inner Sanctum. They were attempting to prevail upon the tzaddikim to return to their guests, who were quite frightened. Constables had arrived, sent by the police with a warning not to alarm the local Russians, who had seen groups of strange figures arriving together with large crowds of hasidim, all pushing to get to the court of the tzaddik. And along with these crowds, the waves of the Dnieper were cresting, blown about by storm winds, which were lifting the straw roofs off the peasants' shacks.

After the delegation of hasidim delivered their message, the oppressive silence that had grown between the two saintly kinsmen was broken, and they agreed to hold the second marriage ceremony after the completion of the seven days of celebration for the first couple.

During those seven feast days in my great-grandfather's court, the trumpet, violin, and drum sounded constantly; and the hasidic music never stopped. But together with the great joy over the nuptials, there was no letup in the sense of dread that had found purchase in the heart of the community. We children were blown about by the storm winds. We ran from one wing of the courtyard and garden to another, wearing heavy winter clothing. We loved the joyful marches of the klezmer band; but, on the other hand, our teeth chattered in terror from every bird that stirred the trees, from the raven's screech, from the whining of cats nearby, and from the howling of dogs far away in the gentiles' neighborhood.

The only area the children were not permitted to enter was the wing where my grandmother, the widow of the tzaddik Rabbi Nahum, his righteous memory a blessing, resided. There the women were keeping the twelve-year-old bride busy with a discussion of women's laws.[18] Despite myself, I was drawn to that area. The bride Malkahle, my aunt whom I loved so much, enchanted me with her sweet smile and the tears in her eyes. But I couldn't figure out the reason for her constant blushing.

On the night of the wedding there was dancing everywhere. I danced with the little girls my age, and the older women formed their own circle dances. My mother, her righteous memory a blessing, who was already mortally ill with the disease that was to take her in the prime of her life, danced the "mitzvah dance"[19] with extraordinary fervor. Everything she did bespoke virtue—this was something she inherited from her mother the Rebbetzin, my grandmother Raheleh, who was famous for her wisdom and goodness. She was the granddaughter of the tzaddik of Apta,[20] the author of *Ohev Yisroel*. And here, too, my mother tried with all the strength she had to bring joy to the bride, so that no tinge of sadness would take hold of her as a result of the raging winds, which blew even more wildly that night than during the previous wedding.

The storm even instilled a certain timidity in the governmental officials who had come to participate in the celebration of the tzaddikim. They loved the gefilte fish and the other delicacies served during the seven days of feasting. Wearing their stately uniforms with brass buttons and leather whips, they walked about solemnly, as if they had both the authority and the ability to quiet the winds and howling, and to put everything in order.

Lowering her eyelids in communion with the magical atmosphere of her childhood, Mother continued her story:

During the entire wedding night, I didn't move from the armchair of my aunt the bride. With her white satin dress, she looked like Queen Esther in her royal garments. The radiance of her face shone by the candlelight in the silver candlesticks. Her beautiful braids were undone by the tearful women surrounding her. They hung loose until her dear thirteen-year-old groom, wearing a sable *shtreimel*, covered them with a gold-embroidered cloth.

Moved by the *badchen's* plaintive singsong exhortations, the bride began sobbing intensely, and my mood also turned heavy and I broke down weeping. But those tears that fell from my eyes and the eyes of the grown-ups did not wash away the oppressive fear that mingled with the holy awe and the abundant joy, until by a miracle the skies cleared.

After the wedding, at the break of dawn, the young couple was carried above the heads of the crowd from the courtyard to the Inner Sanctum. And at that moment tranquility returned. Gentle winds rolled in from the four corners of the earth, the skies shed their black covers, and the howling and shrieking were no longer heard. It was as if the forces of No Good had returned to their abyss, and the wandering souls had found peace.

Then the joy intensified sevenfold and the sounds of singing and music rang out with clarity and purity, as if the messianic era had arrived, and one could truly hear "the voice of the groom and the bride in the cities of Judea and the streets of Jerusalem" along with the "jubilation of grooms in their canopies."[21]

Sounds of thanksgiving drifted along with the leaves in the fresh autumn air from the holy courtyards to the riverbank, accompanying the departing guests and their hosts. After the whistle sounded, and the boat carrying the saintly kinfolk to far-off places set sail, everything settled down. At that moment, people realized that the storm had arisen on account of the abundance of redemptive energy that is likely to blossom at such a special moment, a holy gathering where the living join together with the souls of the saintly departed, where spirits commune under the marriage canopy.

In the end, the attribute of compassion overcame the attribute of severity.

The candles flickered out in the Rebbetzins' dining room, the china lamp grew dim, and the shadows dancing on the flowered wallpaper seemed to be whispering ancient mysteries. Mother's audience had been listening intently and sighed frequently. As she concluded her story, mother too sighed quietly,

"People never stopped talking about that amazing storm, and about the two weddings in the holy courts of my great-grandfather, the tzaddik Rabbi Aharon, his righteous memory a blessing, even in the house of my holy father the Rebbe,[22] after he had settled in Loyev on the Dnieper, establishing his own court in which he followed the ways of his holy ancestors from Chernobyl. In that lovely court, with its orchard and its well in the center, people seemed still to sense that storm of primordial forces. And they also felt the hovering presence of that holy aphorism: 'Our path is that of *tiferet*.'"

By now the melodies had ceased in the Maggid's holy room. And as my father the Rebbe, his righteous memory a blessing, returned from the Maggid's holy room to his Inner Sanctum in the other

courtyard, walking with a briskness expressing holy purpose, he stopped for a few moments in the dining room. As the startled group rose in respect, his voice rang out in ecstatic tones, "The attribute of *tiferet*, compassionate grace, is based on *da'at*, mindfulness. And *da'at* is rooted in *emunah*, faithfulness."[23]

17

CHAPTER

Before and After
the End

Translator's Note: Beginning with pre–World War I reminiscences, this chapter moves forward to events that took place during the war, and concludes with descriptions of the annihilation of Kozienice during World War II. Since Malkah Shapiro moved to Palestine in 1926, her descriptions of Holocaust events are based on survivors' accounts.

This chapter also provides information about the author's birth in 1894, and the family's response to a new girl in the family—when they had been hoping for a boy. Finally, she depicts her own process of retrospection in those moments when her consciousness is flooded with images from her past.—N.P.

Reb Meilekh son of Reb Pinhas[1] was a veteran hasid, a very astute individual, a talmudic scholar and a compassionate father to his children. What does a Jew like him do when he's not able to make ends meet from his many pursuits, even after he has purchased the flour mill in the village of Kucilik?[2] He expresses his worries—that churned like the wheels of his mill in surging waters—in heartfelt prayer, unburdening himself before our Father in Heaven, the compassionate and gracious one.

But when Reb Meilekh laid out his troubles before Heaven, it wasn't like the average Jew; he was a prayer leader who chanted in the synagogue of the holy Maggid of Kozienice, his soul in Eden. Right next to him stood his Rebbe, the tzaddik Rabbi Yerahmiel Moshe, his soul in Eden, the successor to the seat of the holy old Maggid, his righteous memory a blessing. Reb Meilekh found refuge in proximity to his Rebbe's sublimely sweet soul.

The supplications of this universally respected prayer leader so burdened with worries, burst from the innermost place of his heart. They penetrated the hearts of the congregation, helping them to uncover their own deeply buried anxieties[3] and surrender them to their Father in Heaven, just as Scripture says, *"In distress I called on the Lord; the Lord answered me and brought me relief."*[4]

During the High Holidays, on Rosh Hashanah the Festival of Remembrance and on Yom Kippur the Festival of the Tenth Day, he laid out the pleas of his fellow Jews before the blessed Holy One, entreating Him to grace Jacob's seed with a year of light and joy, himself included.

But there were moments when Reb Meilekh forgot his worries altogether during prayer. One such time was the *Kedushat Keter,* the Coronation Sanctus, which begins with the words "[The multitude of angels above, and Your people Israel gathered below] give You a crown."[5] Dancing like a little schoolchild, he would sing a joyous melody, the holy march, which, according to tradition, the holy Maggid of Kozienice, his soul in Eden, heard the ministering angels singing when they were ushering Shmuel Zbitkower[6] into paradise.

And who was Shmuel Zbitkower? He was an affluent Jew, the husband of the hasidic devotee Temerel.[7] Not deeply spiritual, he was in fact an assimilated Jew. So how did he achieve that high standing? It was the merit of a great act of charity that he performed when the Cossacks were in a violent frenzy in Praga on the Vistula, the river that divides Warsaw the capital city into two parts. At that time, when the Cossacks were inflicting a horrific pogrom on the Jews, pillaging and butchering young and old, this Shmuel Zbitkower was moved to set up a barrel filled with gold coins, announcing, "Whoever brings a Jew alive will receive two gold coins, and whoever brings a Jewish body will receive one gold coin." The pogrom ceased immediately. The bodies of those who had been martyred were buried in a Jewish cemetery, and those still alive were spared from the murderous hands of the rampaging Cossacks.

Some time later, our ancestor the holy Maggid, his soul in Eden, was leading services in the large synagogue he had built for the community. At such moments, he would disregard his own frail health as he flung his entire being into his devotions with ecstatic self-surrender. The sweet melodies of his holy prayer carried from the synagogue through the entire town, finally piercing the very Heavens. At that moment, just as he was about to chant the *Kedushah*, which proclaims the coronation of God by the angels above and Israel below, the ministering angels allowed the Maggid to hear the march to which they were ushering that simple Jew into Heaven. In the talmudic aphorism, Zbitkower was one of those who earns paradise in a single moment of virtue.[8]

In the house of my father the Rebbe, his righteous memory a blessing, the tradition of singing that sacred march before the coronation *Kedushah* during High Holiday services was strictly observed. At times the sights and sounds come back to me of that sublime atmosphere in the Maggid's synagogue, filled with its holy congregation all wrapped in their prayer shawls; women in the women's gallery weeping; and both men and women together, focusing their hearts upon our Father in Heaven and proclaiming His sovereignty over the world. At those moments, the image of the prayer leader appears before my eyes, wrapped in his tallit, dancing before the holy ark as he sang the sacred march. I imagine even the birds flying from the tinted glass windows in a blaze of colors to the double vault at the top of the building, adding their voices to the singing holy congregation.

And not only then. On Friday evenings throughout the year, when the Sabbath was being welcomed in the small, ancient *beit midrash*, lit by kerosene lamps hanging from the low ceiling and by

Sabbath candles on the reader's lectern, then too the moving voice of Reb Meilekh the prayer leader rang out with the melodies for *"Lekhah Dodi"*: "Come, my beloved, to greet the bride / Let us welcome Sabbath's presence," together with the congregational chorus, causing those age-old support beams to shake. The entire congregation joined in the sweet melodies: hasidim wrapped in satin caftans, the Sabbath Queen's invited guests; servants and their children, like Shlomo Beryls, who devotedly attended to the needs of the *yoshvim*, the resident scholars committed to study and prayer in the *beit midrash*.

And then there were the townspeople—their memory a blessing, the Lord requite their blood—fine upstanding Jews who were so laden with their cares on weekdays. For example, there was Eliezer Itshe: Every penny that he and his wife earned in their shop came honestly, without cheating their customers, Jew or gentile. Or Reb Zundel the miller with the bass voice, who would bring his hand mill to the *beit midrash* on the day before Passover to grind flour for *shemurah matzah* for the Rebbe's household. And so many others—craftsmen and merchants—fine, upright individuals. On weekdays you would see them in their faded clothes, discussing business with gentile customers in their stores and workshops, or among the peasant wagons on market days together with their wives. You would see them on the commercial streets, on the roadsides, between rows of trees, near the sand dunes by the riverside. Those areas were filled with Jews, but now the Jews are gone and their blood cries out from the ground. From every corner of that holy city the blood of our martyrs cries out; may the Lord requite their blood. Their cries join the weeping of those buried for hundreds of years in the cemetery between the pine trees, with its tree of life and the holy sepulcher of the Maggid, his soul in Eden, and his holy descendants, their righteous memories a blessing.

The faces of the town's Jews, so weighed down with worries and burdens, would radiate joy and thanksgiving on Friday evenings for Sabbath's holy gift of rest and contentment, as they sang "Shake off the dust, arise / Don your garments of splendor, my people," and "May those who despoil you be despoiled / And those who would devour you be far away." Those notes were inserted into the pellucid prayers of my holy father the Rebbe, his righteous memory a blessing, as were the sounds of the young voices of my holy brothers Rabbi Aharonle, his righteous memory a blessing; Rabbi Asher Elimelekh, his righteous memory a blessing, whose entire martyred family rose as a burnt offering on the altar of their Judaism in the Nazi Holocaust; and the sweet voice of the youngest son, Yisrael Elozor of blessed memory, who was later privileged to settle in the Holy Land, on the swampland of the Valley of Zebulun.

That confined space of the ancient *beit midrash* seemed to expand in response to invisible vibrations from the holy pages scattered about in the nearby sacred room of the Maggid, his soul in Eden. It expanded in response to the Sabbath Queen's *Shekhinah*, who was visible in the rays of light coming from the Sabbath candles in their silver candlesticks in those spotlessly clean rooms, in all quarters of the old courtyards where my parents moved after the great fire that struck the town. That Sabbath spirit in those courtyards, suffused with the wonderful aromas of pine and birch trees, with ancient mysteries of holy letters and the sounds of Torah study, still lights our path through all of life's difficulties in this era of the Messiah's birth pangs.

Sometimes on a Sabbath eve as we sing the prayer melodies, I feel myself back in the room of the Maggid's wife the tzaddeket, which in my day served as the women's prayer room. The room was located between the *beit midrash* and the holy room of the Maggid, which for generations had collected the sighs and the prayer slips of Jews in distress. The Maggid's room had stood listening prayerfully for a hundred years, as if waiting for the arrival of the Redeemer, may he come speedily in our day.

I imagine myself between my sisters, the martyred Hannah Goldaleh, and the Rebbetzin of Piaseczno, Rahel Hayyah Miriam of blessed memory, the wife of my uncle Rabbi Kalmish'l, his righteous memory a blessing, who along with his dear children were burnt offerings in the Nazi Holocaust. I am standing next to grandmother, the Rebbetzin Sarah Devorahleh of blessed memory, who is immersed in her prayer sighs for the coming of the

Righteous Redeemer and for the resurrection of the dead; and next to my mother, the tzaddeket Brachaleh, her righteous memory a blessing, with her pure prayer whispers. At that moment my heart is moved by the sounds of prayer and song from the men's section pervading that old room filled with God-fearing women, bnei-tovim, and trustees.[9] Among them were the wife and the modest, pious daughters of the prayer leader Reb Meilekh; and his sisters Rivkaleh, Saraleh Gerona—the wife of the upright shochet Reb Mordechai Noteh, peace be upon him—and their mother Ruchama, peace be upon her. They were wise women, tall of stature; when I was a child I imagined them to be like the daughters of Zelophehad from the Bible, with their energetic spirit and forceful speech. Sometimes I am taken by the feeling of being caught in that unbroken chain. Whether it exists in reality or just in my imagination, it nevertheless gives me both pain and occasional comfort.

On Saturday nights as we took leave of the Sabbath, Reb Meilekh was also one of the lead singers in the hymns sung during the *melaveh malkah,* the meal that escorts the departing Sabbath Queen. Those melodies, which on short summer nights we sang until daybreak, instilled faith in our hearts for the imminence of redemption. And even gentiles who were ill-disposed toward Jews and who were plotting violence were shaken out of their evil intentions when, as they went out to work in their fields or factories, they heard the melodies coming from the house of the "Rabbi Maggid." Their reverential awe for the Maggid, which went back many generations in their own families, was rekindled by the sacred music, awakening a benevolent spirit within them.

When weekday arrived, Reb Meilekh son of Reb Pinchas threw himself into the world of work, his feet carrying him to his flour mill. His large family was a blessing; but the responsibility was a burden, a millstone,[10] not unlike the millstone at his flour mill in the village Kucilik.

Beyond his duty to support his family, his paternal compassion, deeply rooted in his soul, pressed upon him. His sons, God-fearing men and true hasidim, assisted him in his work and bore part of the burden. His daughters, blessed with the spirit of the biblical matriarchs, lovingly shouldered their share. But with all the help it was still a challenge to support his family adequately.

So that sublime Jew, that prince of a man glided through the great sea of Hasidism and made his way through the headaches of his business. He set aside times for Torah study on a regular basis, especially since, along with other devoted hasidim, he was assigned a talmudic tractate on the eighteenth of Kislev, the yahrzeit of the tzaddik Reb Borukh'l, his righteous memory a blessing, and the nineteenth of Kislev, the yahrzeit of the great Maggid Reb Dov of Mezirech, his soul in Eden; he would study his tractate during the long nights of winter.[11] Although Reb Meilekh son of Reb Pinchas was burdened with responsibilities, projects, and worries, his wide, bearded face beamed a warm smile, even after an outburst of angry temper when someone was insolent, whether Jew or gentile.

Most of the gentiles in the district considered themselves his friends. They knew that this Jew was good-hearted, a man of great wisdom. And they knew that he treated his mill employees fairly. When a shipment left with loaded wagons, he even instructed his workers that if fallen upon by thieves in the forest on the way to town, they should hand over his horses and not jeopardize their lives. Ever since that one hijacking when Aharon the wagon driver, concerned for his owner's horses, tried to argue with the thieves and received a bullet in his head, the peasants would help by escorting shipments leaving the mill.

Surviving natives of Kozienice still enjoy telling the story about the time at winter's end when the ice was melting and the wagon got stuck. When the horses had no more strength to drag the wagon loaded with sacks of flour through the icy slush it was mired in, one peasant ran out of his house in the village of Kucilik and began playing on his harmonica. Responding to the lovely harmonica melody, the horses got a new burst of energy and galloped away with the wagon.

During World War I, Reb Meilekh was also held in high esteem by the Austrians after they captured the town and its nearby fortress. The military commander, an intelligent ruler, called for him and enjoyed his wise conversation. By the way, in the bombardment of the town by heavy artillery, not one Jew was injured, and not one of the town's residents was killed; everyone considered it a miracle. We all thought that *"no weapon formed against"* the holy city of the Maggid, his soul in Eden, *"shall succeed,"*[12] but to our utter sorrow, during the recent period of total annihilation, the forces of destruction were given free reign, and the ax swung indiscriminately.

We must not allow ourselves to be overwhelmed by our agony. All our martyred holy ones live forever in our hearts. And Reb Meilekh son of Reb Pinchas stands vividly before our eyes not only as he runs to the *beit midrash* of the Maggid, his soul in Eden, wiping the sweat off his face with his sleeve, and not only in his store on the commercial street bustling with Jews, when the sacks of flour came from the mill in Kucilik, the same store where they also ground flaxseed for food oil. We also see him in his fine house on the street adjacent to Magitowa Street. In that house he stored liquors under license from the tsarist government, before the concessions were taken away from the Jews by the regime's decree. The loving way he would walk with his children, who clung to him as they would to their mother, his helpmeet, would stop people in their tracks and instill a mood of serenity. He even comes to view in the aftermath of the great fire, when Magitowa Street was enveloped in smoldering columns of smoke, and I was walking between the pyres trailing my mother the Rebbetzin, her righteous memory a blessing. Next to her was Nanny Sarah holding my baby sister in her arms, who spread out her hands and said, "No more house."

This six-year-old girl wept in agony, my heart racked with pain. But the tears were held back by the explanation that my holy parents, their righteous memory a blessing, gave: The burning of those holy houses was a divine sign that we were living in the era of the

Messiah's birth pangs, and the righteous Redeemer, standing just out of view, is about to arrive. At that time, when we saw a group of hasidim accompanying Father, his righteous memory a blessing, to a temporary dwelling they had arranged, something akin to pleasure stole into my heart. And in that group was Reb Meilekh son of Reb Pinchas.

There is more. My heart carries deep feelings of love toward Reb Meilekh, on account of the kind words he said just after I came into this world. There was consternation in the house at that time because a girl was born and not a male child after grandfather, the Rebbe Rabbi Elimelekh of Grodzisk, his soul in Eden, had passed away.[13] In particular, Grandmother the Rebbetzin Sarah Devorahleh, her righteous memory a blessing, was very distraught that the name of her father the tzaddik would not be used that year in her esteemed son's house. It seems to me that I remember all this, but of course it's just that I heard snatches of the story as members of the household talked about it in later years.

I can remember, so to speak, that scene by the window in the graceful hall that I loved, that hall that also served as a Sukkah during the harvest festival when the tiled roof was opened, spreading its wings like an eagle.

In that hall by the window with its beautiful drapes, Father the Rebbe, his righteous memory a blessing, is standing and holding the newborn baby on a long decorated pillow. His eyes shining, he gazes intently at the infant's face, furrowing his high forehead. He turns with a warm smile to his friend the hasid Elimelekh, the son of Reb Pinhas the teacher, his memory a blessing, who was one of the veteran hasidim of Grandfather, his soul in Eden, and asks his opinion about the newborn girl. Elimelekh happily gives his encouraging assessment: "There's nothing at all to be sorry about."

Even though he was always distressed that I did not achieve the stature that my honored holy parents, their righteous memories a blessing, had expected of me, I was always grateful to him for his kind words, and it always seemed to me that he retained his faith in this young lady. And he took pleasure when my father the Rebbe examined me as a youngster from time to time, taking the measure of my devotion to truth, the quality of my intellect, and my mastery of Scripture and other classical Jewish texts. Though separated by decades, those sights and sounds often stream in. On Sabbath eves, as we sing the traditional melodies for *"Lekhah Dodi"*—Come my beloved to meet the bride—I imagine hearing the voice of Reb Meilekh son of Reb Pinhas, sweetly intoning his impassioned prayer.

And now, after the catastrophic Holocaust, his image appears before my eyes among all our other martyrs, their righteous memories a blessing, the Lord requite their blood—*"beloved and cherished, never parted in life or in death!"*[14]—with the noble women, our friends and righteous relatives, of blessed memory, the Lord requite their blood, who were violated by impure, murderous hands. And that Reb Meilekh, the Lord requite his blood, just as throughout his life he was a man of abundant faith and a compassionate father to his children, so he was in his last day, according to the stories told by Holocaust survivors. He was brought by the Nazi demons to his last road, clutching to his heart his grandson, the son of his youngest daughter, giving words of comfort. In that manner, they took their last breaths together, in the throes of a horrible death. Only our Father in Heaven, faithful in recompense, can avenge their innocent blood from the evildoers. And it is He who is trustworthy to reward the remnant of Israel with complete redemption, in body and spirit, speedily in our days.

Endnotes

INTRODUCTION

1. See Shaul Stampfer, "Gender Differentiation and Education of the Jewish Woman in Nineteenth-Century Eastern Europe," *Polin* 7 (1992): 63–87; Iris Parush, "Readers in Cameo: Women Readers in Jewish Society of Nineteenth-Century Eastern Europe," *Prooftexts* 14 (1994): 1–23; Don Seeman and Rebecca Kobrin, " 'Like One of the Whole Men': Learning, Gender and Autobiography in R. Barukh Epstein, *Mekor Barukh*," *Nashim: A Journal of Jewish Women's Studies and Gender Issues* 2 (1999): 52–94.
2. See Alina Cala, "The Cult of Tzaddikim among Non-Jews in Poland," *Jewish Folklore and Ethnology Review* 17, nos. 1–2 (1995): 16–19. Cala cites a report that "In the vicinity of Zamosc, Hrubieszow, and Janow one can find many peasant tales about the Magid of Kozenitz." It is interesting that the specific report cited by Cala relates to the Maggid's effective blessing for fertility bestowed on a peasant woman. The report was originally collected around the year 1856. See also David ben Zelig Gersht of Warka, "Khayim-Yisroel Melamed and the Kozhenitser Magid," in *From a Ruined Garden: The Memorial Books of Polish Jewry*, 2nd ed., ed. and trans. Jack Kugelmass and Jonathan Boyarin (Bloomington: Indiana University Press, 1998), 175–179. The reputation of the Maggid of Kozienice in Polish aristocratic circles is confirmed by a passage in *Memoirs of the Countess Potocka*, ed. Casimir Stryienski, trans. Lionel Strachey (New York: Doubleday & McClure, 1900), that mentions "a famous rabbi who lived at Kozieniec" who was known as an expert in "cabalistic ideas" (ibid., 22). The memoirist, who lived from 1776 to 1867, was a grand-niece of the last king of Poland, Stanislaus Augustus Poniatowski (1732–1798).
3. Zvi Halberstam, ed., "*Toldot ha-Maggid mi-Kozienice*," [Appendix], in Yisrael ben Shabbetai Hapstein (the Maggid of Kozienice), *Avodat Yisrael* (Bene Barak: Zvi Halberstam, 1973), lists twenty-three titles, many of which went through a number of editions and printings. The major categories include collections of hasidic homilies, especially *Avodat Yisra'el* on Torah; talmudic novellae on various tractates, especially *Beit Yisra'el*; responsa, including a famous responsum that released a certain *agunah* (chained woman), permitting her to remarry (the Maggid's lenient decision came under attack, but he vigorously defended his views; the controversy grew into a *cause célèbre*, and the exchange of halakhic arguments was published under the title *Agunat Yisra'el*); commentaries on Midrash *Rabbah*; commentaries on kabbalistic works, including Zohar, *Tikunei Zohar*, *Sefer ha-Temunah*, and *Pri Etz Hayyim*.
4. See Nehemia Polen, "Miriam's Dance: Radical Egalitarianism in Hasidic Thought," *Modern Judaism* 12 (1992): 1–21.
5. Yehiel Ya'akov died in an accident at age twenty. The young widow, Sarah Devorah, moved with her small children to White Russia and married another Rebbe, Rabbi Asher Perlow of Stolin (1827–1873), master of the Karlin-Stolin

hasidim. This famous dynasty had begun one hundred years earlier with Rabbi Aharon "The Great" of Karlin (1736–1772). He had been a close friend of Rabbi Yisrael ben Shabbetai Hapstein, the Maggid of Kozienice, when they were both students of Rabbi Dov Baer of Mezhirech. Sarah Devorah lived about seventeen years in White Russia. She returned to Poland and Kozienice in 1884 with her son Yerahmiel Moshe and his wife, Brachah.

6. Avraham Yehudah Tikutzky, *Ha-Mufla be-Doro* (Jerusalem: Makhon Zekher Naftali, 1987), 48.

7. He was the first Hapstein in decades to be the Rebbe of Kozienice. For many years, Rabbi Elimelekh Shapiro of Grodzisk was considered the incumbent Rebbe of Kozienice, but he resided in Grodzisk and visited Kozienice only once a year.

8. I was not able to obtain official birth records from Kozienice, and the published hasidic genealogies are sometimes unclear or in disagreement on birth dates. This birth order was provided by Mrs. Miriam Poker, daughter of Havvah Hapstein (interviewed July 30, 1995, Bene Barak).

9. Nahman Blumenthal, "*Tsu der Geshikhte fun Yidn in Kozienice,*" in *Sefer Zikaron li-Kehilat Kozienice* (Memorial book for the community of Kozienice), ed. Barukh Kaplinsky (in Yiddish and Hebrew) (Tel Aviv: Kozienice Association, 1969), 35. The book was translated into English by Michael Wax and Jack Weinstein (New York: Kozienice Association, 1985). The English edition (*The Book of Kozienice*) is cited as *BK.*

10. The *Universal Jewish Encyclopedia,* s.v. "Israel of Kozienice," states that the naming of a street in memory of the Maggid goes back to 1842. That source gives the name as "Ulica Magida." *BK,* 122 passim, spells the name "Magitowa."

11. Malkah Shapiro, *Be-Lev ha-Mistorin* (Tel Aviv: Nezah, 1955), 119–120.

12. There is an intriguing parallel between the hasidic court as described by Shapiro and the country estates of the Russian nobility. Priscilla Roosevelt, *Life on the Russian Country Estate* (New Haven, Conn.: Yale University Press, 1995), 26, notes that that the latter "constituted an enclosed, self-sufficient idealized world of nature and art." Although there were variations, all estates had common elements, including an "imposing, stylish manor house, decorative service buildings and workshops, formal gardens, and large naturalized park" (ibid., 26). Also suggestive is Roosevelt's observation that "manor houses were material embodiments of lineage and standing" (ibid.).

Of course, the Hapstein court was not in a truly rural area but in the small town of Kozienice. Nevertheless, the basic conception and plan seems to have been remarkably similar to that of the Russian country estate, no doubt on a smaller and less lavish scale. In addition, Shapiro's grandmother owned genuine country estates in Kolodny and Strykowice, described herein, which were operated by her as commercial ventures and were visited by the family in the summertime.

13. Although the date is not given explicitly, it can be inferred from the personal and political events mentioned.

14. Katherine Dalsimer, *Female Adolescence: Psychoanalytic Reflections on Literature* (New Haven, Conn.: Yale University Press, 1986), provides an insightful analysis of the transition from girlhood to womanhood. Her descriptions, based on literary exemplars, offer striking parallels to Shapiro's descriptions of herself as Bat-Zion. In particular, Dalsimer's chapter on preadolescence,

drawing on Carson McCuller's *The Member of the Wedding*, explores the "terrors of new separateness" from parents and the awkwardness and shyness related to puberty, menstruation, and physical development (Dalsimer, *Female Adolescence*, 13–26). Cf. Bat-Zion's distress when she discovers men beginning to look at her (Chapter Eight). The comic–tragic scene in *Member of the Wedding* (quoted in Dalsimer, *Female Adolescence*, 15) in which Frankie, who was then "twelve and five-sixths years old," stands before a mirror, gazing in horror, provides a striking parallel to the mirror scene at the end of Chapter Eight of *The Rebbe's Daughter*.

15. As noted, the author was fourteen years old at the time of her marriage and her husband was even younger, just bar mitzvah (at age thirteen). David Biale, *Eros and the Jews* (New York: Basic Books, 1992), 127–130, describes the old tradition among Ashkenazic Jews to have their children marry at very young ages. Biale notes that the traditional pattern "persisted in Russia during the first half of the nineteenth century" (ibid., 153), but that even in traditional circles, the average marriage age rose dramatically by the early twentieth century (ibid., 162–164). The young age of Shapiro and her husband at the time of their marriage in 1908 indicates the persistence in their family of what was by then a disappearing practice. The bride and groom must have had some acquaintance with Western ways and were no doubt aware of the unusual nature of their marriage. It is safe to assume that this caused considerable discomfort and awkwardness. The trauma of early marriage was a recurrent theme in *Haskalah* critiques of traditional society (see ibid., 150–158). Cf. also Shaul Stampfer, "Marital Patterns in Interwar Poland," in *The Jews of Poland between Two World Wars*, ed. Yisrael Gutman, Ezra Mendelsohn, Jehuda Reinharz, and Chone Shmeruk (Hanover, N.H., University Press of New England, 1989), 173–197, who notes that by the second decade of the twentieth century, "the once-common practice of child marriage was apparently long forgotten" (p. 176).

16. Shapiro mentions her studies with Zeitlin in an interview published (Naomi Gutkind, *"Ha-Rabbanit ha-Soferet," Ha-Tzofeh* [Tel Aviv], 14 February 1969, p. 8,) in the context of a discussion of the dramatic changes that the move to Warsaw occasioned. She states, "This was perhaps a revolutionary step, but I had a strong desire to learn, and I was independent. . . . I must add that my father, his righteous memory a blessing, was no longer alive." In a biographical sketch appended to an anthology of Orthodox Jewish writers—Pinchas Peli, ed., *Emunim Anthology* (Jerusalem: Mossad Harav Kook, 1954), 308—Shapiro noted with evident pride that "During the First World War she completed an advanced course of studies with Hillel Zeitlin in Warsaw, and upon her arrival in the Land . . . she audited classes in Jewish philosophy at the [Hebrew] University in Jerusalem." (I assume the biographical sketch was penned by Shapiro herself.) On Zeitlin, see Arthur Green, "Three Warsaw Mystics," in *Rivkah Shatz-Uffenheimer Memorial*, vol. 2, ed. Rachel Elior and Joseph Dan (Jerusalem: The Hebrew Univeristy, 1996), 1–58 [also *Jerusalem Studies in Jewish Thought* 13 (1996)]; cf. also Shraga Bar Sela, "On the Brink of Disaster: Hillel Zeitlin's Struggle for Jewish Survival in Poland," *Polin* 11 (1998): 77–93. Isaac Bashevis Singer, *Love and Exile: An Autobiographical Trilogy* (New York: Farrar, Straus and Giroux, 1984), 55–57, writes that although Zeitlin "bore within him the religious fervor of the Jews of yore." . . . "It's a fact that the extreme Orthodox didn't look up to him. To them, he was a heretic."

17. Jacob S. Minkin, "Hasidism," *Universal Jewish Encyclopedia.* Cf. Jacob S. Minkin, *The Romance of Hassidism* (New York: Macmillan, 1935), 347–357; the relevant chapter is called "Twilight of the Gods"! Cf. also Gershon C. Bacon, *The Politics of Tradition: Agudat Yisrael in Poland, 1916–1939* (Jerusalem: Magnes Press, 1996), 44.

18. David Assaf, "*Viduyo shel Reb Yitzhak Nahum Tversky mi-Shpikov,*" *Alpayim* 14 (1997): 49–79. My thanks to Arthur Green for bringing this document to my attention.

19. For a description of the painful encounter of one young scion of hasidic nobility with the modern world, see Edward K. Kaplan and Samuel H. Dresner, *Abraham Joshua Heschel* (New York: Yale University Press, 1998). Kaplan notes that in Heschel's family, while there was much tension produced by the inroads of Western culture and ideas, "[o]nly one child apparently rebelled, . . . Gittel [Tova] Perlow, Heschel's first cousin and almost fiancée" (ibid., 60). Tova Perlow emigrated to Palestine, then moved to Belgium and later to Paris, where she completed a doctoral dissertation at the Sorbonne. For the account of her apparent break with Judaism, see ibid., 72.
   Another hasidic heir who abandoned his dynastic legacy and commitment to religious practice was Rabbi Yehezkel Taub of Yablonov (related to the famed Modzitz dynasty). See Yitzhak Alfasi, *Ha-Hasidut ve-Shivat Tziyon* (Tel Aviv: Ma'ariv, 1986), 59, 188, n. 102. Taub was closely associated with Rabbi Yisrael Elozor Hapstein (Malkah Shapiro's brother) in the founding of the settlement eventually called Kefar Hasidim. In this connection, it is worth noting that the celebrated Israeli poet Shin Shalom, whose given name was Shalom Yosef Shapira, was a relative of Malkah Shapiro and lived for several years at Kefar Hasidim about the time Malkah Shapiro was there. Shin Shalom's poetry is suffused with kabbalistic–hasidic themes and at times displays great anguish and ambivalence regarding the abandonment of his dynastic legacy and a traditional lifestyle. See *Encyclopaedia Judaica,* s.v. "Shalom, Shin"; Menachem Ribalow, *The Flowering of Modern Hebrew Literature,* ed. and trans. Judah Nadich (New York: Twayne, 1959), 207–236.

20. Assaf, "*Viduyo shel Reb Yitzhak Nahum,*" 50–51.

21. My understanding of *derekh avodah* is informed by conversations with Zalman Schachter-Shalomi and Arthur Green, both of whom have graciously shared their insights and learning on this and related points.

22. Kalonymos Kalmish Shapiro, *Hakhsharat ha-Avreikhim* (Jerusalem: Vaad Hasidei Piaseczno, 1966), 16–17, and my discussion in *The Holy Fire: The Teachings of Rabbi Kalonymos Shapira, the Rebbe of the Warsaw Ghetto* (Northvale, N.J.: Jason Aronson, 1999), 3–5; Nehemia Polen, "Sensitization to Holiness: The Life and Works of Rabbi Kalonymos Kalmish Shapiro," *Jewish Action,* winter (1989–1990): 30–33. Cf. also Kalonymos Kalmish Shapiro, *Conscious Community: A Guide to Inner Work,* trans. Andrea Cohen-Kiener (Northvale, N.J.: Jason Aronson, 1996).

23. Shapiro would appear to be in agreement with Buber vis-à-vis Scholem in their famous dispute on the essential nature of Hasidism. *The Rebbe's Daughter* suggests that the romantic reading of Hasidism is not just a Westernized overlay that distorts the essence of the movement, as Scholem argued, but really is at the core of what Hasidism is about. See Gershom Scholem, *The Messianic Idea in Judaism* (New York: Schocken Books, 1971).

24. See Shalom Yosef Shapiro, "Eleh Toledot Kfar Hasidim," in *Sefer ha-Tzioniut ha-Datit*, vol. 2, ed. Y. Rafael and S. Z. Shragai (Jerusalem: Mossad Harav Kook, 1977), 204–205. According to this account, the settlement went through several stages. At first the land was purchased privately (without the assistance of the Jewish National Fund) by a group of Kozienice hasidim led by Malkah Shapiro's brother, Rabbi Yisrael Elozor Hapstein, who joined forces with a similar hasidic group led by Rabbi Yehezkel Taub of Yablonov (see n. 19). Economic difficulties and security considerations forced the hasidim to sell their land to the Jewish National Fund and to affiliate with Ha-Po'el Ha-Mizrachi, a religious Zionist organization. Reading between the lines of this account by S. Y. Shapiro (who was a brother-in-law as well as distant cousin of Malkah Shapiro), one senses that for all their love of the Land and commitment to its settlement, the family was initially averse to any political affiliation, even with religious Zionists. See also Samuel Rosenblatt, *The History of the Mizrachi Movement* (New York: Mizrachi Organization of America, 1951), 39–40.
25. There is a dedication page: The book is dedicated to the memory of the author's late daughter, Rahel Hutner, "her soul in Eden, by her grieving mother."
26. See, however, Yaffa Eliach, *Hasidic Tales of the Holocaust* (New York: Oxford University Press, 1982). Eliach's foreword emphasizes women as protagonists and storytellers in her collection (ibid., xxi–xxii).
27. Cf. Avrom Fleishman, *Figures of Autobiography* (Berkeley: University of California Press, 1983), 1–39. Note especially Fleishman's statement that autobiography "is not only volatile in its changes but so profuse in its variety of forms as to make no urgent claim for a place among the genres" (ibid., 38). By contrast, Carolyn A. Barros, *Autobiography: Narrative of Transformation* (Ann Arbor: University of Michigan Press, 1998), celebrates the changing character of autobiography over time as pointing to its most essential contribution to culture: "Autobiography is about transformation. . . . [It] declares that change itself changes" (ibid., 209). A good discussion of this issue in the context of traditional Jewish society in the early modern period is found in Jacob J. Schacter, "History and Memory of Self: The Autobiography of Rabbi Jacob Emden," in *Jewish History and Jewish Memory: Essays in Honor of Yosef Hayim Yerushalmi*, ed. Elisheva Carlebach, John M. Efron, and David N. Myers (Hanover. N.H.: Brandeis University Press and University Press of New England, 1998), 428–452.
28. Philippe Lejeune, *On Autobiography, Theory and History of Literature*, vol. 52, ed. and with a foreword by Paul John Eakin, trans. Katherine Leary, (Minneapolis: University of Minnesota Press, 1989), 4.
29. Ibid., 11–14. Emphasis in original. The significance of the title page is its liminal status: It is attached to the text, and yet it points to the real world "outside the text."
30. Ibid., 12.
31. Ibid., 31–51.
32. See n. 9.
33. Members of the Shapiro family also contributed to the book.
34. Polen, *The Holy Fire*. It was, in fact, my work on that book that led me to discover the writings of Malkah Shapiro and to place them in a meaningful context. For technical reasons, the romanized spelling of his last name differs slightly from hers.
35. Tikutzky, *Ha-Mufla Be-Doro*, 70.

36. Lejeune, *On Autobiography*, 46–47.
37. Ibid., 6–7.
38. In several crucial respects, Shapiro's memoir paints a different picture from the one that emerges from the Kozienice memorial book (see n. 9). For example, Yissokhor Lederman recalls that the Rebbe's daughters "took secret lessons in Yiddish, Hebrew and Russian from the educated soldiers serving in the Smolensker regiment in our town" (*BK*, 127–128). This appears to conflict with Shapiro's depiction of the girls' home schooling enthusiastically organized by their parents. Similarly, Lederman states that the Rebbe's daughters helped found the town's first clandestine *Haskalah* library, in 1905—the precise year in which this memoir is set. He writes, "we—*bes-medresh* students, . . . and the *rebbe's* daughters—would read Peretz and Mapu, study Nakhman Krochmal and A. H. Weiss" (ibid., 127). At a later point in the book, Lederman links the "Kozienice Rabbi's daughter" with the founding of the first Jewish library in town, "under the eyes of the Rebbe and his disciples" (ibid., 309). Note that in this second account, Lederman gives the year as 1907. Rather than attempting to choose between Lederman's memory and Shapiro's, it is preferable to simply appreciate that each one is giving his or her version. On the other hand, there are large areas of convergence between Shapiro's memoir and the portrayals in *BK*. For a discussion of memorial books and their historical significance, see the introduction to Kugelmass and Boyarin, eds., *From a Ruined Garden*, 1–48. Kugelmass and Boyarin assess the political, social, and psychological tensions that are reflected in the "architecture of memory" constructed by the Yizkor books. Yaffa Eliach, in *There Once Was a World: A 900-Year Chronicle of the Shtetl of Eishyshok* (Boston: Little, Brown, 1998), 521–522, notes the importance of the "first public, coed library in the history of Eishyshok" as an a sign of, and catalyst for, cultural change from tradition to modernity. It is interesting that the library in Eishyshok, which opened around the same time as that in Kozienice (which was not public), had a similar collection, weighted toward the classics of the Hebrew Enlightenment.
39. Roy Pascal, *Design and Truth in Autobiography* (Cambridge, Mass.: Harvard University Press, 1960), 180–181; cf. also Elizabeth W. Bruss, *Autobiographical Acts: The Changing Situation of a Literary Genre* (Baltimore: Johns Hopkins University Press, 1976).
40. Paul John Eakin, *Fictions in Autobiography: Studies in the Art of Self-Invention* (Princeton, N.J.: Princeton University Press, 1985), 277–278, acknowledges at the end of his study that while the autobiographical self is constructed, it is not fictional. The self is finally a "mysterious reality"; whether that self is invented or discovered is "beyond our knowing, for knowledge of the self is inseparable from the practice of language."
41. Pascal, *Design and Truth in Autobiography*, 195.
42. My thinking on the meditative quality of Shapiro's writing has benefited greatly from conversations with my colleague and friend Menachem Rotstein. I wish to thank Dr. Rotstein for graciously sharing his insights.
43. The best known autobiography of a Jewish woman is that of Glikl bas Judah Leib (Gluckel of Hameln), recently analyzed by Natalie Zemon Davis, *Women on the Margins: Three Seventeenth-Century Lives* (Cambridge, Mass: Harvard University Press, 1995); see ibid., 220–221, n. 1 to p. 6, for publication and translation history.

44. Published by the Indiana University Press (Bloomington), 1989. This topic is also treated most insightfully by Biale, "Eros and Autobiography," in *Eros and the Jews*, 151–158.
45. Note that this pattern is the precise reverse image of the Christian pattern laid down in Augustine's *Confessions*, in which a period of sin and confusion precedes a religious conversion, followed by a life of spiritual triumph—taking one's place at the Father's table.
46. Shapiro's fully embracing appreciation of the world of her childhood distinguishes her from other writers deeply rooted in the world of tradition, such as S. Y. Agnon, whose attitude, as Band put it, stood "between nostalgia and nightmare." See Arnold Band, *Between Nostalgia and Nightmare* (Berkeley: University of California Press, 1968). Shapiro's effort to link herself to the world of her childhood in an apparently unconditional manner sets her apart from another woman writer who left the shtetl, Devorah Baron. See Anne Lapidus Lerner, "Lost Childhood in East European Hebrew Literature," in *The Jewish Family: Metaphor and Memory*, ed. David Kraemer (New York: Oxford University Press, 1989), 95–112; Ruth Adler, "Dvora Baron: Daughter of the Shtetl," in *Women of the Word: Jewish Women and Jewish Writing*, ed. Judith R. Baskin (Detroit: Wayne State University Press, 1994), 91–110. See also Anita Norich's remarks on the autobiographical writings of Esther Singer Kreitman—sister of Isaac Bashevis Singer—in "The Family Singer and the Autobiographical Imagination," *Prooftexts* 10 (1990): 91–107.
47. Caroline Walker Bynam, *Fragmentation and Redemption: Essays on Gender and the Human Body in Medieval Religion* (New York: Zone Books, 1992), 32.
48. Ibid., 40.
49. For a discussion of traditional attitudes that largely denied women access to classical Jewish literature, see Stampfer, "Gender Differentiation and Education," 63–87. See also Parush, "Readers in Cameo," 1–23; Iris Cameo, "The Politics of Literacy: Women and Foreign Languages in Jewish Society of 19th-Century Eastern Europe," *Modern Judaism* 15 (1995): 183–206. One nineteenth-century figure who did not conform to traditional norms for women and text study was Rayna Batya, granddaughter of Rabbi Hayyim of Volozhyn and wife of Rabbi Naftali Zevi Yehudah Berlin ("Neziv"). Passionately devoted to Torah study, she evidently felt trapped by the limited role assigned to her. We have no writings from her hand; what we know of her thoughts and feelings is found in the writings of her nephew: Rabbi Barukh Epstein, *Mekor Barukh* (Vilna: n.p., 1928). For analysis, see Don Seeman, "The Silence of Rayna Batya: Torah, Suffering, and Rabbi Barukh Epstein's 'Wisdom of Women,' " *The Torah u-Madda Journal* 6 (1995–1996): 91–128; Seeman and Kobrin, " 'Like One of the Whole Men.' "
50. Cf. Scholem's famous remarks on the "exclusively masculine character of Kabbalism": Gershom Scholem, *Major Trends in Jewish Mysticism* (New York: Schocken, 1971), 37–38. On women in *heikhalot* literature, see Rebecca Macy Lesses, *Ritual Practices to Gain Power: Angels, Incantations and Revelation in Early Jewish Mysticism* (Harrisburg, Pa.: Trinity Press International, 1998), 372: "Women are primarily obstacles to the purity men must attain in order to adjure angels or ascend to heaven." For early Ashkenazic Hasidism, see Judith R. Baskin, "From Separation to Displacement: The Problem of Women in Sefer Hasidim," *Association for Jewish Studies Review* 19 (1994): 1–18. For Beshtian

Hasidism, see Ada Rapoport-Albert, "On Women in Hasidism, S. A. Horodecky and the Maid of Ludmir Tradition," in *Jewish History: Essays in Honour of Chimen Abramsky*, ed. Ada Rapoport-Albert and Steven J. Zipperstein (London: P. Halban, 1988), 495–525; Polen, "Miriam's Dance."

51. Estelle C. Jelinek, ed., "Introduction: Women's Autobiography and the Male Tradition," in *Women's Autobiography* (Bloomington: Indiana University Press, 1980), 15.

52. Ibid., 17 f.

53. Although the fire is never discussed in a sustained manner, it was a highly traumatic event in Shapiro's early childhood and remained a pivotal memory throughout her life; see esp. Chapter Seventeen herein, in which fragmentary recollections of the fire are juxtaposed with images of the destruction of the townspeople in the Holocaust.

    Dan Miron, *The Image of the Shtetl and Other Studies of the Modern Jewish Literary Imagination* (Syracuse, N.Y.: Syracuse University Press, 2000), 1–48, points out the recurrence of fire accounts in shtetl narratives. He argues that, in addition to the actual frequency and severity of fires, the theme serves as a trope, a metaphor for fragility and vulnerability that harks back to the historical memory of the destruction of the Temple in Jerusalem.

54. Estelle C. Jelinek, *The Tradition of Women's Autobiography* (Boston: Twayne, 1986), 128–147.

55. Shapiro's publications, including *Mi-Din le-Rahamim*, had a mixed reception. While the *haredi* (ultra-Orthodox) press passed over her work in silence, the religious-Zionist press (in such journals as *Ha-Tzofeh*) was warmly receptive, celebrating the phenomenon of the "Rebbetzin writer." The secular Israeli press, to the extent that it took notice of her work at all, was rather guarded and cool. A good illustration of this is a review of an earlier work, *Shneinu ba-Maginim*, published in 1952, that also has stories from the world of Polish Hasidism alongside stories of *Eretz Yisra'el*. The review by K. Aharon Bertini, "Review of Malkah Shapiro, *Shneinu ba-Maginim*," *Gilyonot* 28 (1953): 106–107, enthusiastically embraces the stories that are set in *Eretz Yisra'el*, describing the building of the Land. As for the stories set in pre–World War I Poland, however, Bertini disparages their quality and dismisses their authenticity. He excoriates Shapiro for describing a static world without change, in stories in which the plot is either "extremely defective or absent entirely." He chides her for depicting a hasidic milieu of sublime spirituality while avoiding the tensions provoked by corporeal appetites and desires. Furthermore, he professes astonishment bordering on disbelief that such an idyllic world ever really existed, especially at a time when Hasidism (so he says) was in a state of deterioration, so much so that writers such as Peretz and Berdichevsky were already picking through its ruins for usable fragments to create a literature of hasidic neoromanticism, which did not correspond to any living reality. Since her stories are set in the period of Hasidism's decline, she ought to have depicted that decline.

    Bertini recognized that the book is grounded in the author's experiences, but he apparently missed the fact that the family described is the author's own and that the young protagonist is the writer herself as a child. We cannot blame him for not having seen through the author's camouflage. But had he realized that the stories are autobiographical, one hopes that he would have granted her the right to her own experiences, to remembering her early years in the way she remembered them, instead of taking her work to be an artistic distortion and a manifestation of false consciousness.

The entire question of the reception of women Hebrew-language authors by a largely male critical establishment is broached by Amalia Kahan-Carmon. In her view, "literary critics have measured women's writings in Hebrew by inadequate means and so declared that writing itself to be inadequate." I am quoting here the summary of her views by Naomi Sokoloff, "Modern Hebrew Literature: The Impact of Feminist Research," in *Feminist Perspectives on Jewish Studies*, ed. Lynn Davidman and Shelly Tenenbaum (New Haven, Conn.: Yale University Press, 1994), 237. See also Zierler's analysis of Eli Schweid's and Hillel Barzel's critiques of Devorah Baron: Wendy Zierler, "Yokheved Bat-Miriam's Female Personification of Erets Israel," *Prooftexts* 20 (2000): 117–118; and, in an essay on Yiddish poetry by women, Hellerstein's remark that "A critical consensus of poetic quality is defined as much by unacknowledged assumptions about gender as well as by explicit debates about language, aesthetics, philosophy, psychology, and politics." Kathryn Hellerstein, "Translating as a Feminist: Reconceiving Anna Margolin," *Prooftexts* 20 (2000): 195–196.

56. On Glikl bas Judah Leib, see n. 43; on Dvorah Baron (1887–1956), see n. 46; also Wendy Zierler, " 'In What World?': Devorah Baron's Fiction of Exile," *Prooftexts* 19 (1999): 127–150. While a rabbi's daughter, Baron did not come from a hasidic milieu, and her stories are clearly intended to be read as fiction, despite some strong autobiographical elements. An important memoir, again from a non-hasidic milieu, is that of Pauline Wengeroff, *Rememberings: The World of a Russian-Jewish Woman in the Nineteeth Century*, ed. and with an afterword by Bernard D. Cooperman, trans. Henny Wenkart (Bethesda: University Press of Maryland, 2000). (Shulamit Magnus is also publishing a translation of Wengeroff.)

The closest parallel to *The Rebbe's Daughter* of which I am aware is the memoir of Ita Kalish, a great-granddaughter of the famed Rabbi Mendel of Warka; her father's name was also Mendel. Kalish's Hebrew-language memoir is called *Etmoli* (Tel Aviv: Hakibutz Hameuchad, 1970); an English excerpt was published as "Life in a Hassidic Court in Russian Poland toward the End of the 19th and the Early 20th Centuries," *Yivo Annual* 13 (1965): 264–278. Kalish's memoir, although similar in many ways to Shapiro's work, displays much more ambivalence about hasidic life and traditional piety. Furthermore, Kalish's work is an engaging chronicle of people and events that recounts incidents from different periods of her life but does not focus in a sustained manner on her inner world as a child.

Both Kalish and Shapiro were transitional figures, with one foot in the old world of piety and tradition and the other in modernity. Having begun life in the former, they could speak of it with vividness and authority, but it was their entry into modernity that enabled them to write their minds. Still, it must have taken great courage and extraordinary reserves of energy and will. To get some idea of the difficulties they faced, one must review the classic writers on women and literary production, such as Virginia Wolff and Tillie Olson. To this must be added the special hurdles faced by a hasidic Jewish woman writing and publishing in Hebrew. Finally, Shapiro faced the (at best) ambivalent attitude of the Orthodox community regarding belletristic writing in general. The basic question is, Of what value is style in writing in a world where all that matters is Torah and mitzvot?

One traditional figure who did find positive spiritual value in literary activity was Rabbi Abraham Isaac Kook; see Ya'akov Even Hen, "Ha-Sifrut ba-Hashkafato shel ha-Rav Kook," *Mabua* 28 (5756/1996): 66–78.

SOME WORDS ABOUT THE TRANSLATION

1. Scheindlin remarks on the quality of the present tense to evoke a dreamlike atmosphere in his review of A. B. Yehoshua's *A Journey to the End of the Millennium*. Yehoshua's English translator, Nicholas de Lange, decided to transfer the Hebrew verbs into the past tense, a move that Scheindlin sees as less than ideal. See Raymond P. Scheindlin, "Ascetic Ashkenaz Puts Sensuous Sephardic Culture on Trial," *Forward*, 15 January 1999, pp. 11–12. The issue of translating Hebrew narrative present is also discussed by Hillel Halkin, "On Translating the Living and the Dead: Some Thoughts of a Hebrew-English Translator," *Prooftexts* 3 (1983): 79.
2. Halkin, in his Sholem Aleichem translations, was faced with a similar challenge, but resolved it in a somewhat different way. See Sholem Aleichem, *Tevyeh the Dairyman and the Railroad Stories*, trans. and with an introduction by Hillel Halkin (New York: Schocken, 1987), xxxviii–xl.
3. On this issue, see Halkin, "On Translating the Living and the Dead," 86; also Arthur Green, "On Translating Hasidic Homilies," *Prooftexts* 3 (1983): 66–67. Cf. also Robert Alter, *Hebrew and Modernity* (Bloomington: Indiana University Press, 1994), 1–22.

CHAPTER ONE

1. The month of Kislev in the Jewish calendar corresponds approximately to December in the Gregorian calendar. Hanukkah begins on the twenty-fifth of Kislev.
2. Hebrew: *Admor*. I have generally translated it as "Rebbe."
3. Throughout this work, family members are often referred to with diminutives— here, adding "le" to Moshe. David Assaf, *"Viduyo shel Reb Yitzhak Nahum Tversky mi-Shpikov,"* *Alpayim* 14 (1997): 50, n. 4, writes that "terms of endearment and diminutives were characteristic of Chernobyl Hasidism in its many branches."
4. The quotation is from the Babylonian Talmud *Shabbat* 21b. Rashi explains there that the Tarmodians sold kindling for fires and went about in the streets later than the general populace, as their wares might be needed (cf. Soncino 91, n. 8). Tarmod, or Tadmor, is known by the Latin name Palmyra and is a city in an oasis in the Syrian desert. *Jewish Encyclopedia*, s.v. "Palmyra"; Marcus Jastrow, *A Dictionary of the Targumim, the Talmud Babli and Yerushalmi, and the Midrashic Literature* (rpt.; New York: Judaica Press, 1989), s.v. "Tadmor."
5. This second (slightly paraphrased) quotation, from *Shabbat* 31a, is part of a well-known aggadic passage in which an individual tries to provoke the

saintly Hillel to anger by asking him a series of foolish questions, one of which is, "Why are the eyes of the Tarmodians bleared?" The unflappable Hillel responds that the sand blows into their eyes and weakens their vision (cf. Rashi on *Shabbat* 31a).

6. The first talmudic passage, read in a homiletic–hasidic fashion, is combined with the second passage. The term "Tarmodian" is understood metaphorically to designate a type of personality rather than a geographical place of origin. The Hanukkah lights are meant to rectify the traces of "Tarmodian" character within each individual. Cf. Yisrael ben Shabbetai (the Maggid of Kozienicer), *Avodat Yisrael* (Bene Berak: Zvi Halberstam, 1973), 13a, *Derush le-Hanukkah*: "The inner meaning of the Tarmodians' loss of vision is that their eyes are shut, unable to gaze at holiness. This is because they 'dwell amidst the sand.' This means that they are in a world of separation and fragmentation, symbolized by sand because sand does not stick together, each grain being separate from its fellow. But the whole purpose of Hanukkah is to draw down supernal light, to enlighten those who walk in darkness, to open the eyes of the blind, so that they will see that God is their creator."

7. In the hasidic court, the *meshamesh ba-kodesh* performs personal services for the Rebbe, in contrast to the *gabbai*, who serves as an administrator.

8. Hebrew: *tzei ha-shittah*. *Shittah* (pl. *shittim*) is "acacia," a tree found in subtropical desert regions (such as the Negev in Israel) but not in Poland. Recall that according to the Book of Exodus, acacia was used by the Israelites in constructing the Tabernacle, in particular the Ark of the Covenant. Employing the Hebrew *shittah* is consistent with Shapiro's propensity to borrow terminology from the biblical Sanctuary and apply it to her father's court. But what tree *did* she intend by *shittah*? Given that pine, oak, and chestnut are all mentioned explicitly by their expected Hebrew terms, my best guess is that Shapiro intends birch. Residents of Kozienice seem to have had a particular love for the birch groves that graced the town. In the preface to *The Book of Kozienice*, Goldstein writes, "Kozienice, as [a] provincial town, was surrounded with the most beautiful, dense forests. Pine trees so tall and stoistic [sic] in their splendor. And young trees just coming up, so green and fresh. Extremely picturesque was the small birch forest. So unique among the vast pine trees. Tall, white trunks, branches covered with silver-green leaves. And when the sun set on them and the wind caressed the shimmering leaves, it seemed like crystal bells ringing, whispering gently." Sabina Weinstock Goldstein, preface to *Sefer Zikaron li-Kehilat Kozienice* (Memorial book for the community of Kozienice), ed. Barukh Kaplinsky (in Yiddish and Hebrew) (Tel Aviv: Kozienice Association, 1969), vii. The book was translated into English by Michael Wax and Jack Weinstein (New York: Kozienice Association, 1985). The birches were still a striking feature of Kozienice when I visited in April 1999.

9. Strykowice and Zwolen are towns about twenty-two miles south of Kozienice and about twenty-five miles west of Radom.

10. This street was named in honor of the Kozienicer Maggid, Rabbi Yisrael Hapstein (1737–1814), Bat-Zion's ancestor and the lineage's founder.

11. A set of rabbinic benedictions said at the start of the day in preparation for the day's Torah study. The blessings express the thought that study of Torah is both a privilege and an obligation.

12. Saadiah Gaon (882–942), scholar and philosopher, was the foremost rabbinic figure of his day and leader of Babylonian Jewry.
13. This section of the Pentateuch (Gen. 47:28–50:26) is read annually around the time of Hanukkah or shortly thereafter. The author here is portraying her father's breadth of learning beyond what was standard for a traditional rabbi of the period. In particular, knowledge of Arabic would have been more typically expected of a scholar of the *Haskalah* type or someone with Western academic training, but not a hasidic Rebbe.
14. Nahmanides, "*Sha'ar ha-Gemul*," in *Kitvei Ramban*, vol. 2, ed. Charles Chavel (Jerusalem: Mossad Horav Kook, 1966), 295–296, explains that there are two Edens: the physical, terrestrial one, located in an actual place on earth, and the supernal one, located in the sefirotic realm. Later kabbalists revised this notion in the direction of incremental spirituality, so that even the lower Eden is nonphysical, a heavenly paradise for souls after death where they retain the personality configuration and emotional attachments they had on earth. The upper Eden, however, is essentially unattached to any residue of earthly life; its spirituality involves intellectual apprehension of the deity. See Zohar 2:136a. Cf. Moshe Idel, "The Journey to Paradise," *Jerusalem Studies in Jewish Folklore* 2 (1982): 9, n. 9. Isaiah Tishby, *The Wisdom of the Zohar*, vol. 2 (New York: Littman Library/Oxford University Press, 1989), 749–751, 773, n. 17, writes that for the author of the Zohar, the earthly Garden of Eden is a "staging-post or training ground for the soul in its journey." See also Moshe Cordovero, *Pardes Rimmonim* (Jerusalem: Mordecai Atiah, 1962), 31:2; Rabbi Shneur Zalman of Liady, *Tanya, Iggeret ha-Kodesh* 17.
15. Hannah Twersky (1810–1892) was one of the children of Rabbi Mordecai Twersky of Chernobyl (1770–1837), son of the lineage's founder, Rabbi Menahem Nahum, author of *Me'or Eynayim*. According to a genealogy of the Chernobyl dynasty—Aharon David Twersky, *Sefer Ha-Yahas Mi-Chernobyl ve-Ruzhin*, (1938; rpt., Brooklyn: Beit Hillel, 1990), 13 f.—there were a total of eleven children, eight sons and three daughters. Each of the sons became a noted Rebbe with his own dynasty, but of the daughters, only Hannah appears to have achieved a position of leadership. She married Rabbi David Horodetzky and was the grandmother of the scholar Samuel Abba Horodetzky. There is some confusion regarding Hannah's second name. The *Sefer Ha-Yahas*—an apparently meticulous and exhaustively researched family history by a family member—lists her full name as Hannah Hayyah, not Hannah Havvah (ibid., 22). Similarly, S. A. Horodetzky, *Ha-Hasidut ve-Toratah* (Tel Aviv: Dvir, 1944), 96, gives his grandmother's name as Hannah Hayyah. Also listing her name as Hannah Hayyah are Moshe Feinkind, *Froyen-Rebeyyim un Berimte Persenlikhkeiten in Poylen* (in Yiddish) (Warsaw: privately published, 1937), 26–30; Levi ha-Levi Grossman, *Shem u-She'erit* (Jerusalem: Bezalel, 1989), 36; Shlomo Ashkenazi, *Ha-Isha ba-Aspaklaryat ha-Yahadut*, vol. 2, 2nd ed. (Tel Aviv: Zion, 1979), 56–57; and Neil Rosenstein, *The Unbroken Chain: Biographical Sketches and Genealogy of Illustrious Jewish Families from the 15th–20th Century*, vol. 2, rev. ed. (New York: CIS, 1990), 1186, 1240. On the other hand, Harry M. Rabinowicz, *The World of Hasidism* (Hartford, Conn.: Hartmore House, 1970), 205, gives her name as Hannah Havvah, as does Yitzhak Alfasi, *Ha-Hasidut* (Tel Aviv: Sifriyat Ma'ariv, 1977), 241, and Shapiro herein. However, at least with regard to Shapiro, it is possible that we have a simple typographical

error, as in Chapter Two herein, she herself gives the name as Hannah Hayyah. For a discussion of women leaders in Hasidism, see Nehemia Polen, "Miriam's Dance: Radical Egalitarianism in Hasidic Thought," *Modern Judaism* 12 (1992): 1–21.

16. *Talmidah hakhamah:* the feminine form of the traditional term for an accomplished talmudic scholar. It would have been highly unusual to apply it to a woman in this period.

17. Hebrew: *yoshvim.*

18. Since the death of the Maggid in 1814.

19. Hebrew: *Hozeh.* Rabbi Jacob Isaac Horowitz (1745–1815) , a charismatic tzaddik known for his clairvoyant powers. He was one of the founding fathers of Hasidism in Poland. See Rabinowicz, *The World of Hasidism,* 99–101.

20. The Jewish experience of conscription into the Russian army is succinctly summarized by Michael Stanislawski, *Psalms for the Tsar* (New York: Yeshiva University Library, 1988), 11–12: "Historians, memoirists, and scores of fiction writers . . . have described in great detail the travails of the Jews in the tsarist army, their religious persecution, forced conversion, physical torture, and the like (as well as their attempts to dodge the draft)." While by the twentieth century some of the worst policies had been abolished—such as the induction of children for a period of conscription lasting twenty-five years—it was still the case that Jews who tried to maintain their religious observances might be subjected to constant torments. Young hasidic men, therefore, developed (often desperate) stratagems to avoid induction.

21. Because of their noxious odors, tanneries were considered repulsive places. Talmud *Yoma* 11b classifies tanneries with outhouses as buildings upon which one does not place a mezuzah; Mishnah *Bava Batra* 25a mandates that they must be located at least fifty cubits outside the town limits. Similarly, the occupation of tanner was considered among the least desirable. Talmud *Kiddushin* 82b states: "The world cannot function without perfumers or tanners. Happy is one whose occupation is perfumer; woe to one whose occupation is tanner."

22. The tsarist regime is here equated with Jacob's nemesis in the Bible, Esau. On this typological symbolism, see Gerson D. Cohen, *Studies in the Variety of Rabbinic Cultures* (Philadelphia: Jewish Publication Society, 1991), 243–269.

23. Hebrew: *kodesh.* It is standard hasidic practice to appropriate biblical terms referring to the sancta and apply them to the tzaddik and his environment. Here the original reference is to the inner area of the desert tabernacle erected by Moses; see Exod. 26:33.

24. Isa. 1:4

25. Most of the chapters of Isa. 40–66 are in this category.

26. This is a play on a rabbinic epigram; see Rashi on Gen. 24:42.

27. Hebrew: *Erev Hanukkah.* The word *"erev"* is also used in conjunction with other festive and holy days: *Erev Shabbat, Erev Pesah.* The day before a holy day has its own special character. It is usually a time of intense preparation and anticipation, and—at least by the afternoon—already begins to take on the mood of the day that follows.

28. The memorial book of Vurke (Warka) records the practice of preparing goose fat for Passover use on Hanukkah. See Jack Kugelmass and Jonathan Boyarin, eds. and trans., *From a Ruined Garden: The Memorial Books of Polish Jewry,* 2nd

ed. (Bloomington: Indiana University Press, 1998), 175–179. It is interesting that the context of this reference is a story about the Maggid of Kozienice.

29. This passage exemplifies Shapiro's depiction of nature as an arena of kabbalistic forces resonating sympathetically with human intentionality and devoted action. Here, the stormy wind is no doubt to be understood as the will of the tzaddik (her father), whose sacred service seeks to break through the limitations of the physical condition, here represented by the walls of the courtyard. The entire passage is alive with what Idel calls the "magical model" in Hasidism: "The world depends upon the higher powers, the spiritual force that is attracted below by the very body of the *Zaddik* and by his religious acts, as well as by his knowledge of the secrets of Torah." These ideas draw on earlier motifs from the Kabbalah of Rabbi Cordovero, especially the belief that the "term *Zaddik* [refers] to the extraordinary individual who is able to perform ritual in a manner that changes the course of nature." Moshe Idel, *Hasidism: Between Ecstasy and Magic* (Albany: State University of New York Press, 1995), 70. Note further Idel's discussion of the terms *"berakhah"* (blessing) and *"hamshakhah"* (drawing down spiritual energy). In the hasidic school of the Great Maggid (of which Kozienice was a part), these are magical processes, "a way to attract the infinite divine as energy here below in a contracted form" (ibid., 72). See also Seth Brody, "'Open to Me the Gates of Righteousness': The Pursuit of Holiness and Non-Duality in Early Hasidic Teaching," *Jewish Quarterly Review* 89, nos. 1–2 (1998), 3–44. Finally, Shapiro links this supernatural transformation of nature to the festival of Hanukkah by invoking the language ("wonders and miracles") of the blessings and hymns recited at the candle lighting.

30. Prov. 22:5. I translate the verse in line with the intention here, which follows a passage in the Talmud (*Ketubbot* 30a), "Everything is in the hands of heaven, except for cold drafts (that is, humans are fully responsible if they catch cold by carelessly exposing themselves to the cold)." The talmudic rendering of the verse is, of course, a midrashic homily. Standard versions have: "Thorns and snares are in the way of the crooked man; one who guards his soul shall be far from them."

CHAPTER TWO

1. This refers to Kosciuszko's uprising against the Russians in 1794. Colonel Berek Joselewicz led a Jewish legion in the uprising.
2. Hebrew: *yehudim yafim;* translation of the Yiddish expression *sheine yidden.* See glossary.
3. The heroine of the apocryphal book bearing her name. When the Land of Israel was invaded by an enemy army under the leadership of Holofernes, the beautiful Judith enters the enemy camp, wins the general's favor, and eventually murders him, enabling the Jews to rout the enemy.
4. Cf. *Shabbat* 112b. This classical rabbinic epigram conveys the thought that the stature of successive generations manifests decay and devolution, so that the ancients are far superior to those alive today and that we cannot hope to duplicate the achievements of the great figures of antiquity. For a discussion of this notion as well as the contrasting notion of progressive growth, see

Shnayer Z. Leiman, "Dwarfs on the Shoulders of Giants," *Tradition* 27, no. 3 (1993): 90–94; Louis Jacobs, "Hasidism and the Dogma of the Decline of the Generations," in *Hasidism Reappraised*, ed. Ada Rapoport-Albert (London: Littman Library, 1996), 208–213.

5. While the men take flight and hide in fear, it is the women who, under the leadership of Pereleh, defy the enemy's threat and whose shouts and prayers are effective in saving the community. Note that the story displays Pereleh's leadership role while her father was still alive. A longer and more detailed version of this story is found in Malkah Shapiro, *Shneinu ba-Maginim* (Tel Aviv: Agudat ha-Sofrim-Dvir, 1952), 66–75.

6. This is a good example of how a hasidic Rebbe might frame popular folk practices within a context of kabbalistic symbolism, bestowing upon them a depth of meaning and significance.

7. Hebrew: *mesim leylot ka-yamim;* a talmudic expression (*Mo'ed Katan* 25b) describing a righteous person devoted to Torah study night and day. For a hasidic interpretation of the phrase, see Rabbi Moshe Eliakim Beriyah Hapstein, *Da'at Moshe*, vol. 2 (1879; rev. ed. Jerusalem: Keren le-hadpasat sifre bet Kozienice, 1999), 629.

8. Ps. 136.

9. Ps. 136:1.

10. Ps. 30:2.

11. Ps. 30:1.

CHAPTER THREE

1. The biblical prohibition of wearing garments made of wool and linen (see Deut. 22:11). In generally avoiding wool altogether, the family practiced a supererogatory piety; by the letter of the law, it is perfectly permissible to wear garments of wool, as long as one is certain that no linen is mixed in. The total avoidance of wool is a stringency characteristic of many hasidim. Part of this extreme concern may be rooted in a hasidic tradition that prayers offered by an individual wearing *sha'atnez* are blocked and not accepted in Heaven. Note that the family did seem to wear simple, unsewn garments made of wool (e.g., shawls and scarves). See Aaron Wertheim, *Law and Custom in Chassidism* (in Hebrew) (Jerusalem: Mossad Harav Kook, 1960), 193–195.

2. Gen. 48:16.

3. Hebrew: *le-kater*, "to offer incense." The practice of burning a piece of clothing as a prophylactic against the Evil Eye is discussed in Yedida Stillman, "The Evil Eye in Morocco," *Hebrew University Folklore Research Center Studies*, vol. 1, ed. Dov Noy and Issachar Ben-Ami (1970), 85–86. As described by Stillman, the practice involves obtaining threads from a garment of the perpetrator of the Evil Eye, a variation of the procedure described here. Cf. also Joachim Schoenfeld, *Shtetl Memoirs: Jewish Life in Galicia under the Austro-Hungarian Empire and in the Reborn Poland: 1898–1939* (Hoboken, N.J.: Ktav, 1985), 41–42.

4. With reference to Hayyim, the Hebrew word *"rofe'"* sometimes appears in scare quotes. Hayyim, apparently not a licensed physician, is most likely a feldsher, a type of paramedic or folk doctor. Typically drawn from the lower

classes and sometimes barely literate, feldshers generally practiced in the countryside rather than in cities. By the late nineteenth and early twentieth centuries, feldsher education had undergone improvements and was becoming professionalized. Nevertheless, feldshers still suffered from low prestige and were often stigmatized as quacks by full-fledged physicians. See Samuel C. Ramer, "The Transformation of the Russian Feldsher, 1864–1914," in *Imperial Russia 1700–1917*, ed. Ezra Mendelsohn and Marshall S. Shatz (De Kalb, Ill.: Northern Illinois University Press, 1988), 136–160; and Samuel C. Ramer, "Who Was the Russian Feldsher?" *Bulletin of the History of Medicine* 50 (1976): 213–225. Cf. also Edward Kossoy and Abraham Ohry, *The Feldshers* (Jerusalem: Magnes Press, 1992). For the sake of consistency, my translation omits the author's occasional use of scare quotes.

5. Stillman (note 3, above) records the practice in Morocco (and transferred to Israel) "to burn alum as well as a special grass called *b'kher* (cf. the classical Arabic verb *bakhkhara*, "to fumigate"). While it is burning special words are recited" Yedida Stillman, "The Evil Eye in Morocco," *Hebrew University Folklore Research Center Studies*, edited by Dov Noy and Issachar Ben-Ami, Vol. I (1970), 85.

6. This is an example of the hasidic Rebbe's open acceptance of a folk practice that many strict traditionalists would no doubt find objectionable for theological reasons. Rabbi Menashe Sutthon, *Kenesia le-Shem Shamayim* (Jerusalem: published privately, 1874) , rails against the practice of Jewish women to offer incense and sacrifice to demons to cure a sick person; in Sutthon's view, this widespread practice is idolatry, pure and simple. See H. J. Zimmels, *Magicians, Theologians and Doctors* (London: E. Goldston, 1952), 83–85.

7. The deliberate making of an imperfection on a sculpted object is generally practiced to avoid any violation of the second commandment of the Decalogue, the making of graven images. Steven Schwartzchild, "Aesthetics," in *Contemporary Jewish Religious Thought*, ed. Arthur A. Cohen and Paul Mendes-Flohr (New York: Free Press, 1987), 1–6, calls this "the theology of the slashed nose." Similarly, Lionel Kochan, "The Unfinished and the Idol: Toward a Theory of Jewish Aesthetics," *Modern Judaism* 17, no. 2 (1997): 125–131, argues that the avoidance of perfect images reflects an aesthetic of incompleteness, consistent with Judaism's belief in the fluidity of time and an open, undetermined future. Here the Rabbi's concern is the false appearance created, but his action is strikingly reminiscent of the slashing of the nose.

8. See *Ketubbot* 5:5.

9. The Yiddish suffix "-sh" is yet another diminutive of endearment, as is the "-ke" in Yisrael Elozor'ke in the next paragraph.

10. Josh. 1:8.

11. Aharon was concerned about whether he was devoting all his time to Torah study. His father replied that the crucial factor was not the amount of time spent, but the intentionality that accompanies it. If the study is conducted with sacred devotion and aimed toward service of God, then the student is transformed by Torah's light, and everything he does or says radiates that light. The person's very self becomes Torah. By *being* Torah, one is truly engaged in Torah day and night, thus fulfilling the verse in Joshua. Rabbi Yerahmiel Moshe's words are a moderate expression of the hasidic approach to Torah study; in early formulations, the quest for *devekut* (meditative communion)

totally overshadows the cognitive aspects of study. See Jacob Weiss, "Torah Study in Early Hasidism," in *Studies in Eastern European Jewish Mysticism*, ed. David Goldstein (Oxford: Littman Library, 1985), 56–68.

12. The most general and inclusive of the set of rabbinic blessings to be recited before partaking of food. The formula in its entirety is: "Blessed are You, Lord our God, King of the universe, through whose word everything came to be."

13. The Rabbi is referring to the mystical notion that the holidays of the Jewish calendar are not only times of historical remembrance but also moments of alignment with transtemporal patterns of spiritual energy that the sensitive person may tap into and receive. Thus Hanukkah is the time to receive anew the gifts of light and clear vision.

14. Ps. 30:2, 4.

15. The ceremony of name addition effects a positive transformation in the fate of a person who has been decreed by heaven to die. Changing or adding a name confounds the Angel of Death, since the person named on the decree no longer exists. See J. D. Eisenstein, *Ozar Dinim u-Minhagim* (New York: Hebrew Publishing Company, 1917), 428, s.v. *"Shinui ha-Shem"*; Jacob Z. Lauterbach, "The Naming of Children in Jewish Folklore, Ritual and Practice" in *Studies in Jewish Law, Custom and Folklore*, selected by Bernard J. Bamberger (New York: Ktav, 1970), 62–63. The author was named "Reizel Malkah" at birth. (Her full name is found on her wedding invitation, a copy of which is reproduced in Abraham Tikotski, *Ha-Mufla Be-Doro: Ha-Admor ha-Rav ha-Kadosh ha-Saraf, Rebbe Aharon Yehiel mi-Kozienice zatsal* (Jerusalem: Makhon Zekher Naftali, 1987), 70. The name Bat-Zion, "daughter of Zion," is significant on several levels of meaning. As the name added during her illness, it redirected her fate from death to life, as we learn here. But the name also underscores the importance of Zion and the Holy Land in her life; indeed, most members of her family who stayed in Poland perished in the Holocaust. It was by emigrating to Palestine, by becoming a "daughter of Zion" in 1927 that the author saved her life. Finally, by using the name Bat-Zion for the memoir's main character, the author—who gives her name on the title page as Malkah Shapiro— is able to suppress the fact that the work is autobiographical, the story of her own youth. See Phillipe Lejeune, "Autobiography in the Third Person," *New Literary History* 9, no. 1 (1977): 28–50.

16. According to the *aggadah*, Serah was chosen to gently break the news to Jacob that Joseph was still alive. Accompanying herself on the harp, she sang a beautiful melody, "Joseph, my uncle is alive. . . ." As a reward for her sensitivity and wisdom, Jacob blessed her with eternal life, and she entered Paradise alive. See Louis Ginzberg, *Legends of the Jews*, vol. 2 (Philadelphia: Jewish Publication Society of America, 5730/1969), 115–116.

17. See Zohar 3:167b, and the extensive discussion in Chava Weissler, *Voices of the Matriarchs* (Boston: Beacon Press, 1998), 76–88.

CHAPTER FOUR

1. Ps. 91:13.
2. Ps. 91:9.
3. Ps. 91:11–12

4. Ps. 91:15.
5. Hebrew: *ha-Rabbanit mi-Ta'am.* Many towns had two parallel rabbinic figures: the official Crown Rabbi and the traditional Rabbi. See David H. Weinberg, *Between Tradition and Modernity* (New York: Holmes & Meier, 1996), 55; Gershon Bacon, "Warsaw-Vilna-Budapest: On Joseph Ben-David's Model of the Modernization of Jewry," *Jewish History* 11 (1997): 111, n. 16. Not surprisingly, relationships between the two kinds of Rabbis were often tense. It is thus interesting that here the Crown Rebbetzin visits with the family of the hasidic Rebbe of the town. According to Barukh Kaplinsky, ed., *Sefer Zikaron li-Kehilat Kozienice* (Memorial book for the community of Kozienice) (in Yiddish and Hebrew) (Tel Aviv: Kozienice Association, 1969), 43, the Crown Rabbi from 1896 to 1914 was Ya'akov Hirsch Weinberg. The memorial book was translated into English by Michael Wax and Jack Weinstein as *The Book of Kozienice* (New York: Kozienice Association, 1985).
6. *Novoe Vremia* was a pro-bureaucracy Petrograd newspaper. See Heinz-Dietrich Lowe, *The Tsars and the Jews: Reform, Reaction and Anti-Semitism in Imperial Russia 1772–1917* (Langhorne, Pa.: Harwood Academic, 1993), 336.
7. Tzvi Elimelekh Shapiro of Dinow, [Second Essay for the months of Kislev and Tevet], in *Benei Yissakhar* (New York: Hayyim u-Verkhah, 1975), 43d, presents the hasidic objections to card playing. In his view, cards are an expression of Hellenistic culture against which the Maccabees fought. The lights of Hanukkah are meant to dispel the darkness brought on by such Hellenistic practices. He observes that the Hebrew word for "playing card" (*kelaf*) is related to the kabbalistic term *"kelipah"* (shell, husk, peeling; dark force). He further notes that the gematria of *"kartin"* (Yiddish: playing cards) equals that of Satan!
8. The author is delicately revealing that Hannah Goldah has been married and is now divorced. In Jewish law (*halakhah*), a single woman need not cover her hair. Once married, however, a woman covers her hair for the rest of her life, even if widowed or divorced. See Shulchan Arukh, *Even Ha-Ezer* 21:2; *Bet Shmu'el* #5. Hannah Goldah's divorce is mentioned in Neil Rosenstein, *The Unbroken Chain: Biographical Sketches and Geneaology of Illustrious Jewish Familes from the 15th–20th Century,* vol. 2 (rev. ed.; New York: CIS Publishers, 1990), 1198, 1221. Rosenstein gives the husband's name as Avraham Yehoshua Heschel Twersky of Kiev, son of Yeshaya Twersky of Makarov.
9. This is Rabbi Kalonymos Kalmish Shapiro (1889–1943), later to become the Rebbe of Piaseczno and author of *Esh Kodesh,* among other works. See Nehemia Polen, *The Holy Fire: The Teachings of Rabbi Kalonymos Shapira, the Rebbe of the Warsaw Ghetto* (Northvale, N.J.: Jason Aronson, 1994). Kalonymos Kalmish and (Rahel) Hayyah Miriam were second cousins twice removed.
10. A translation of the Pentateuch into Yiddish, incorporating much aggadic and folkloric material, by Jacob ben Isaac Ashkenazy (c. 1590–1618). This work of traditional piety was widely popular with Ashkenazi Jewish women. See Shmuel Niger, "Yiddish Literature and the Female Reader," trans. and abridg. Sheva Zucker, in *Women of the Word: Jewish Women and Jewish Writing,* ed. Judith Baskin (Detroit: Wayne State University Press, 1994), 76.
11. Leah Reizel Hapstein Rabinowicz (b. 1862), daughter of Sarah Devorah Shapiro and her first husband, Rabbi Yehiel Ya'akov Hapstein (father of the incumbent Rebbe Rabbi Yerahmiel Moshe, Bat-Zion's father). Leah was married to Nathan David Rabinowicz of Parczew, a descendant of the Ya'akov

Yitzhak, "the Holy Jew" of Przysucha, the founder of the "new way" of Polish Hasidism.

12. Rabbi Yisrael Perlow of Stolin (1870–1921), son of Sarah Devorah Shapiro and her second husband, Rabbi Asher Perlow of Stolin the Second.

13. Ps. 30:2–3. Ps. 30 is particularly associated with Hanukkah, as its superscription reads "A psalm of David. A song of dedication of the House [Hanukkat ha-bayit]."

14. Literally: "This is Hanukkah." The name emerges from a verse in Scripture (Num. 7:84; cf. 7:88), referring to the culmination of the dedication offerings for the altar of the tabernacle in the days of Moses, "This was the dedication offering for the altar from the chieftains of Israel upon its being anointed." With respect to Hanukkah, the name suggests that the last day of the festival is its capstone and climax; indeed, in hasidic thought, Z'ot Hanukkah is considered a kind of final coda for the celebration of the New Year and a time for receiving its blessings with great joy. Cf. Elimelekh of Dinov, Bnei Yisaskhar, 92a–b, sec. 2; also R. Yerahmiel Yisra'el Yitzhak of Aleksandrow, Yismah Yisra'el, vol. 1 (Bene Brak: Aleksandrow Hasidim Publishing Institute, 1999), 138.

15. For the idea of the sun sawing a path in the heavens, see Bere'shit Rabbah 6:7 (Soncino, 46–47).

16. The parenthetical explanation is in the Hebrew text. Since the last day of Hanukkah is the culmination of the High Holiday season (see n. 16), the thirteen divine attributes of mercy—central to the High Holiday liturgy—are symbolically evoked by that precise number of birds.

17. The phrase comes from the familiar "Lekha Dodi" hymn by R. Shlomo Alkabetz, sung at the service of welcoming the Sabbath. See Reuven Kimelman, "Mavo' le-Lekhah Dodi u-le-Kabbalat Shabbat," Jerusalem Studies in Jewish Thought 14 (1998): 422, n. 154. For a hasidic understanding of the phrase, see Rabbi Kalonymos Kalman Epstein of Cracow, Ma'or va-Shemesh, vol. 2 (1842; rev. ed. Jerusalem: Even Yisra'el, 1992), 640 (Parashat Nisavim).

18. From the Nishmat prayer from the morning service for Sabbath and festivals. The Hebrew phrase "min ha-olam ve-ad ha-olam," here translated "from eternity to eternity," is biblical; cf. Ps. 106:48, Neh. 9:5, and 1 Chron. 16:36. In rabbinic Hebrew, especially as understood in a kabbalistic–hasidic context, it might better be translated "from the lowest world to the highest world."

The hasidic custom of chanting the Nishmat prayer on Z'ot Hanukkah is recorded in Seder Hadlakat Ner Hanukkah Lefi Nusah Raboteinu ha-Kedoshim mi-Koidinov (Bene Brak: Siah Avot, 5755/1995), 20–21.

19. Ps. 30:2.s

20. This is Rabbi Mordecai Twersky of Loyev (1843–1909)—father of the author's mother, Brachah Tzippora Gitl—known as "the Loyever Rebbe." He was a great-great-grandson of the famed Rabbi Menahem Nahum of Chernobyl, author of Me'or Eynayim.

CHAPTER FIVE

1. As noted earlier, Hannah Goldah must cover her hair because she had once been married.

2. Rachel's tomb in Bethlehem is a cultic center for individuals (largely women) seeking healing and fertility. According to Susan Starr Sered, "A Tale of Three Rachels, or the Cultural Herstory of a Symbol," *Nashim* 1 (5758/1998): 5–41, the cult is essentially a product of the nineteenth century, especially its last decades. In another article, "Rachel's Tomb: The Development of a Cult," *Jewish Studies Quarterly* 2 (1995): 103–148, Sered points out that in the late nineteenth century, the red threads wrapped around Rachel's tomb were a "general cure-all," used as a charm against such diseases as German measles and scarlet fever, and were not specifically associated with fertility. That is consistent with Nehamaleh's statement here.

3. *Va-yikra' Rabbah* 9:3.

4. Rabbi Jacob Isaac Horowitz of Lublin (1745–1815); see Chapter 1, n. 19.

5. Rabbi Jacob Isaac Rabinowicz (1765–1814), disciple of the Seer of Lublin (see n. 4) who broke from his Rebbe to found a new way of Polish Hasidism, de-emphasizing miracles and stressing intellectual attainment and ascetic piety.

6. This phenomenon offers a remarkable parallel to what Bilu has called "the symbolic transfer of saints from Morocco to Israel and their reinstallation in the new country." See Yoram Bilu, "Dreams and the Wishes of the Saint," in *Judaism Viewed from Within and from Without: Anthropological Studies*, ed. Harvey E. Goldberg (Albany: State University of New York Press, 1987), 285–313.

7. Gen. 48:7. As noted earlier, the author's middle daughter, named Rahel, died during the author's lifetime and this book is dedicated to her memory. At the time of her death, she headed the Office for Children and Youth in Israel's Ministry of Welfare. A memorial book was published after Rahel's death, titled *Rahel Hutner: Mukdash Le-Zikhrah ba-Yom ha-Shanah ha-Rishon le-Petiratah* (Jerusalem: State of Israel Department of Social Services, 1967).

8. The allusion is to Jacob's deathbed words to Joseph in Gen. 48:7: "*And as for me, when I came from Padan, Rachel died on me in the land of Canaan on the way, when yet there was a kibrat of land to come unto Efrat; and I buried her there on the way to Efrat, the same is Bethlehem.*" The unusual word "*kibrat*" occasions a midrashic comment from Rabbi Moses ha-Darshan, cited by Rashi: "The time of Rachel's death was the dry season when the ground is riddled and full of holes like a sieve (*kevarah*)."

9. The Hebrew text has "twenty *mil*." Here as elsewhere, Shapiro is no doubt using a Hebrew analog for a Yiddish, Russian, or Polish word, not a precise equivalent; the word "*mil*" intends the Russian *verst*. Twenty *verst* are about thirteen miles.

10. The fifteenth day of the month of Shevat; the New Year for Trees, celebrated by eating fruits associated with (and, if possible, grown in) the Holy Land. In the Hebrew calendar, Tu b'Shevat falls less than two months after Hanukkah, in late winter.

11. The Hebrew text has "*pinones ve-havalzus*," words that I could not find in any Hebrew dictionary. After much inquiry I discovered that these terms appear in an archaic dialect spoken in the old Yishuv in Tiberias whose vocabulary was drawn from Ladino, Arabic, and Hebrew. The dialect was called *Teveryait*-—"Tiberian." A similar dialect prevailing in Mezhah (Kefar Tavor), which drew more heavily on Yiddish, was called *Mezha'it*. Thistle and fennel seeds were commonly used as seasoning for cooking in old Tiberias and were sold in the souk for that purpose. For this information I am indebted to Tamar

Aronson and her informants in Israel, especially Carmela Lachish and Atara Finkelstein of Tiberias.

12. Num. 6:24–27.
13. See Maimonides, *Mishneh Torah*, Laws of Mourning 14:2, who states that escorting one's guests is a greater mitzvah than hosting them. On the custom of blessing one's departing guests with the Priestly Blessing, see the sources collected in Yosef Yizhak Lerner, *Sefer ha-Bayit* (Jerusalem: Sha'arei Ziv Institute, 1995), 479–480. Joseph Hayyim ben Elijah Al-Hakam, *Siddur Od Yosef Hai*, ed. Yosef Hayyim Mizrahi (Jerusalem: published by the editor, 1995), 701–708, incorporating the liturgical traditions and customs of Rabbi Joseph Hayyim al-Hakko of Baghdad (1833–1909), presents a brief service to be recited when accompanying a departing guest, including the Priestly Blessing.
14. The kabbalists taught that *Eretz Yisra'el* is the mystical centerpoint of the universe, corresponding to the sefirah of *Malkhut*. On this see Moshe Idel, "The Land of Israel in Medieval Kabbalah," in *The Land of Israel: Jewish Perspectives*, ed. Lawrence A. Hoffman (Notre Dame, Ind.: University of Notre Dame Press, 1986), 170–187. In this passage, the symbolic centerpoint of land is linked with another point that is central in the world of Hasidism, that of the Rebbe's court. See Arthur Green, "The Zaddik as Axis Mundi," *Journal of the American Academy of Religion* 45, no. 3 (1977): 327–347.

CHAPTER SIX

1. The Sabbath on which the lectionary reading includes Exod. 15, the Song at the Sea. It is customary to scatter food for the birds on this Sabbath. One folk legend has it that the birds joined the Israelites in singing the Song, for which we express our appreciation by supplying them with bread crumbs or other food. Another aggadic explanation traces the gratitude to a favor that the birds did for the Israelites in connection with the story of the manna in Exod. 16. For more details, see J. D. Eisenstein, *Ozar Dinim u-Minhagim* (New York: Hebrew Publishing, 1928), 402–403, s.v. "*Shabbat Shirah*."
2. *The Gates of Zion*, a kabbalistic anthology of prayers and liturgies, replete with Lurianic symbolism, edited by Nathan Hannover and first published in 1662.
3. Exod. 15:20. "And Miriam took the timbrel in her hand: But where did the Israelites get timbrels and dance-instruments in the desert? The answer is that the righteous women of that generation were confident that God would perform miracles and mighty deeds for them at the time of the exodus from Egypt, so they prepared timbrels and dance-instruments in advance and brought them along." This footnote was written by Shapiro and appears in the Hebrew text. The comment is found in Rashi on Exod 15:20 and is based on *Mekhilta*, with the interesting variation that the *Mekhilta* speaks of "tzaddikim," righteous men, while Rashi has "zidkoniot," righteous women; and it is Rashi's version that Shapiro follows on this point.
4. Exod. 15:27: "*And they came to Elim, where there were twelve springs of water and seventy palm trees; and they encamped there beside the water.*"
5. Num. 11:7.
6. Num. 11:31–32.
7. Exod. 15:1.

8. Some halakhic authorities look askance at this custom, considering it a violation of Sabbath laws. Once again, the author portrays her father as affirming
   the positive religious value of folk custom in the face of such qualms. See
   Rabbi Yehiel Michel Halevi Epstein, *Arukh ha-Shulhan, Hilkhot Shabbat* 324:3,
   who records the criticism but defends the custom in precisely the terms used
   here, "A Jewish custom has the force of Scripture."
9. "Unruly or misbehaved." In this context, the word refers to a period in the
   winter months during which some Jews fast on Mondays and Thursdays, as a
   supererogatory act of piety. The period covers the weeks with Sabbaths on
   which the following Torah sections are read: *Shemot, Va-'era', Bo', Be-shallah,
   Yitro,* and *Mishpatim* (Exod. 1:1–24:18). The first letters of the names of these
   parshiyot form the word *"shovavim."*
10. Exod. 16:14.
11. Exod. 15:21. This is the Song of Miriam, not that of Moses, which differs slight-
    ly in its phrasing (Exod. 15:1). On hasidic understandings of the significance
    of the difference, see Nehemia Polen, "Miriam's Dance: Radical Egalitarianism
    in Hasidic Thought," *Modern Judaism* 12 (1992): 1–21.

CHAPTER SEVEN

1. The fifteenth day of the month of Shevat, the New Year for trees; the Jewish
   Arbor Day. The day falls in late winter or early spring.
2. Hebrew: *Tzaar ba'alei hayyim.* Causing pain and suffering to animals is considered a serious sin, based on Exod. 23:5, as explained by the Talmud, *Bava
   Metzi'a* 32a–33a. From Deut. 11:15, the Talmud derives the principle that farm
   animals must be fed before humans may partake of food.
3. See Chapter Three, n. 1. Note that the Crown Rebbetzin wore wool.
4. Hebrew: *ha-halonot ha-shekufim-atumim.* The phrase appears in 1 Kings 6:4,
   and I have translated in accord with the rabbinic interpretation that the windows of Solomon's Temple were constructed narrow on the inside and wide
   on the outside to serve as beacons of light for the world outside, but that there
   was no need to gather light for the Temple itself. See Midrash *Leviticus Rabbah*
   31:7 (on Lev. 24:2; Soncino, 401–402); Rashi and *Yalkut Shimoni* on 1 Kings 6:4.
   The Maggid of Kozienice in his *Avodat Yisrael, Parashat Terumah,* s.v. *"Ve-
   no'adeti lekha sham"* (Exod. 25:22) understands the symbolism of the windows
   as alluding to the kind of tzaddik who surrenders his selfhood and accomplishments back to the Divine. See Yisrael ben Shabbetai (the Maggid of
   Kozienice), *Avodat Yisrael* (Bene Berak: Zvi Halberstam, 1973). Through that
   negation of self, he is able to be a clear channel of light and blessing for all the
   world. Given the prominence of the Maggid and his teachings in Malkah
   Shapiro's writings, it is likely that she has this understanding in mind when
   she describes the Maggid's synagogue as having windows that were
   shekufim-atumim.
5. Only in the messianic era will the full bouquet of the fruit of *Eretz Yisra'el* be
   manifest. See Mishnah *Sotah* 9:12; Sifra on Lev. 26:3.
6. In kabbalistic-hasidic fashion, the Rebbe is invoking *gematria,* numerical letter
   equivalents, to demonstrate a correspondence between particular Hebrew
   words—whose meaning he expounds—and the groups of nuts that he counts

out in specified amounts. The Hebrew *dai* is spelled with the letter *dalet*—*gematria* (four), and *yod* (ten) for a total of fourteen. *Tov* is *tet* (nine), *vav* (six), and *bet* (two), totaling seventeen.

7. Sg. 4:13–14. The Song of Songs, understood to express the mutual love of God and Israel, is chanted at twilight's entry into Sabbath.

CHAPTER EIGHT

1. As a young woman who had reached her twelfth birthday, she was now a bat mitzvah.

2. That is, the wife of Rabbi Israel Shapiro of Grodzisk (see n. 4). Feigenu (Nehamah Feige Perlow) was born around 1873 to Sarah Devorah Shapiro and her second husband, Rabbi Asher Perlow the second of Stolin. She was thus a half-sister to Rabbi Yerahmiel Moshe Hapstein and to the just-mentioned "Aunt Leahnu." Her son Avraham Elimelekh Shapiro was betrothed to Bat-Zion (Malkah Shapiro); they were to marry about two years after the time in which this memoir is set.

3. Hebrew: *la-tet et eyneyem bah;* a variant of a rabbinic phrase that often refers to gazing with erotic desire. See, for example, *Sanhedrin 75a; Gittin 58a.*

4. Rabbi Israel Shapiro of Grodzisk (1874–1942), husband of Rebbetzin Feige Shapiro and Bat-Zion's future father-in-law.

5. The visualization of one's breath as forming the letters of prayer is a practice mentioned in hasidic sources. See Rabbi Kalonymos Kalman Epstein of Cracow (d. 1823), *Ma'or va-Shemesh,* vol 1. (1842, rpt. Jerusalem: Even Yisra'el, 1992), 222–225, *Parashat Yitro,* s.v. "*Va-Yotze' Moshe.*"

6. Hebrew: *tefilat shav;* "a prayer in vain." See *Berachot 54a.*

7. At the end of this prayer, it is customary to insert a biblical verse chosen to correspond to the individual's Hebrew name in the following manner: The first letter of the verse corresponds to the first letter of one's name, and the verse's last letter corresponds to the last letter of one's name. Lists of such verses are provided in many prayer books. The custom is based on the belief that after death, the soul is in such a state of confusion and disorientation that it does not even remember its own name. The recitation of the verse ensures that the individual will recall his name, will respond to angelic calls for that name, and will thus be able to begin the process that will eventually lead to entry into Heaven.

8. Ps. 41:14. In this instance, the English translation preserves the pattern of first letter/last letter correspondence between name and verse (B – B/N – N). Note that the narrator informs the reader that Bat-Zion has other names, but she does not specify them.

9. The text has a transcription in Hebrew characters of Russian *Vi brishni.*

10. This *aggadah* is found in *Sotah* 36b; cf. Louis Ginzberg, *Legends of the Jews,* vol. 2 (Philadelphia: Jewish Publication Society, 5728/1969), 72.

11. Deut. 32:7.

12. The Rebbe is thinking here of *Binah* as one of the ten *sefirot,* the divine manifestations of kabbalistic theosophy. *Binah* is the third *sefirah,* the last of the upper triad, representing the divine intellect, and the opening to the more humanly accessible seven lower *sefirot,* which represent the emotional life of the divine realm. *Binah* is often referred to as the "Supernal Mother."

13. See *Shabbat* 133b; *Sotah* 14a; *Tana de-Be Eliyahu Rabbah* 26. The Rebbe's universalizing words "to every people, every person, every creature" are adumbrated in the last source cited.

14. Hayyim Selig Slonimski, founder and editor of the Hebrew-language journal *Ha-Zefirah*. Slonimski was a moderate *maskil*. Nevertheless, some of his scientific and historical views were controversial in traditional circles, and it is certainly of interest that the Rebbe would engage in an exchange of views with him.

Slonimski wrote a number of articles on astronomical and calendrical topics for *He-Asif*, including discussions of the views of Maimonides; but I was not able to locate the precise passage cited here. See *He-Asif* 1 (1884), 228–232; 3 (1886), 390–393; 4 (1887), 233–244. On Slonimski's role in propagating knowledge of modern science to Russian Jewry, see Isaac Goldberg, "Chaim Selig Slonimski: 19th Century Popularizer of Science," in *Shmuel K. Mirsky Memorial Volume*, ed. Gersion Appel, Morris Epstein, and Hayim Leaf (Jerusalem: Sura Institute, 1970), 247–261.

15. Rabbi Ya'akov Noson Weisman (c. 1832–1916), Rabbi of Turov (a small town east of Pinsk), emigrated to the Land of Israel and served as rabbi in Tiberias. He was the author of *Mahshavot be-Etzah*; see Avraham Yizhak Bromberg, *Mi-Gedolei ha-Hasidut: Beit Kozienice* (Jerusalem: Beit Hillel, 1982), 147–149.

16. Hebrew: *tokhahat geluyah ve-ahavah mesuteret*. See Nahmanides, *Torah Commentary*, Introduction.

17. The Rebbe (Rabbi Yerahmiel Moshe) is referring to Rabbi Israel Shapiro of Grodzisk (see n. 4).

18. Literally: "the four cubits of *halakhah* (Jewish law)," reflecting the fact that in the rabbinic period, the sacred space of the Jerusalem temple has been transformed from an actual spatial locus into the conceptual domain of talmudic legal categories. See *Berachot* 8a.

19. Ps. 139:6.

20. Eccles. 7:23.

21. See Yisrael ben Shabbetai Hapstein (the Maggid of Kozienice), *Avodat Yisrael* (Bene Berak: Makhon Nofet Tsufim, 1996), 223, 267; commentary to *Avot* 4:5. Cf. Isaiah Shohet of Odessa, *Sefer Tehilim . . . im Perush Asifat Amarim* (1884; rpt. New York: n.p., 1953), gloss on Ps. 139:6.

22. For Leah, see Chapter Four, n. 11. She was a half-sister to Rebbetzin Feige Shapiro and sister-in-law to the Rebbe Rabbi Yerahmiel Moshe Hapstein, who was a child of Sarah Devorah and her first husband, Rabbi Yehiel Ya'akov.

23. This is the mitzvah of *niddah*, menstrual separation.

24. The oft-cited rabbinic teaching is that *hasidei umot ha-olam* have a portion in Paradise; see *Tosefta Sanhedrin* 13:2; Maimonides, *Mishneh Torah*, Laws of Kings 8:11.

25. Mishnah *Avot* 4:25 (in the name of Elisha ben Avuyah). The mishnah contrasts this with learning as an old person, which is like writing with ink on smudged paper.

26. This elides what is generally taken to be the talmudic view that, although women receive reward for the study of Torah, they do not receive as much reward as men, since men's study is mandatory and women's study is optional (see *Avodah Zarah* 3a; *Sotah* 21a). The encouragement of women's Torah study is a recurrent theme in this work. For the view of Malkah Shapiro's brother-in-law, see Rabbi Kalonymos Kalmish Shapira, *Esh Kodesh*

(Jerusalem: Vaad Hasidei Piaseczno, 1960), 183, discussed in Nehemia Polen, "Miriam's Dance: Radical Egalitarianism in Hasidic Thought," *Modern Judaism* 12 (1992): 1–21.

27. Once again, this is creative rereading of the Talmud's line of argument, which the author presents in a manner far more supportive of women's study of Torah than the original passage (*Sotah* 21a) might otherwise suggest.

28. Prov. 6:23.

29. Prov. 6:22.

30. Sg. 8:7. BT *Sotah* 21a.

31. Maimonides, *Mishneh Torah*, Laws of Sanctification of the New Moon, 5:1. Cf. *The Code of Maimonides*, book 3, treatise 8, trans. Solomon Gandz (New Haven, Conn.: Yale University Press, 1956), 22.

32. *Code of Maimonides*, 6:1; cf. pp. 26–27.

33. Cf. Louis Jacobs, "Tobacco and the Hasidim," *Polin* 11 (1998): 25–30.

CHAPTER NINE

1. Rabbi Joshua Falk, *Sefer Me'irat Einayim, Hoshen Mishpat* 3:13, citing Rabbi Jacob Weil. My thanks to Rabbi Nahum Eisenstein for this reference.

2. Deut. 4:15. This verse is understood to mean that one must be careful to preserve one's health. While this verse is the one generally cited in informal discussions of this topic, the early sources actually cite Deut. 4:9; see *Shevu'ot* 36a; Maimonides, *Mishneh Torah*, Laws of Murder 11:4.

3. The hasidic teaching turns on a pun to shift the Maimonidean philosophical statement on the noncorporeal nature of the deity into an ethical dictum that anyone enmeshed in the physical cannot comprehend divinity.

4. The verse intended is Gen. 19:11; it is slightly misquoted and conflated with 19:4. The reference is to the Sodomites who have gathered around Lot's house.

5. Travel by foot was undoubtedly dictated by economic necessity, but there was also the sense that going by foot was more appropriate for a journey that was actually a religious pilgrimage. As in all pilgrimages, much of the spiritual work was done on the road, in anticipation and preparation for the audience with the Rebbe. There was also a powerful social element, since journeys to the Rebbe were almost always made with other hasidim. On the return trip, the group would share experiences and attempt to more fully comprehend and crystallize the teachings they had heard. According to Rabbi Kalonymos Kalman Epstein of Cracow, *Ma'or va-Shemesh*, vol. 2 (1842; rpt., Jerusalem: Even Yisra'el, 1992), 607–608 *Parashat Ki Tetze*, the spiritual interaction with fellow seekers on a pilgrimage is central to the work of repentance in the period preceding the High Holidays. According to this teacher (one of the foremost early leaders of Hasidism in Poland), the notion that the spiritual work of repentance is essentially social and must be accomplished with others is a fundamental innovative insight of the hasidic movement. Cf. also Elliot R. Wolfson, "Walking as a Sacred Duty" in *Hasidism Reappraised*, ed. Ada Rapaport-Albert (London: Littman Library, 1996), 180–207.

6. A town about thirty miles west of Kozienice and the residence of Sarah Devorah's grandfather Rabbi Hayyim Meir Yehiel Shapiro (1789–1849),

known as the Seraph of Mogielnica, famous for his ecstatic prayer and para-normal powers. Hayyim Meir Yehiel was a grandson of the Maggid of Kozienice.

7. Corrected on the basis of Malkah Shapiro, *Be-Lev ha-Mistorin* (Tel Aviv: Nezah, 1955), 21. The printed text here reads: *"yatzanu et ha-ir le-Kozienice"* (we left the town to Kozienice), which makes no sense in context.

8. The reference is to Rabbi Hayyim Meir Yehiel (see n. 6).

9. This is Pereleh Hapstein Shapiro (d. 1849). One of the outstanding women per-sonalities of Hasidism, a charismatic and ascetic. Pereleh is the central figure in a story told in Chapter Two herein. I hope to write more about her; for now, see Nehemia Polen, "Miriam's Dance: Radical Egalitarianism in Hasidic Thought," *Modern Judaism* 12 (1992): 1–21.

10. Simon Schama, *Landscape and Memory* (New York: Vintage Books, 1995), 181, writes of the dominant position of Jews in the business of harvesting lumber from Polish forests. Their customers included the British Navy. Cf. Shapiro's account here with Schama's portrait of "hard-boiled Scotsmen in freshly pow-dered wigs haggl[ing] with Polish Jews in sable-rimmed hats, corkscrew side-curls, and long black coats over the price of oak and fir" (ibid.).

11. Temerel Bergson, wife of Berek Dov Bergson, followers of the Maggid of Kozienice. Their philanthropy supported hasidic causes, and their business enterprises employed many hasidim, including some famous Rebbes, such as Rabbi Simha Bunem of Przysucha and Rabbi Isaac of Warka. Berek Bergson's father was Shmuel Zbitkower (1758-1801), known as the "Rothschild of Polish Jewry." One of Temerel Bergson's descendants was the philosopher Henri Bergson. See Harry M. Rabinowicz, *The World of Hasidism* (Hartford, Conn.: Hartmore House, 1970), 98, 107; Raphael Mahler, *Hasidism and the Jewish Enlightenment* (Philadelphia: Jewish Publication Society, 1985), 188–189.

12. Hebrew and Aramaic: *Nehar Dinur*. The term comes from Dan. 7:10. In aggadic literature, the River of Fire brings forth every day a choir of angels that praise God and then cease to exist. The river itself arises from the sweat of angelic *Hayyot* who bear God's throne. Cf. *Bere'shit Rabbah* 78:1 and *Hagigah* 15a. In modern Hebrew, the term refers to the Milky Way.

13. This is a fragment of the *Kiddush Levanah*, the blessing of Sanctification of the Moon, found in the Talmud (*Sanhedrin* 42a) and part of the liturgy to this day; see *ArtScroll Siddur* [Rabbinical Council of America edition], trans. Nosson Scherman (Brooklyn: Mesorah, 1985), 612. The blessing links the monthly renewal of the moon to the eschatological hope for Israel's renewal and restoration.

14. Cf. Zech. 9:9.

15. Because of their significance in light of kabbalistic symbolism, the hairs of one's beard are sacred. Many Rebbes would never trim their beards, and some would not even touch the beard for fear of pulling out a hair. Strands of hair that do fall out are reverently deposited in a sacred book. In Kabbalah, there are thir-teen strands of the beard of Supernal Man, corresponding to the thirteen divine attributes of mercy. The motif appears frequently in hasidic works. See, e.g., Rabbi Shneur Zalman of Liady, *Likkutei Torah* (New York: Kehot, 1996), 27, *Parashat 'Emor* (Leviticus); Epstein, *Ma'or va-Shemesh*, vol. 1, 371, *Parashat 'Emor*.

16. A section of the Pentateuch, corresponding to Exod. 10–13. The Pentateuch is divided into fifty-three such sections, *parshiyot*. Since the *parshiyot* are read

serially, generally one per week and annually at about the same time of year, naming a parashah is a convenient way to designate a particular week of the calendar. Parashat Bo' typically falls in midwinter, roughly in January.

17. The Seraph of Mogielnica passed away in 1849. After the passing of Rabbi Moshe Eliakim Beriyah Hapstein (son of the founder of the lineage) in 1828, the Seraph was considered the Rebbe in Kozienice as well as Mogielnica. See Zvi Halberstam, *Toldot ha-Maggid mi-Kozienice* [Appendix], in Yisrael ben Shabbetai Hapstein (the Maggid of Kozienice), *Avodat Yisrael* (Bene Barak: Zvi Halberstam, 1973), 38; *Encyclopedia of Hasidism Personalities* (Jerusalem: Mossad Harav Kook, 1986), 611. Similarly, after the passing of the Seraph, his son, Rabbi Elimelekh of Grodzisk (1816–1892), was considered Rebbe of Kozienice as well as Grodzisk. The accession of Rabbi Yerahmiel Moshe Hapstein (Bat-Zion's father) to the seat at Kozienice was thus a return of leadership to the Hapstein branch of the family.

18. The origins of this theme are traced in Gershom Scholem, "The Tradition of the Thirty-Six Hidden Just Men" in his *The Messianic Idea in Judaism* (New York: Schocken, 1978), 251–256.

19. On messianic speculation concerning 1860 (as well as 1840), see Abraham G. Duker, "The Tarniks (Believers in the Coming of the Messiah in 1840)," in *The Joshua Starr Memorial Volume* (New York: Conference on Jewish Relations, 1953), 191–201, cited in Stephen Sharot, *Messianism, Mysticism and Magic* (Chapel Hill: The University of North Carolina Press, 1982), 275, n. 52.

In this connection it is useful to recall that 1861 was the year serfdom was abolished in Russia, an event of great moment and consequence. On the revolutionary atmosphere in Poland at the time, see Piotr S. Wandycz, "The Fateful Year 1861," in his *The Lands of Partitioned Poland: 1795–1918* (Seattle: University of Washington Press, 1996), 161–167.

20. *Sanhedrin* 98a.

21. See Sanhedrin 98b; cf. Meir Waxman, "*Heblei Mashiah*," in *Messianism in the Talmudic Era*, ed. Leo Landman (New York: Ktav, 1979), 442–444.

CHAPTER TEN

1. The poem "*Ish Hasid Hayah*" by Jesse ben Mordecai (thirteenth century) tells the story of a poor, pious scholar whose family is rescued from starvation by Elijah. Selling his services at the market for a fabulous sum (which he gives to the poor man), Elijah erects a palatial structure with the assistance of angelic helpers. Cf. *Mahzor Vitry*, vol. 1, ed. S. Hurwitz (Nuremberg: J. Bulka, 1923; rpt. Jerusalem: n.p., 1988), 184–185. On Elijah legends in general, see Aharon Wiener, *The Prophet Elijah in the Development of Judaism* (London: Routledge & Kegan Paul, 1978); Samuel M. Segal, *Elijah: A Study in Jewish Folklore* (New York: Behrman's Jewish Book House, 1935).

2. Deut. 23:15.

3. The *Shema*, often said to be the Jew's central affirmation of faith, is found in Deut. 6:4–9. Here the reference is to the *Keri'at Shema she-al ha-Mittah*, said at bedtime, offering reassurance and protection against the terrors of the night.

4. On strikes and antigovernment agitation during this period, especially after the events of Bloody Sunday, see Adam B. Ulam, *Russia's Failed Revolutions* (New York: Basic Books, 1981), 163 f.

5. Although Shapiro wrote 1904, the Duma was actually established in 1905.
6. Rabbi Elimelekh Shapiro of Grodzisk, father of Sarah Devorah Shapiro. His yahrzeit is 1 Nisan, two weeks before Passover. Grodzisk is about twenty-four miles southwest of Warsaw, and Mogielnica is about forty-eight miles south of Grodzisk.
7. Rabbi Hayyim Meir Yehiel Shapiro of Mogielnica is the son of Pereleh Hapstein Shapiro (see Chapter Nine, n. 9).
8. Wheat to be used to bake matzot mitzvah, matzahs for the special rite of matzah eating during the Seder, must be kept from all contact with water from the time of harvesting until the time of baking. The wheat handled in this manner is called *shemurah* (safeguarded), as is the resultant flour and the final product, the matzah used at the Seder. See Shulchan Arukh, *Orach Chayyim* 453:4; see also Chapter Thirteen, herein.
9. "Excellence and faithfulness—are His who lives forever." An angelic hymn in praise of God found in the Merkavah text *Heikhalot Rabbati* (chap. 26); incorporated in the High Holiday service of the Ashkenazi rite, and every Sabbath in hasidic congregations. The hymn and its background are discussed in Gershom Scholem, *Major Trends in Jewish Mysticism* (New York: Schocken, 1971), 58–59.
10. Hebrew: *efodei hazeihen;* probably a translation of the Yiddish *brusttuch,* "breast-cloth," worn for purposes of modesty within fashionable dresses. See Giza Frankel, "Notes on the Costume of the Jewish Woman in Eastern Europe," *Journal of Jewish Art* 7 (1980): 50–57. My thanks to Chava Weissler for help in locating this article.

CHAPTER ELEVEN

1. Kozienice has a large palace with extensive gardens and grounds near the center of town, designed by the architect Franciszek Placidi in the baroque style, with later renovations by Jan Fontana (*Kozienice: Informacja Turystyczna*, n.p., n.d.). During the latter part of the eighteenth century, the site was a summer residence for Stanislaw Augustus Poniatowski (1732–1798), the last king of Poland. After the partition of Poland and the transfer of Kozienice to the tsarist empire, the palace came under Russian control. In the late nineteenth and early twentieth centuries it was called the "Garski Palace," after the Russian noble family that owned it. The palace was severely damaged during World War II and was reconstructed after the war, though without restoration of the original ornate features. It now houses the town's municipal offices. The palace annex is the home of the Kozienice Regional Museum. See Katarzyna Oczkowicz and Krzysztof Reczek, *Kozienice: The Town and the Region*, trans. Krzysztof Korkosz (Regional Museum in Kozienice, n.d.) and Barukh Kaplinsky, ed., *Sefer Zikaron li-Kehilat Kozienice* (Memorial book for the community of Kozienice) (in Yiddish and Hebrew) (Tel Aviv: Kozienice, 1969), 42. The book was translated into English by Michael Wax and Jack Weinstein (New York: Kozienice, 1985). Note the prewar photograph of the palace on p. 33 of the Yiddish and Hebrew edition.
2. This is the Zagadzsanka, a tributary of the Vistula.
3. Ps. 104:9.

4. As noted earlier, the Maggid of Kozienice died in 1814. If the gentleman was 100 in 1905, he would have been about 9 in 1814.
5. The reference is to the approach of Passover, especially the seventh day of the festival, when the crossing of the sea is celebrated. There is also an allusion to the hope for the speedy advent of the messianic redemption.
6. The talmudic aphorism at *Berakhot* 19a is "A person should not open his mouth to Satan"—that is, a person should not speak in a manner that might give Satan ideas about ways to cause mischief.
7. Ps. 116:6.
8. Gen. 18:14.

CHAPTER TWELVE

1. The Hebrew draws on the language of Sg. 2:9 as well as the rabbinic phrase *se'or she-ba'isa*, "the sourdough leavening" that makes dough rise—understood symbolically as the Evil Urge that drives humans to acts of arrogance and wickedness. See *Berakhot* 17a.
2. See Chapter Six herein.
3. Peter Stolypin, minister of the interior, was later appointed prime minister; see Adam B. Ulam, *Russia's Failed Revolutions* (New York: Basic Books, 1981), 212. Shapiro's chronology is not accurate here: Stolypin was actually assassinated on September 1, 1911.
4. See Chapter Nine, n. 19.
5. The Hebrew is a slight variation on Isa. 3:5.
6. The Maggid was actually the great-great-grandfather of the incumbent Rebbe. The Hebrew *saba* (behind which undoubtedly hovers the Yiddish *zeide*) is used somewhat loosely as a term of endearment for the family's founder, a loving and intimate title for the paterfamilias.
7. According to Giza Frankel, "Notes on the Costume of the Jewish Woman in Eastern Europe," *Journal of Jewish Art* 7 (1980): 50–57, *binda* is an alternate term for *sterntichl*, a coronet for the head decorated with pearls and precious stones. Frankel notes that it could be both a symbol and a repository of a family's wealth—as we see here.
8. She was the wife of Rabbi Elazar Hapstein, father of Rabbi Yehiel Ya'akov Hapstein, Sarah Devorah's first husband.
9. The notion that Diaspora synagogues will be transported to *Eretz Yisra'el* is found in *Megillah* 29a. This is combined here with the kabbalistic–hasidic teaching that the tzaddik defines his own domain of sacred space, a kind of extraterritorial Holy Land. See, for example, Zohar 1:155b–156a. Cf. Arthur Green, "The Zaddik as Axis Mundi," *Journal of the American Academy of Religion* 45, no. 3 (1977): 327–347.
10. Celebration, feast. In hasidic tradition, the anniversary of the death of a tzaddik is celebrated as a joyous occasion by his descendants and followers, since on that date the tzaddik is elevated to a new dimension of Heavenly bliss and proximity to God.
11. Hebrew: *Rosh Hodesh Nisan*; the yahrzeit of Sarah Devorah's father (see Chapter Ten, n. 5).
12. Gen. 27:27.

13. The author is highlighting the devout practices of the women of the family, which one might tend to associate more stereotypically with pious men. Her point is precisely that, in her family, women as well as men adopted self-imposed restrictions and partial fasts such as avoidance of meat on Mondays and Thursdays, days when *Tachanun*—an added section of petitionary and penitential prayers—is recited. Similarly, taking meals in silence suggests that eating food was a spiritual discipline and that meals were times for meditative reflection rather than the simple satisfaction of appetite and light banter. In general, the women are portrayed as leading lives of inwardness, focused devotion, self-sacrifice, and intellectual engagement (in addition to tending to their household tasks!). For the theoretical background of food praxis, see Louis Jacobs, "Eating as an Act of Worship in Hasidic Thought," *Studies in Jewish Religious and Intellectual History Presented to Alexander Altmann*, ed. S. Stein and R. Loewe (University: University of Alabama Press, 1979), 157–166; Louis Jacobs, "The Uplifting of Sparks in Later Jewish Mysticism" in *Jewish Spirituality from the Sixteenth-Century Revival to the Present*, ed. Arthur Green (New York: Crossroad, 1994), 99–126.

14. Drawing on the language and imagery of Sg. 2:9, midrashically associated with the advent of messianic redemption.

CHAPTER THIRTEEN

1. Hebrew: *mayim she-lanu.* According to the Talmud and Codes, water for matzah baking must not be drawn during daylight hours, for fear that it will have been warmed by the sun and the heat will hasten fermentation, a process that is incompatible with matzah production. It is, therefore, required that water be drawn around the time of dusk. The water is placed in earthenware jugs, covered with a cloth for protection, and carefully stored overnight in a cool place until the following day, when it may be mixed with Passover flour to bake matzahs. See *Pesahim* 42; Shulchan Arukh, *Orach Chayyim* 455:1.

2. All flour ground for baking Passover matzot must be kept from contact with water from the time of grinding until the time of the actual matzah baking (when the flour is mixed with water, kneaded quickly, and immediately placed into the oven for baking). An added level of stringency is required for wheat to be used to bake matzot mitzvah, matzot for the special rite of matzah eating during the Seder. Such wheat must be kept from all contact with water from the time of harvesting until the time of baking. The wheat handled in this manner is called *shemurah* (safeguarded), as is the resultant flour and the final product, the matzah used at the Seder. See Shulchan Arukh, *Orach Chayyim* 453:4. The production of *shemurah* matzah thus demands an extraordinary level of care and awareness at every stage. In the hasidic milieu, as depicted here, however, there is still one more element: that of kabbalistic–hasidic intentionality, which links physical action with mystical meaning by means of Hebrew word and letter symbolism.

3. This undoubtedly refers to the number of grains in the jug, which were selected one by one. There may have been a kabbalistic significance to this amount.

4. Using kabbalistic–hasidic tropes, the Rebbe is setting up a multitiered correspondence between the production of the *shemurah* flour, the symbolic mean-

ing of the associated Hebrew words, and the Jewish people's religious destiny. The ideas presented here are based on Passover homilies of the author's ancestor the Maggid of Kozienice. See Yisrael ben Shabbetai (the Maggid of Kozienice), *Avodat Yisrael* (Jerusalem: A. Weinstock, 1984), 127, "*Le-Shabbat ha-Gadol.*" The Maggid explains that the distribution of wheat to the poor is a way of activating and purifying the twenty-two letters of the Alef Bet for sacred use in Torah study and prayer. Furthermore, the tzaddik is responsible for reaching out to those in need of spiritual assistance as well as those needing material help.

5. Her brother is quoting a famous passage in Mishnah *Avot* (*Pirkei Avot*) 5:26, which in its original context means, study the Torah at all times, from all angles. By playfully applying the passage to the turning mill, he is inviting his sister to operate the mill herself.

6. The steward is playing on a talmudic passage (*Berachot* 34b) that speaks of "wine guarded within the grape from the six days of creation," which will be drunk at the feast for the righteous at the end of days.

7. The keys had gone through the process of *libun*, in which a metal object is heated by fire to the point of glowing. The object is thereby made kosher, or—as in this instance—kosher for Passover.

8. Depending on the object, this process may involve immersion into boiling water (see the previous note for another method). In this instance, the effort was supererogatory. Reserved solely for Passover use, the utensils would not have become disqualified, because they were set aside and stored away from the time of the previous year's Passover. This is an example, then, of the exceptional strictness with which the Rebbe and his family prepared for Passover.

9. The use of the *gartl* at this time indicates that the process of returning the books to the Rebbe's house was itself a sacred event.

10. Both of these works deal with advanced meditative practices. *Brit Menuhah* presents "meditations on the inner lights sparkling from the various vocalizations of the Tetragrammaton." Gershom Scholem, *Kabbalah* (Jerusalem: Keter, 1974), 65. *Pri Etz Chayyim* is a book of Lurianic teachings on prayer and *kavanot* (mystical meditation) as transmitted by Luria's foremost disciple, R. Hayim Vital. See Scholem, *Kabbalah*, 446.

11. *Ilan ha-Kadosh* was no doubt a version of *Ilan ha-Gadol* (The great tree), a large chart depicting the structure of creation as it progresses from the Infinite (*Ein Sof*) on downward, based on the Lurianic system of Four Worlds (see next note). Scholem, *Kabbalah*, 119–120.

12. For an explanation of the Four Worlds of Kabbalah, see Scholem, *Kabbalah*, 119. Briefly, the worlds represent stages of the emanative process, in the direction of greater crystallization and concretization (beginning with Emanation, which is essentially united with the Infinite). As listed here, the order is reversed, from most concrete and corporeal to the most abstract and spiritual.

13. The Babylonian talmudic scholar Samuel was reputed to have been an expert at astronomical calculations, especially with respect to the new moon. See *Rosh Hashanah* 20b.

14. Rabbi Yerahmiel Moshe Hapstein's father (the author's paternal grandfather) was Rabbi Yehiel Ya'akov Hapstein. Born c. 1846, he died in 1866, before his twentieth birthday. His great piety led him to perform several ritual ablutions

each day. One such ablution in the summer led to his accidental drowning in the river Staw (also called the Zagozdzonka, see n. 16); the date was 30 Sivan. See Zvi Halberstam, *"Toldot ha-Maggid mi-Kozienice"* [Appendix], in Yisrael ben Shabbetai (the Maggid of Kozienice), *Avodat Yisrael* (Bene Barak: Zvi Halberstam, 1973), 57; Avraham Yizhak Bromberg, *Mi-Gedolei ha-Hasidut: Beit Kozienice* (Jerusalem: Beit Hillel, 1982), 142. Note that Yerahmiel Moshe was born in 1860, so when his father died he was about six years old.

15. See Chapter Eight, n. 15.
16. The Zagozdzonka River, a tributary of the Vistula, runs through the town of Kozienice. For the most part it is languid but there are several dams where the water rushes over at great speed. One such dam, just east of the old Jewish cemetery, forms a large pond behind it. As the water courses over the dam and the spillway beyond, it roars with considerable force and the sound can be heard for a great distance downstream. Beyond the dam, the waters once again become quite placid; and the river, now more accurately described as a brook, runs through a grassy ravine behind old farm buildings. I found this spot during my visit to Kozienice in April 1999. Secluded and not visible from main roads, the area still retains a pristine beauty. On the day of my visit in mid-spring, this refreshingly serene spot was bursting with wildflowers and cherry blossoms. The watercourse just beyond the pond was apparently called the "River Staw"; *"staw"* is the Polish word for "pond."
17. See Chapter Eleven, n. 1.
18. In the sefirotic system, Heaven is *Tiferet* and earth is *Malkhut;* they are united through the ninth sefirah, *Yesod,* associated with the tzaddik. See G. Scholem, "Tsaddik: The Righteous One," in his *On the Mystical Shape of the Godhead* (New York: Schocken, 1991), 88–139. The letters of the Tetragrammaton represent the sefirot; the third letter of the Name, *vav,* is the supernal link channeling the energies of the upper sefirot into the final *heh,* representing *Malkhut* or *Shekhinah.* Here as before, the ideas expressed are found in Hapstein, *Avodat Yisrael,* 125, "Le-Shabbat ha-Gadol," "Be-Gemara."
19. Emphasis in the original. The allusion is probably to Num. 21:14–16.
20. Note that the author contradicts herself here. Earlier and later in this chapter, she says the sketch was made by the Maggid of Kozienice.

CHAPTER FOURTEEN

1. Alluding to Sg. 2:9, traditionally understood as a messianic passage.
2. The author here is recalling a time that took place after 1905, the setting of this memoir. Rahel Hayyah Miriam Hapstein was to marry Kalonymos Kalmish Shapiro, the Rebbe of Piaseczno. They were third cousins once removed. Havvah Hapstein married Rabbi Shalom Yosef Shapiro, her fourth cousin. Given that Malkah Shapiro married her half first cousin, Rabbi Avraham Elimelekh Shapiro, it is remarkable to observe the level of dynastic inbreeding that prevailed this family. As noted earlier, Hannah Goldah was divorced from Avraham Yehoshua Heschel Twersky of Kiev. See Neil Rosenstein, *The Unbroken Chain: Biograhical Sketches and Genealogy of*

Illustrious Jewish Families from the 15th–20th Century, 2 vols. (rev. ed. New York: CIS Publishers, 1990).

3. Hebrew: *yihudei devekut kedushah*, contemplations on permutations of the divine name. The practice has a mystical aim—ecstatic communion with the One—as well as a theurgic goal—the channeling of divine energy to bestow blessing here on earth. Both aims are part of the role of the hasidic tzaddik. See Moshe Idel, *Hasidism: Between Ecstasy and Magic* (Albany: State University of New York Press, 1995). For the practice of *yihudim* in the Lurianic context, see Lawrence Fine, "The Contemplative Practice of Yihudim in Lurianic Kabbalah," in *Jewish Spirituality from the Sixteenth-Century Revival to the Present*, ed. Arthur Green (New York: Crossroad, 1994), 64–98.

4. The Hebrew incorporates a fragment of Mal. 3:20: *"The sun of righteousness [shall shine] with healing [in its wings]."*

5. Ps. 114:1.

6. In aggadic and mystical literature, a Heavenly partition that screens the manifest presence of God from His angelic retinue; see *Hagigah* 15a.

7. Hebrew: *se'or she-be-isah* (the leavening of the dough); used in the Talmud (*Berachot* 17a) as a trope for the Evil Urge (*yezer ha-ra*).

8. According to the Midrash, all creation was silent at the time of the Revelation at Sinai; cf. *Shemot Rabbah* 29:9.

9. See Exod. 15:27.

10. Cf. Isa. 8:14; Jer. 13:16.

11. Ps. 118:5.

12. These sentences are based on a homily of the Kozienicer Maggid. See Yisrael ben Shabbetai Hapstein (the Maggid of Kozienice), *Avodat Yisrael* (Jerusalem: A. Weinstock, 1984), 127, *"Le-Shabbat ha-Gadol."* The Maggid explains that the way to "choose life" is to infuse one's words of prayer with true intention.

13. A slight variation of Prov. 18:21.

14. Deut. 30:19.

15. Hebrew: *'or ha-ganuz*; the primordial light of the first day of Creation, hidden away (according to the *aggadah*) because it was so powerful and sublime; see *Hagigah* 12a; *Bere'shit Rabbah* 3:6; *Zohar* 1:31b–32a. A collection of sources with helpful discussion can be found in Daniel Matt, *Zohar: The Book of Enlightenment* (New York: Paulist Press, 1983), 210–214.

16. As found in Exod. 6:6–7, *"I will free you . . . and deliver you. . . . I will redeem you. . . . I will take you."* The explanation linking the four cups with these four expressions is found in *Yerushalmi Pesahim* 37b.

17. Ps. 114:4, 7–8.

18. *Seder Olam* 5. On the significance of Miriam's well in Kozienice Hasidism, see Hapstein, *Avodat Yisrae*, 187–189, *"Parashat Hukkat,"* *"Az yashir Yisrael."* Cf. also Gershom Scholem, *"Shekhinah*: The Feminine Element in Divinity," in his *On the Mystical Shape of the Godhead* (New York: Schocken, 1991), 188.

19. The Hebrew word here, *"hometz,"* is related to *"hametz"* (leaven), the substance to be avoided on Passover. See n. 7.

20. Sg. 4:15.

21. Cf. Sg. 7:2.

22. Zech. 8:12.

23. Sg. 7:6.

24. Citation in original. See Hapstein, *Avodat Yisrael*, "*Be-Midrash Hazita.*"
25. Sg. 7:2.

CHAPTER FIFTEEN

1. Hebrew: *Ha-Kitrug she-nikhshal.* A "*kitrug*" is an indictment in the Heavenly Court brought by an angelic adversary of the Jewish people, usually prompted by a Jewish misdeed or shortcoming, which serves as a pretext for accusations that Israel is unworthy and ought to be judged severely in the New Year. Unpleasant premonitory effects of the indictment are often felt below on the terrestrial plane, such as the loss of the prayer leader's voice in the story. A *kitrug* may be countered with good deeds, especially charity, as well as with the intercessory blessing of a tzaddik.
2. According to a tradition that was widespread among Polish hasidim, the Kozienicer Maggid heard a certain sublime melody for *Kedushat Keter* when Shmuel Zbitkower, a Warsaw industrialist who had used his wealth to save many Jews from a massacre, was ushered into Heaven by the ministering angels. For more on Zbitkower and the folk tradition about the angelic song, see Chapter Seventeen. See also Chapter Nine, n. 11
3. See Chapter Seven, n. 4.
4. This *selihah* is by Rabbi Gershom ben Judah, known as Rabbeinu Gershom Me'or ha-Golah ("Light of the Diaspora"; 960–1028).

CHAPTER SIXTEEN

1. Gen. 27:28.
2. Brachah Tzippora Gitl Twersky, who narrates the inner story, was born c. 1861. From the description here and throughout the story, one receives the impression of a child about five or six years of age. This would date the wedding to 1866 or 1867. See the next note.
3. Rabbi Yissachar Dov Rokeah (Yashkar Bereleh) of Belz, third Belzer Rebbe, son of Rabbi Yehoshua Rokeah, was born in 1854 and died in 1926. If, as customary in these circles, the groom was about age thirteen at marriage (see further in the story), this would date the wedding to about 1867, consistent with the date suggested in n. 2. Neil Rosenstein, *The Unbroken Chain: Biographical Sketches and Genealogy of Illustrious Jewish Families from the 15th–20th Century*, vol. 2, rev. ed. (New York: CIS Publishers, 1990), 1204, has an entry for Rabbi Aharon Twersky's granddaughter Batya (daughter of Rabbi Yeshaya Meshulam Zusia, son of Rabbi Aharon Twersky of Chernobyl), and notes that she was the (first) wife of Yissachar Dov Rokeah, the Rebbe of Belz. All this is consistent with the information supplied by the story. However, Rosenstein gives Batya's second name as "Ruchama," not Nehama as here. He lists her date of death as 1884. In *Sefer Ha-Yahas Mi-Chernobyl ve-Ruzhin*, a genealogy of the Chernobyl dynasty by Aharon David Twersky (Lublin, 1938; rpt. Brooklyn: Beit Hillel, 1990), 115, her name is listed as Batya Rahuma.
4. Rosenstein, *The Unbroken Chain*, 114, 117, notes that Yissachar Dov's brother, Rabbi Aryeh Leibush Rokeah, was married to another granddaughter of Rabbi

Aharon Twersky of Chernobyl—Malkah, daughter of Rabbi Menahem Nahum, son of Rabbi Aharon. David Assaf, "*Viduyo shel Reb Yitzhak Nahum Tversky mi-Shpikov*," 14 *Alpayim* (1997): 49–79, discusses yet a third marriage between the Belz and Chernobyl dynasties, that of Rabbi Isaac Nahum Twersky of Shpikov (1888–1942) with Batsheva, the daughter of the Rabbi Yissachar Dov in the text. Isaac Nahum wrote a "confession" detailing his anguish at the deteriorated state of hasidic life in his day.

The theme of the story—the clash of spiritual cultures between the two families—sheds light on Nahum's confession. At least as perceived by the Chernobyl side, there was tension between the relatively open and moderate Twerskys, on the one hand, and the spiritually and politically militant Rokeah dynasty from Belz, on the other hand. Historians confirm that Belz remained rigidly traditionalist and isolationist into the twentieth century. See Mendel Piekarz, *Ideological Trends of Hasidism in Poland During the Interwar Period and the Holocaust* (Jerusalem: Bialik Institute, 1990), 23–24.

5. Cf. 1 Kings 18:44.
6. The Hebrew terms are taken from Isa. 30:15. The continuation of the verse is significant for the context: "*Your victory shall come about through calm and confidence.*"
7. See *Ketubbot* 17a.
8. The *badchen* (jester) at a hasidic wedding has a far more weighty task than simply providing comedy and laughter, though that is certainly not lacking in his routine. A major aspect of the *badchen's* task is to remind the couple of its responsibility as a link in an illustrious lineage. The presence of deceased ancestors and of children yet unborn is evoked, and the couple's own mortality is alluded to. Aspects of hasidic life and even family idiosyncrasies are often gently satirized. The entire act, if done well, is laced with witty and deft allusions to biblical and rabbinic texts and moves the couple and the guests from laughter, to tears, to wistful spiritual longing, and back again to laughter.
9. *Kiddushin* 41a.
10. Amalek is considered the archetype of the anti-Semite. See Exod. 17:8–16; Deut. 25:17–19.
11. See Chapter Nine, n. 12.
12. The *yichud* room is a private area set aside for the bride and groom to retire to after the wedding ceremony. The door must be locked behind them and no one else is to be present, although two witnesses stand guard outside the door. This opportunity for intimacy is the final stage of the wedding ceremony. Consummation rarely takes place in the *yichud* room; the law stipulates that the *opportunity* for consummation is the capstone of the wedding.
13. Rapoport-Albert notes that hasidic weddings often provided an opportunity for tzaddikim to discuss basic religious issues and communal policies. These discussions sometimes turned into heated arguments. Thus weddings might rather ironically become occasions for provoking and revealing a "high level of tension and hostility" between the courts. One example is the famous wedding at Ustila, at which Rabbi Ya'akov Yitzhak of Psyscha was nearly excommunicated. A still earlier occurrence was a wedding in Berditchev in 1802. See Ada Rapoport-Albert, "Hasidism after 1772: Structural Continuity and Change" in her *Hasidism Reappraised* (London: Littman Library, 1996), 121.
14. The world of evil and demonic forces is a skewed mirror image of the divine world. This world, the domain of Satan, is often referred to as *Sitra Ahra*, the

Other Side, or as here, the Left Side. See G. Scholem, "Sitra Ahra: Good and Evil in the Kabbalah," *On the Mystical Shape of the Godhead* (New York: Schocken, 1991), 56–87; Elliot Wolfson, "Left Contained in the Right: A Study in Zoharic Hermeneutics," *AJSReview* 11 (1986): 27–52.

15. Variation on Ps. 20:7.
16. *Bere'shit Rabbah* 12:15; Rashi on Gen. 1:1.
17. Understood kabbalistically as the harmonious combination of severity (*din, gevurah*) and love (*hesed*).
18. The reference is undoubtedly to *hilkhot niddah*, laws relating to menstrual impurity and conjugal separation.
19. A dance in which close relatives (including the new relatives by marriage) dance with the bride. The dancing partners are separated by a long chain of napkins knotted together or by a *gartl*. This is the only time when male as well as female relatives are permitted to dance with the bride, and the moment has a special poignancy and sanctity.
20. Abraham Joshua Heschel of Apta (1748–1825).
21. This is the language of the *Sheva Brachot*, the Seven Blessings recited at a wedding; see *Ketubbot* 8a.
22. This is Brachah's father, Rabbi Mordecai Twersky (see Chapter Four, n. 20).
23. What is meant here may be gleaned from an essay Malkah Shapiro wrote in memory of her daughter Rahel Hutner. She states, "[D]a'at is that quality which brings into convergence all the divine attributes employed in the governance of the world. . . . *Da'at* . . . imparts the strength to curb one's impulses and imparts stature to the individual, through the posture of compassionate grace (*Tiferet*) which is grounded in one's physical nature but is simultaneously attached to the sublime and the spiritual." The essay appears in a collection of appreciations and remembrances that appeared after her daughter's death, titled *Rahel Hutner: Mukdash Le-Zikhrah ba-Yom ha-Shanah ha-Rishon le-Petiratah* (Jerusalem: State of Israel Department of Social Services, 1967).

CHAPTER SEVENTEEN

1. Meilekh is a diminutive of Elimelekh. The author writes this person's name in various forms: Reb Meilikh bereb Pinhas ("bereb" means "son of"); Reb Meilikh reb Pinhas, with the "be-" of "bereb" clipped off, as it might be in speech; Reb Meilikh bereb Pinhas's, adding a pleonastic possessive suffix. Sometimes she writes Elimelekh, rather than the diminutive Meilikh. Elimelekh's last name was Freilich. The Freilichs were a large and prominent family in Kozienice; see Barukh Kaplinsky, ed., *Sefer Zikaron li-Kehilat Kozienice* (Memorial book for the community of Kozienice) (in Yiddish and Hebrew) (Tel Aviv: Kozienice Association, 1960), 216–225. The book was translated into English by Michael Wax and Jack Weinstein (New York: Kozienice Association, 1985). I was not able to ascertain the exact year of Elimelekh Freilich's birth, but it must have been around 1870.
2. Polish: *Kociolki;* a village about four kilometers south of Kozienice.
3. The Hebrew—*sefunei temunei da'agoteihem*—draws in part on Deut. 33:19: "*treasures concealed in the sand.*"

4. Ps. 118:5.
5. The history of this symbolism is superbly traced in Arthur Green, *Keter: The Crown of God in Early Jewish Mysticism* (Princeton, N.J.: Princeton University Press, 1997).
6. Zbitkower was a major industrialist and financier (see Chapter Nine, n. 11). A major supplier to the Polish army, he was the patriarch of the Bergson family, which controlled much of Warsaw's banking. Raphael Mahler, *Hasidism and the Jewish Enlightenment* (Philadelphia: Jewish Publication Society, 1985), 188–189. As Joseph Marcus notes in *Social and Political History of the Jews of Poland, 1919–1939* (Berlin: Mouton, 1983), 75–76, the prominent Bergson family included a Nobel prize winner for literature (Henri Bergson). An important essay on Zbitkower is by the Polish–Jewish historian Emmanuel Ringelblum, "Samuel Zbitkower: An Economic and Social Leader in Poland at the Time of the Partition,"n.s. *Zion* 3 (1938): 246–266; 4 (1938): 337–355. Ringelblum discusses the folk tradition of Zbitkower's efforts in halting a pogrom (ibid., 256–257). While raising some questions about details, his conclusion is that the story is essentially authentic. The story first appeared in print in Polish in 1872–1873. The aspect of the story concerning the Maggid of Kozienice and the angelic song that accompanied Zbitkower's entry into paradise is discussed by Ringelblum, ibid., n. 45. Ringelblum's informant heard the story from the masters of the Sanz hasidic dynasty, where it was attributed to Rabbi Naftali of Ropczyce, who heard it from the Kozienicer Maggid himself.

   Zbitkower's daughter-in-law Temerel (also known as Tamar and Temer'l) Bergson was a devoted follower of the Maggid of Kozienice and a major supporter of Hasidism in Poland. (It is tempting, by the way, to see Henri Bergson's notion of *élan vital* as possibly influenced by his hasidic heritage, in particular the notion of *hiyyut*, "vital spiritual energy.")
7. Temerel was actually Shmuel Zbitkower's daughter-in-law. See the previous note, and Chapter Nine, n. 11.
8. Cf. *Avodah Zarah* 10b.
9. Hebrew: *gabbai'ot;* women in charge of charitable activities such as tending the sick, dowering poor brides, and providing hospitality for wayfarers.
10. A talmudic expression for the responsibility of being a family breadwinner is "a millstone around the neck"; see *Kiddushin* 29b.
11. It is customary to study an entire tractate of the Talmud in memory of the departed, especially a departed Rebbe. Such study is considered meritorious for the soul. At the time of the Rebbe's yahrzeit, the tractate is concluded in a public celebration known as a *siyum,* and a feast is held. In this case, the Rebbes were Barukh of Medzibozh (c. 1756–1810), grandson of the Baal Shem Tov, and Dov Baer, the Maggid of Mezirech (1704–1772), successor to the Baal Shem Tov.
12. Cf. Isa. 54:17.
13. Rabbi Elimelekh Shapiro of Grodzisk (actually the author's great-grandfather) passed away on 1 Nisan 1892; Malkah Bat-Zion was born two years later in 1894.
14. 2 Sam. 1:23.

FAMILY TREE

BAAL SHEM TOV d.1760
DOV BAER, THE MAGGID OF MEZHIRECH d.1772

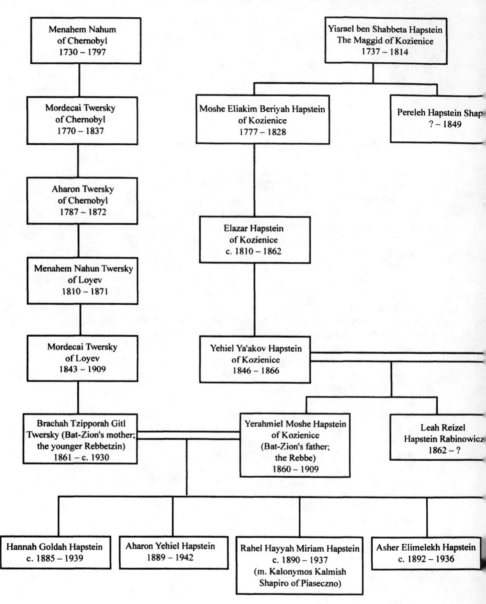

```
Menahem Nahum
of Chernobyl
1730 – 1797

Mordecai Twersky
of Chernobyl
1770 – 1837

Aharon Twersky
of Chernobyl
1787 – 1872

Menahem Nahun Twersky
of Loyev
1810 – 1871

Mordecai Twersky
of Loyev
1843 – 1909

Brachah Tzipporah Gitl
Twersky (Bat-Zion's mother;
the younger Rebbetzin)
1861 – c. 1930
```

```
Yisrael ben Shabbeta Hapstein
The Maggid of Kozienice
1737 – 1814

Moshe Eliakim Beriyah Hapstein
of Kozienice
1777 – 1828

Pereleh Hapstein Shap
? – 1849

Elazar Hapstein
of Kozienice
c. 1810 – 1862

Yehiel Ya'akov Hapstein
of Kozienice
1846 – 1866

Yerahmiel Moshe Hapstein
of Kozienice
(Bat-Zion's father;
the Rebbe)
1860 – 1909

Leah Reizel
Hapstein Rabinowicz
1862 – ?
```

```
Hannah Goldah Hapstein
c. 1885 – 1939

Aharon Yehiel Hapstein
1889 – 1942

Rahel Hayyah Miriam Hapstein
c. 1890 – 1937
(m. Kalonymos Kalmish
Shapiro of Piaseczno)

Asher Elimelekh Hapstein
c. 1892 – 1936
```

Dates are based on the best information available. Some pre-twentieth-century birthdates are variously reported and should be considered approximate.

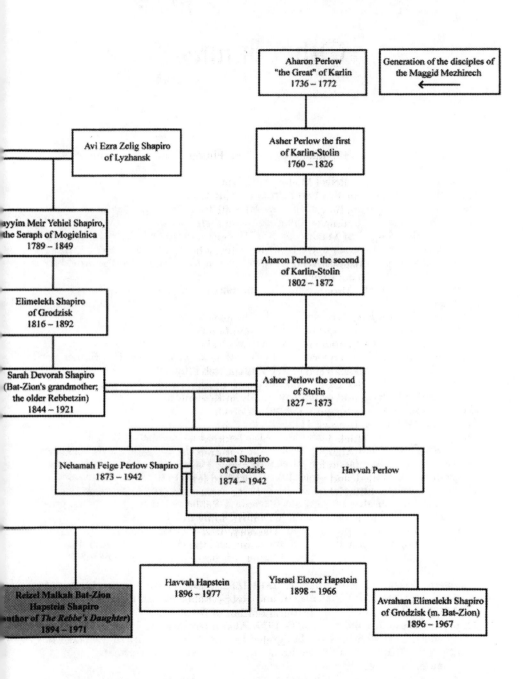

List of Family Members and Other Figures

Baal Shem Tov. d. 1760. Rabbi Israel ben Eliezer. Founder of the hasidic movement.

Bat-Zion. See Hapstein, Reizel Malkah Bat-Zion.

Brachaleh. See Hapstein, Brachah Tzipporah Gitl Twersky.

Brachanu. See Hapstein, Brachah Tzipporah Gitl Twersky.

Devorah of Safed. Longtime family guest from *Eretz Yisra'el*.

Dov Baer, the Maggid of Mazhirech. d. 1772. Successor to Dov Baer, the Maggid of Mezhirech. Successor to the Baal Shem Tov, whose court attracted a circle of remarkable personalities, who in turn set the foundation for the world of Hasidism down to our own time.

Elazar the assistant. Also referred to as Elazar the Litvak and Elazar the melammed.

Elimelekh ben Pinhas, Reb. See Freilich, Elimelekh.

Esther Reizel. Apprentice girl to the Hapstein family.

Feigenu, Rebbetzin of Grodzisk. See Shapiro, Nehamah Feige Perlow.

Freilich, Elimelekh. Also referred to as Reb Meilekh ben Pinhas, Reb Elimelekh ben Pinhas, Reb Meilekh son of Reb Pinhas, Reb Elimelekh son of Pinhas, and Elimelekh. Devoted hasid and follower of the Rebbe Yerahmiel Moshe. Member of a large and prominent family in Kozienice.

Grodzisker Rebbe. See Shapiro, Rabbi Elimelekh.

Hannah Havvah. See Twersky, Hannah Hayyah.

Hapstein, Aharon Yehiel. 1889–1942. Also referred to as Aharon Yehiel'sh, Reb Areleh, and Rabbi Aharonl. Brother of Bat-Zion. In adult life, a charismatic Rebbe with a reputation for miracle working. He focused on the needs of the poor, less educated, and other disenfranchised Jews in the interwar period.

Hapstein, Asher Elimelekh. c. 1892–1936. Also referred to as Reb Asher Elimelekh'l. Brother of Bat-Zion. Became a Rebbe noted for his gentle, gracious personality. Perished with his entire family in the Holocaust.

Hapstein, Brachah Tzipporah Gitl Twersky. 1861–c. 1930. Also referred to as Brachaleh, Brachanu, Rebbetzin Brachanu, and the younger Rebbetzin. Wife of Yerahmiel Moshe, the Rebbe. Mother of Bat-Zion. Descendent of Rabbi Menahem Nahum of Chernobyl.

Hapstein, Elazar of Kozienice. c. 1810–1862. Also referred to as Elazar of Kozienice, tzaddik Rabbi Elazar, and Rebbe Rabbi Elazar. Grandson of the Maggid of Kozienice and great-grandfather of Bat-Zion.

Hapstein, Hannah Goldah. c. 1885–1939. Also referred to as Hannale, Hannah Goldeleh. Sister of Bat-Zion. Emigrated to *Eretz Yisra'el;* returned to Poland in the late 1930s for a family wedding and was killed in the German bombardment of Warsaw in September 1939.

Hapstein, Havvah. 1896–1977. Also referred to as Havvaleh. Sister of Bat-Zion. Married her relative Shalom Yosef Shapira. Moved to *Eretz Yisra'el* and joined

Kefar Hasidim. Devoted to a life of farming, she remained in Kefar Hasidim until her death.

Hapstein, Moshe Eliakim Beriyah of Kozienice. 1777–1828. Son of the Maggid of Kozienice and great-great grandfather of Bat-Zion. Author of many hasidic books.

Hapstein, Rahel Hayyah Miriam. c. 1890–1937. Also referred to as Hayyah Miriam'l. Sister of Bat-Zion. Future wife of Kalonymos Kalmish Shapiro (the Piaseczner Rebbe).

Hapstein, Reizel Malkah Bat-Zion. 1894–1971. Also referred to as Bat-Zion and Malkah Shapiro. Daughter of the Rebbe Yerahmiel Moshe and Rebbetzin Brachah Tzippora Gitl. Author of this memoir.

Hapstein, Sarah Devorah. See Shapiro, Sarah Devorah.

Hapstein, Yehiel Ya'akov of Kozienice. 1846–1866. First husband of Sarah Devorah Shapiro. Great-grandson of the Maggid of Kozienice and grandfather of Bat-Zion.

Hapstein, Yerahmiel Moshe. 1860–1909. Also referred to as Rebbe Rabbi Yerahmiel Moshele and Moshenu. Rebbe of Kozienice. Husband of Brachah Tzipporah Gitl and father of Bat-Zion. Descendent of the Kozienicer Maggid.

Hapstein, Yisrael ben Shabbetai. 1737–1814. The Maggid of Kozienice (the Kozienicer Maggid). Hasidic master and patriarch of the Hapstein dynasty. A founding father of Hasidism in Poland.

Hapstein, Yisrael Elozor. 1898–1966. Also referred to as Yisrael Elozor'l and Yisrael Elozor'ke. Brother of Bat-Zion. Moved to *Eretz Yisra'el*. A founder of Kefar Hasidim, where he worked to develop farming and was involved in the draining of swamps that harbored malaria.

Havvanu. See Perlow, Havvah.

Hayyah. Sarah Devorah's mother. Wife of Rabbi Elimelekh Shapiro of Grodzisk. A descendent of Rabbi Jabob Isaac, the "Holy Jew" of Przysucha.

Hayyim, Dr. A feldsher who was a close friend of and attended to the Hapstein family.

Hutner, Rahel. Malkah Shapiro's middle daughter, who married the talmudic scholar Rabbi Yehoshua Hutner. At the time of her death, in 1966, she headed the Office for Children and Youth in Israel's Ministry of Welfare.

Kalmish'l. See Shapiro, Kalonymos Kalmish.

Kozienicer Maggid. See Hapstein, Yisrael ben Shabbetai.

Kozienicer Rebbitzin Tzipporah. A scion of Rabbi Naftali of Ropczyce, she was the wife of Rabbi Elazar Hapstein.

Leahnu of Parczew. See Rabinowicz, Leah Reizel Hapstein.

Maggid of Kozienice. See Hapstein, Yisrael ben Shabbetai.

Malkah. The Hapstein's house manager.

Meilekh son of Reb Pinhas. See Freilich, Elimelekh.

Nanny Sarah. An old and trusted member of the Hapstein household.

Older Rebbetzin. See Shapiro, Sarah Devorah.

Pereleh. See Shapiro, Pereleh Hapstein.

Perlow, Aharon "the Great" of Karlin. 1736–1772. A disciple of the Maggid of Mezhirech; founder of the Karlin-Stolin dynasty.

Perlow, Aharon the second of Karlin-Stolin. 1802–1872. Grandson of Rabbi Aharon "the Great" Perlow. Author of *Bet Aharon*.

Perlow, Asher the first of Karlin-Stolin. 1760–1826. Son of Rabbi Aharon "the Great" Perlow.

Perlow, Asher the second of Stolin. 1827–1873. Son of Rabbi Aharon Perlow the second of Karlin-Stolin. Second husband of Sarah Devorah Shapiro.

Perlow, Havvah. Also referred to as Havvahnu. Daughter of Sarah Devorah Shapiro, sister to Rebbe Yerahmiel Moshe Hapstein, and Bat-Zion's aunt.

Perlow, Yisrael of Stolin. Also referred to as Rabbi Yisrael'nu. After the death of his father, he was invested as Rebbe of Stolin at the age of five. Know by some as the "Yenuka" (wonder child) of Stolin.

Rabinowicz, Leah Reizel Hapstein. b. 1862. Also referred to as Leahnu, and Rebbetzin Leah'nu of Parczew. Daughter of Sarah Devorah Shapiro, sister of the Rebbe Yerahmiel Moshe, and Bat-Zion's aunt.

Sarah Devorahleh. See Shapiro, Sarah Devorah.

Shapiro, Avraham Elimelekh. 1896–1967. Future husband of Bat-Zion. Emigrated to *Eretz Yisra'el* and lived first in Haifa and then Jerusalem. Published hasidic works from the Grodzisk and Karlin-Stolin traditions.

Shapiro, Elimelekh. 1816–1892. Also referred to as tzaddik Reb Elimelekh and the Grodzisker Rebbe. Grandson of Pereleh Hapstein Shapiro and father of Sarah Devorah Shapiro. Renowned Hasidic master.

Shapiro, Hayyim Meir Yehiel. 1789–1849. "The Seraph" of Mogielnica. A popular charismatic Rebbe noted for ecstatic prayer and fervent piety.

Shapiro, Israel of Grodzisk. 1874–1942. Also referred to as Rabbi Yisraelnu, the Rebbe of Grodzisk. Direct descendent of the Maggid of Kozienice through the Maggid's daughter, Pereleh Hapstein Shapiro. Husband of Nehama Feige Perlow and future father-in-law of Bat-Zion. Killed in the Holocaust; as he was led to the gas chambers, he exhorted his community to sanctify the Divine Name by surrendering their lives with joy and the singing of "I Believe."

Shapiro, Kalonymos Kalmish. 1889–1943. The Piaseczner Rebbe. Son of Rabbi Elimelekh Shapiro and future husband of Bat-Zion's sister Rahel Hayyah Miriam. Author of *Esh Kodesh*. Also referred to as Rabbi Kalmish'l and Kalonymos Kalmish Shapiro of Piaseczno.

Shapiro, Malkah. See Hapstein, Reizel Malkah Bat-Zion.

Shapiro, Nehamah Feige Perlow. 1873–1942. Also referred to as Feigenu and the Rebbetzin Feigenu of Grodzisk. Daughter of Sarah Devorah Shapiro, sister of the Rebbe Yerahmiel Moshe, and future mother-in-law of Bat-Zion.

Shapiro, Pereleh Hapstein. d. 1849. Also referred to as Pereleh and Perel. Daughter of Rabbi Yisrael ben Shabbetai Hapstein, the Maggid of Kozienice. Wife of Rabbi Avi Ezra Zelig Shapiro of Lyzhansk. Matriarch of Shapiro branch of Kozienice dynasty. Great-grandmother of Sarah Devorah Shapiro (the older Rebbetzin).

Shapiro, Sarah Devorah. 1844–1921. Also referred to as Sarah Devorahleh, Rebbetzin Sarah Devorahleh, and the older Rebbetzin. Matriarch of the Hapstein household. Mother of the Rebbe Yerahmiel Moshe and grandmother of Bat-Zion and of Avraham Elimelekh Shapiro, Bat-Zion's future husband.

Twersky, Aharon of Chernobyl. 1787–1872. Oldest son of Rabbi Mordecai Twersky of Chernobyl and grandson of the founder of the dynasty, Menahem Nahum Twersky.

Twersky, Brachah Tzipporah Gitl. See Hapstein, Brachah Tzipporah Gitl Twersky.

Twersky, Hannah Hayyah. Also referred to as Hannah Havvah. Great-great-aunt of Rebbetzin Brachah Tzipporah Gitl and granddaughter of the founder of the Twersky dynasty.

Twersky, Menahem Nahum of Chernobyl. 1730–1797. Also referred to as Rabbi Nahum.Founder of the Twersky hasidic dynasty. Author of the classic hasidic *Me'or Eynayim.* Disciple of the Baal Shem Tov and the Maggid of Mezhirech.

Twersky, Menahem Nahum of Loyev. 1810–1871. Son of Rabbi Aharon Twersky of Chernobyl and great-grandfather of Bat-Zion.

Twersky, Mordecai of Chernobyl. 1770–1837. Son of Menahem Nahum Twersky of Chernobyl. Established an impressive court and attracted thousands of followers. After his death, his eight sons all established courts in different towns.

Twersky, Mordecai. 1843–1909. The Loyever Rebbe. Also referred to as Mordecai Twersky of Loyev. Father of Brachah Tzippora Gitl Twersky and grandfather of Bat-Zion.

Yerahmiel Moshe. See Hapstein, Yerahmiel Moshe.

Yisrael'nu, Rabbi of Stolin. See Perlow, Yisrael.

Yisraelnu, the Rebbe of Grodzisk. See Shapiro, Rabbi Israel.

Younger Rebbetzin. See Hapstein, Brachah Tzipporah Gitl Twersky.

Glossary

Admor. Acronym for *Adoneinu Moreinu ve-Rabeinu* (our Master, our teacher, our rabbi); a standard honorific term for a hasidic master. I have generally translated *Admor* as Rebbe.

apprentice girl. A young girl, typically needy or orphaned, taken in by the Hapstein family and made part of the household. Working for room and board, the apprentice girl was given the opportunity to learn domestic skills, such as embroidery and crocheting.

Ayin ha-ra. The Evil Eye.

baal teshuvah. A person who returns to religious piety after having lapsed from strict observance.

bat mitzvah. A girl's entry into the status of Jewish religious obligation and maturity. According to rabbinic law as found in the Mishna, Talmud, and Codes, this takes place at age twelve. Boys reach legal maturity at age thirteen.

beit midrash. Hall for Torah study, often used for prayer services as well.

ben-tovim (fem: bas-tovim; pl. bnei-tovim). A well-bred person born of a old, respected family; often used when the family has fallen on hard times.

Congress Poland. A region of Poland created in 1815 by the Congress of Vienna and granted limited autonomy within the Russian Empire. The region, which included Warsaw and its environs, was considered to be the core of old Poland.

Crown Rabbi (Hebrew: *ha-Rav mi-Ta'am*). A governmental official appointed to fulfill clerical tasks—such as registering births, marriages, and deaths—and to officiate at life-cycle events. The essential job skill was facility in Russian, which many traditional rabbis did not possess. Some Crown Rabbis had little Judaic knowledge at all, whereas others received their rabbinic training at a government-authorized rabbinical seminary; their rabbinic learning was considered inferior to the old-style *yeshiva*-trained Rabbi or hasidic Rebbe. As representatives of the hated czarist regime, they were often viewed with suspicion by the Jewish populace.

da'at (mindfulness). In Kabbalah, the connection between the upper *sefirot* of intellect and the lower *sefirot* of emotion.

devekut. Communion with God; attainment of union or near-union with the Divine by means of ecstatic prayer and meditation. The central ideal of the hasidic religious life.

dybbuk. The soul of a dead person that has possessed the body of a living person.

Eretz Yisra'el. The Land of Israel. This is a religious designation, in contrast to *Medinat Yisra'el*, the State of Israel.

ezrat nashim. A room or area set aside for women's prayer.

feldsher. A paramedic or folk doctor.

gabbai. The Rebbe's administrative assistant; an appointee in charge of synagogue ritual.

gartl. A long black sash or belt, usually made of satin mesh, worn by hasidim during prayer and other sacred occasions. It separates the upper, more holy, part of the body from the lower part.

Hallel. Ps. 113–118 recited or sung as a liturgical unit during festival services and other sacred celebrations.

hametz. Bread or other food prohibited during Passover because it is leavened.

He-asif. Hebrew-language annual that focuses on Jewish history, culture, and religion. Published in Warsaw (1884–1893).

heder. Traditional one-room school focusing on religious subjects; typically held in the teacher's home.

Humash. A volume containing either one or all five of the Five Books of Moses (Pentateuch), often with classical rabbinic commentaries by Rashi, Ibn Ezra, and Nahmanides (among others).

Inner Sanctum. The master's private chambers, used for study, contemplation, and audiences. The term is borrowed from the Holy of Holies of the Tabernacle (Exod. 26:33).

kapote. A long black caftan or frock worn by hasidim.

kazatzke. A lively dance of Cossack origin, often performed at weddings.

kelipot (sing. kelipah). Literally, shells or husks; forces of darkness, demonic powers.

kodesh. The Master's receiving room or office. See Inner Sanctum.

Kol Nidrei. Solem declaration chanted at the start of Yom Kippur services.

Litvak. A Jew from Lithuania or White Russia. The Litvak stereotype was that of an overly rationalistic individual, often with an acerbic, curmudgeonly exterior. In the Polish-Jewish world, the Litvak's Yiddish accent was immediately noticeable.

Ma'ariv. Evening prayer.

Maggid. Preacher; ofen applied to a hasidic master known for his homiletic skills.

maskil (pl. maskilim). An adherent of the *Haskalah*, a movement advocating the modernization of Jewish society and culture on the basis of scientific rationalism. A mood of mutual suspicion and hostility often prevailed between adherents of the *Haskalah* and Hasidism.

melammed. A teacher or tutor of children for sacred studies.

melaveh malkeh. The Saturday evening meal that escorts the departing Sabbath Queen.

meshamesh ba-kodesh. A valet, aide, or personal attendant who performs personal services for the Rebbe; it is an envied position because of the proximity to the Master.

Mincha. Afternoon prayer.

netilat yadayim. Ritual hand washing at the start of the day and before partaking of bread at meals.

niddah. A woman in the state of menstrual impurity.

p'tchah. Jellied calves' foot.

peyos. Long sidelocks, worn by hasidic boys and men in fulfillment of Lev. 19:27.

pilpul. Talmudic argumentation characterized by keen dialectics.

Polesia. "The region in the western part of Russia around the Pripet Marshes, with the town of Pinsk in its centre, and stretching westward almost to the town of Brest-Litovsk, eastward to the town of Mozyr, and northwards to the approaches of Minsk, while to the south it includes the northern portion of Volhynia." Wolf Zeev Rabinowitsch, *Lithuanian Hasidism* (New York: Schocken, 1970), xiii.

porets. The Polish nobleman; stereotypically viewed as cruel, capricious, and rash.

sefirah (pl. sefirot). In Kabbalah, a stage of Divine self-manifestation. There are ten *sefirot.*

Selichot. Petitionary prayers in preparation for the High Holidays.

Seraph. A celestial being; sometimes applied figuratively to a hasidic master noted for fervor and ecstatic prayer.

sha'atnez. A mixture of wool and linen, prohibited for clothing. See Deut. 22:11.

Shalom Aleikhem. Pen name of Shalom Rabinovitz (1859–1916), great Yiddish author and humorist.

Shehecheyanu. "Blessed are You, Lord our God, King of the universe, who has kept us alive, sustained us, and enabled us to reach this season." The benediction is recited when eating seasonal fruits for the first time within any one year, as well as other special occasions.

sheine yidden. Literally, beautiful Jews. In the hasidic world, the term refers to Jews of impeccable piety and religious devotion who serve as inspiring exemplars for the community.

Shekhinah. Indwelling Divine Presence; the feminine Presence of God.

Shemoneh Esrei. The central rabbinic prayer; the "Eighteen Blessings," also known as the *Amidah,* the Standing Prayer, or *Tefillah.*

shochet. Ritual slaughterer of animals for kosher food consumption.

shtreimel. A fur-edged hat, worn as a garment of distinction by hasidim, especially on Sabbaths and holidays.

stern tichl. A turbanlike head cover worn with a brooch gathering the front; it has a certain air of elegance.

talmidah hakhamah (masc. talmid hakham). A tamudic scholar.

tiferet. Compassionate grace. The sixth *sefirah,* understood kabbalistically as the harmonious combination of severity (*din, gevurah*) and love (*hesed*).

tzaddik (fem. tzaddeket; pl. tzaddikim). Righteous or saintly individual. In Hasidism, the word tzadik designates the community's leader, its spiritual heart who mediates contact with the divine realm and serves as the conduit of heavenly grace and blessing.

tzitzit. Fringes attached to the corners of garments in fulfillment of Num. 15:37–41.

veteran hasidim. Old-time members of a hasidic community; trusted members of the court's inner circle.

yahrzeit. Anniversary of a person's death, usually marked by religious observances.

yihudim. Meditative practices involving permutations and combinations of the divine names, intended to channel and unite various aspects of divine energy, based on the theology of Lurianic Kabbalah.

yoshvim. Permanent residents of the hasidic court whose ongoing presence in the *beit midrash* provided a core group continually devoted to study and prayer.

Bibliography

Adler, Ruth. "Dvora Baron: Daughter of the Shtetl." In *Women of the Word: Jewish Women and Jewish Writing*, edited by Judith R. Baskin, 91–100. Detroit: Wayne State University Press, 1994.

Aescoly, Aaron Ze'ev. *Hasidism in Poland*. Jerusalem: Magnes Press, 1998.

Alfasi, Yitzhak, ed. *Encyclopedia of Hasidism: Personalities* (in Hebrew). Jerusalem: Mossad Harav Kook, 1986.

Alfasi, Yitzhak. *Ha-Hasidut ve-Shivat Tziyon*. Tel Aviv: Ma'ariv, 1986.

—— *Ha-Hasidut*. Tel Aviv: Sifriyat Ma'ariv, 1977.

Al-Hakam, Joseph Hayyim ben Elijah. *Siddur Od Yosef Hai*. Jerusalem: Yosef Hayyim Mizrahi, 1995.

Alter, Robert. *Hebrew and Modernity*. Bloomington: Indiana University Press, 1994.

Ashkenazi, Shlomo. *Ha-Isha ba-Aspaklaryat ha-Yahadut*. 2d ed. 2 vols. Tel Aviv: Zion, 1979.

Assaf, David. " 'Money for Household Expenses': Economic Aspects of the Hasidic Courts." In *Studies in the History of the Jews in Old Poland in Honor of Jacob Goldberg*, edited by Adam Teller, 14–50. Jerusalem: Magnes Press, 1998.

—— "Viduyo shel Reb Yitzhak Nahum Tversky mi-Shpikov." *Alpayim* 14 (1997): 49–79.

Bacon, Gershon C. *The Politics of Tradition: Agudat Yisrael in Poland, 1916–1939*. Jerusalem: Magnes Press, 1996.

—— "Warsaw-Vilna-Budapest: On Joseph Ben-David's Model of the Modernization of Jewry." *Jewish History* 11 (1997): 102–112.

Band, Arnold. *Between Nostalgia and Nightmare*. Berkeley: University of California Press, 1968.

Bar Sela, Shraga. "On the Brink of Disaster: Hillel Zeitlin's Struggle for Jewish Survival in Poland." *Polin* 11 (1998): 77–93.

Baron, Salo W. *The Russian Jew under Tsars and Soviets*. 2nd ed. New York: Schocken, 1987.

Barros, Carolyn A. *Autobiography: Narrative of Transformation*. Ann Arbor: University of Michigan Press, 1998.

Baskin, Judith R. "From Separation to Displacement: The Problem of Women in Sefer Hasidim." *Association for Jewish Studies Review* 19 (1994): 1–18.

Benjamin, Walter. *Illuminations*. Edited and with an introduction by Hannah Arendt. Translated by Harry Zohn. New York: Harcourt, Brace & World, 1955.

Bertini, K. Aharon. "Review of Malkah Shapiro, *Shneinu ba-Maginim*." *Gilyonot* 28 (1953): 106–107.

Biale, David. *Eros and the Jews*. New York: Basic Books, 1992.

Bilu, Yoram. "Dreams and the Wishes of the Saint." In *Judaism Viewed from Within and from Without: Anthropological Studies*, edited by Harvey E. Goldberg, 285–313. Albany: State University of New York Press, 1987.

Brody, Seth. " 'Open to Me the Gates of Righteousness': The Pursuit of Holiness and Non-Duality in Early Hasidic Teaching." *Jewish Quarterly Review* 89, nos. 1–2 (1998): 3–44.

Bromberg, Avraham Yizhak. *Mi-Gedolei ha-Hasidut: Beit Kozienice*. Jerusalem: Beit Hillel, 1982.

Bruss, Elizabeth W. *Autobiographical Acts: The Changing Situation of a Literary Genre.* Baltimore: The Johns Hopkins University Press, 1976.

Byman, Caroline Walker. *Fragmentation and Redemption: Essays on Gender and the Human Body in Medieval Religion.* New York: Zone Books, 1992.

Cala, Alina. "The Cult of Tzaddikim among Non-Jews in Poland," *Jewish Folklore and Ethnology Review* 17, nos. 1–2 (1995): 16–19.

Cohen, Gerson D. "Esau as Symbol in Early Medieval Thought." In *Studies in the Variety of Rabbinic Cultures.* Philadelphia: Jewish Publication Society, 1991.

Cordovero, Moshe. *Pardes Rimmonim.* Jerusalem: Mordecai Atiah, 1962.

Dalsimer, Katherine. *Female Adolescence: Psychoanalytic Reflections on Literature.* New Haven, Conn.: Yale University Press, 1986.

Danziger, Yerahmiel Israel Isaac of Aleksandrow. *Yismah Yisra'el.* Bene Berak: Aleksandrow Hasidim Publishing Institute, 1999.

Davis, Natalie Zemon. *Women on the Margins: Three Seventeenth-Century Lives.* Cambridge, Mass.: Harvard University Press, 1995.

Duker, Abraham G. "The Tarniks (Believers in the Coming of the Messiah in 1840)." In *The Joshua Starr Memorial Volume.* 191–201. New York: Conference on Jewish Relations, 1953.

Eakin, Paul John. *Fictions in Autobiography: Studies in the Art of Self-Invention.* Princeton, N.J.: Princeton University Press, 1985.

Eisenstein, J. D. *Otzar Dinim u-Minhagim.* New York: Hebrew Publishing Company, 1917.

Eliach, Yaffa. *Hasidic Tales of the Holocaust.* New York: Oxford University Press, 1982.

——— *There Once Was a World: A 900-Year Chronicle of the Shtetl of Eishyshok.* Boston: Little, Brown, 1998.

Epstein, Barukh. *Mekor Barukh.* Vilna: n.p., 1928.

Epstein, Kalonymos Kalman of Cracow. *Ma'or va-Shemesh.* 1842. Rev. ed., Jerusalem: Even Yisra'el, 1992.

Epstein, Lisa. *Caring for the Soul's House: The Jews of Russia and Health Care 1860–1914.* Ann Arbor, Mich.: UMI Dissertation Services, 1995.

Epstein, Yehiel Michel ha-Levi. *Arukh ha-Shulhan.* 8 vols. 1901–1929. Reprint, Tel Aviv: Yatzo Sifrei Kodesh, n.d.

Even Hen, Ya'akov. "Ha-Sifrut ba-Hashkafato shel ha-Rav Kook." *Mabua* 28 (1996): 66–78.

Feinkind, Moshe. *Froyen-Rebeyyim un Berimte Persenlikhkeiten in Poylen* (in Yiddish). Warsaw: published by the author's children, 1937.

Fine, Lawrence. "The Contemplative Practice of Yihudim in Lurianic Kabbalah." In *Jewish Spirituality from the Sixteenth-Century Revival to the Present,* edited by Arthur Green, 64–98. New York: Crossroad, 1994.

Fleishman, Avrom. *Figures of Autobiography.* Berkeley: University of California Press, 1983.

Frankel, Giza. "Notes on the Costume of the Jewish Woman in Eastern Europe." *Journal of Jewish Art* 7 (1980): 50–57.

Ginzberg, Louis. *Legends of the Jews.* 7 vols. Philadelphia: Jewish Publication Society of America, 5730/1969.

Goldberg, Isaac. "Chaim Selig Slonimski: 19th-Century Popularizer of Science." In *Shmuel K. Mirsky Memorial Volume,* edited by Gersion Appel, Morris Epstein, and Hayim Leaf, 247–261. Jerusalem: Sura Institute, 1970.

Goldstein, Sabina Weinstock. Preface to *The Book of Kozienice*. Revised by Samuel Goldstein. Translated by Michael Wax and Jack Weinstein. New York: Kozienice Association, 1985.

Green, Arthur, ed. *Jewish Spirituality from the Sixteenth-Century Revival to the Present*. New York: Crossroad, 1994.

Green, Arthur. *Keter: The Crown of God in Early Jewish Mysticism*. Princeton, N.J.: Princeton University Press, 1997.

———— "On Translating Hasidic Homilies." *Prooftexts* 3 (1983): 63–72.

———— "Three Warsaw Mystics." In *Rivkah Shatz-Uffenheimer Memorial, Volume II*, edited by Rachel Elior and Joseph Dan, 1–58. Jerusalem: The Hebrew University of Jerusalem, 1996. [*Jerusalem Studies in Jewish Thought* 13 (1996), 1–58.]

———— "The Zaddik as Axis Mundi." *Journal of the American Academy of Religion* 45, no. 3 (1977): 327–347.

Grossman, Levi ha-Levi. *Shem u-She'erit*. Jerusalem: Bezalel, 1989.

Halberstam, Zvi. *Toldot ha-Maggid mi-Kozienice*. Bene Barak: author, 1973.

Halkin, Hillel. "On Translating the Living and the Dead: Some Thoughts of a Hebrew-English Translator." *Prooftexts* 3 (1983): 73–90.

Hannover, Nathan. *Sha'arei Ziyyon*. N.p., 1662.

Hapstein, Moshe Eliyakim Beriah. *Da'at Moshe*. 2 vols. Jerusalem: Keren le-hadpasat sifre bet Kozienice, 1999.

Hapstein, Yisrael ben Shabbetai (the Maggid of Kozienice). *Avodat Yisrael*. Bene Berak: Makhon Nofet Tsufim, 1996.

———— *Avodat Yisrael*. Bene Berak: Zvi Halberstam, 1973.

———— *Avodat Yisrael*. Jerusalem: A. Weinstock, 1984.

Hapstein, Yisrael Elozor. *Sefer Avodat Elozor*. Tel Aviv: Va'ad Hasidei Kozienice be-Eretz Israel, 1976.

Hellerstein, Kathryn. "Translating as a Feminist: Reconceiving Anna Margolin." *Prooftexts* 20 (2000): 191–208.

Horodezky, Samuel Abba. *Ha-Hasidut ve-Toratah*. Tel Aviv: Dvir, 1944.

Hurwitz, S., ed. *Mahzor Vitry*. 1923. Nuremburg: J. Bulka, 1923. Reprint, Jerusalem: n.p., 1988.

Idel, Moshe. "The Journey to Paradise." *Jerusalem Studies in Jewish Folklore* 2 (1982): 7–16.

———— *Hasidism: Between Ecstasy and Magic*. Albany: State University of New York Press, 1995.

———— "The Land of Israel in Medieval Kabbalah." In *The Land of Israel: Jewish Perspectives*, edited by Lawrence A. Hoffman, 170–187. Notre Dame, Ind.: University of Notre Dame Press, 1986.

Jacobs, Louis. "Eating as an Act of Worship in Hasidic Thought." In *Studies in Jewish Religious and Intellectual History Presented to Alexander Altmann*, edited by S. Stein and R. Loewe, 157–166. University: University of Alabama Press, 1979.

———— "Hasidism and the Dogma of the Decline of the Generations." In *Hasidism Reappraised*, edited by Ada Rapoport-Albert, 208–213. London: Littman Library, 1996.

———— "Tobacco and the Hasidim." *Polin* 11 (1998): 25–30.

———— "The Uplifting of Sparks in Later Jewish Mysticism." In *Jewish Spirituality from the Sixteenth-Century Revival to the Present*, edited by Arthur Green, 99–126. New York: Crossroad, 1994.

Jelinek, Estelle C. *The Tradition of Women's Autobiography*. Boston: Twayne Publishers, 1986.

——— "Women's Autobiography and the Male Tradition." In *Women's Autobiography*, edited by Estelle C. Jelinek, 1–20. Bloomington: Indiana University Press, 1980.

Kalish, Ita. *Etmoli*. Tel Aviv: Hakubutz Hameuchad, 1970.

——— "Life in a Hassidic Court in Russian Poland toward the End of the 19th and the Early 20th Centuries." *Yivo Annual* 13 (1965): 264–278.

Kaplan, Edward K., and Samuel H. Dresner. *Abraham Joshua Heschel*. New York: Yale University Press, 1998.

Kaplinsky, Barukh, ed. *The Book of Kozienice*. Revised by Samuel Goldstein. Translated by Michael Wax and Jack Weinstein. New York: Kozienice Association, 1985.

——— *Sefer Zikaron li-Kehilat Kozienice* (Memorial book for the community of Kozienice; in Yiddish and Hebrew). Tel Aviv: Kozienice Association, 1969.

Kimelman, Reuven. "*Mavo le-Lekhah Dodi u-le-Kabbalat Shabbat.*" *Jerusalem Studies in Jewish Thought* 14 (1998): 394–454.

Kochan, Lionel. "The Unfinished and the Idol: Toward a Theory of Jewish Aesthetics." *Modern Judaism* 17, no. 2 (1997): 125–131.

Kossoy, Edward, and Abraham Ohry. *The Feldshers*. Jerusalem: Magnes Press, 1992.

Kozienice: Informacja Turystyczna. N.p, n.d.

Kugelmass, Jack, and Jonathan Boyarin, eds. and trans. *From a Ruined Garden: The Memorial Books of Polish Jewry*. 2d ed. Bloomington: Indiana University Press, 1998.

Lauterbach, Jacob Z. "The Naming of Children in Jewish Folklore, Ritual and Practice." In *Studies in Jewish Law, Custom and Folklore*. Selected by Bernard J. Bamberger. New York: Ktav, 1970.

Leiman, Shnayer Z. "Dwarfs on the Shoulders of Giants." *Tradition* 27, no. 3 (1993): 90–94.

Lejeune, Philippe. "Autobiography in the Third Person." *New Literary History* 9, no. 1 (1977): 28–50.

——— *On Autobiography*. Edited by Paul John Eakin. Translated by Katherine Leary. Minneapolis: University of Minnesota Press, 1989.

Lerner, Ann Lapidus. "Lost Childhood in East European Hebrew Literature." In *The Jewish Family: Metaphor and Memory*, edited by David Kraemer, 95–112. New York: Oxford University Press, 1989.

Lerner, Yosef Yizhak. *Sefer ha-Bayit*. Jerusalem: Sha'arei Ziv Institute, 1995.

Lesses, Rebecca Macy. *Ritual Practices to Gain Power: Angels, Incantations and Revelation in Early Jewish Mysticism*. Harrisburg, Pa.: Trinity Press International, 1998.

Lowe, Heinz-Dietrich. *The Tsars and the Jews: Reform, Reaction, and Anti-Semitism in Imperial Russia, 1772–1919*. Langhorne, Pa.: Harwood Academic Publishers, 1993.

Mahler, Raphael. *Hasidism and the Jewish Enlightenment*. Philadelphia: Jewish Publication Society, 1985.

Marcus, Joseph. *Social and Political History of the Jews of Poland, 1919–1939*. Berlin: Mouton, 1983.

Matt, Daniel. *Zohar: The Book of Enlightenment*. New York: Paulist Press, 1983.

Menahem Nahum of Chernobyl. *Me'or Eynayim*. New Square, N.Y.: Me'or ha-Torah Institute, 1998.

Minkin, Jacob. *The Romance of Hassidism*. New York: Macmillan, 1935.

Mintz, Alan. *"Banished from Their Father's Table": Loss of Faith and Hebrew Autobiography*. Bloomington: Indiana University Press, 1989.

Miron, Dan. *The Image of the Shtetl and Other Studies of the Modern Jewish Literary Imagination*. Syracuse, N.Y.: Syracuse University Press, 2000.

Nahmanides, Moses. *Sha'ar ha-Gemul*. In *Kitvei Ramban*. 2 vols., edited by Charles Chavel, 264–311. Jerusalem: Mossad Harav Kook, 1966.

Niger, Shmuel. "Yiddish Literature and the Female Reader." In *Women of the Word: Jewish Women and Jewish Writing*, edited by Judith Baskin, 70–90. Translated and abridged by Sheva Zucker. Detroit: Wayne State University Press, 1994.

Norich, Anita. "The Family Singer and the Autobiographical Imagination." *Prooftexts* 10 (1990): 91–107.

Oczkowicz, Katarzyna, and Krzysztof Reczek. *Kozienice—The Town and the Region*. Translated by Krzysztof Korkosz. Kozienice: Regional Museum in Kozienice, n.d.

Parush, Iris. "The Politics of Literacy: Women and Foreign Languages in Jewish Society of 19th-Century Eastern Europe. *Modern Judaism* 15 (1995): 183–206.

——— "Readers in Cameo: Women Readers in Jewish Society of Nineteenth-Century Eastern Europe." *Prooftexts* 14 (1994): 1–23.

Pascal, Roy. *Design and Truth in Autobiography*. Cambridge, Mass.: Harvard University Press, 1960.

Patterson, David. "On Translating Modern Hebrew Literature." *Journal of Jewish Studies* 50 (1999): 139–146.

Peli, Pinchas, ed. *Emunim Anthology*. Jerusalem: Mossad Harav Kook, 1954.

Piekarz, Mendel. *Ideological Trends of Hasidism in Poland during the Interwar Period and the Holocaust* (in Hebrew). Jerusalem: Bialik Institute, 1990.

Polen, Nehemia. "Aspects of Hasidic Life in Eastern Europe before World War II." In *Critical Issues of the Holocaust*, edited by Alex Grobman and Daniel Landes, 63–71. New York: Rossel, 1983.

——— "Coming of Age in Kozienice: Malkah Shapiro's Memoir of Youth in the Sacred Space of a Hasidic Zaddik." In *Celebrating Elie Wiesel: Stories, Essays, Reflections*, edited by Alan Rosen, 123–140. Notre Dame, Ind.: University of Notre Dame Press, 1988.

——— *The Holy Fire: The Teachings of Rabbi Kalonymos Shapira, the Rebbe of the Warsaw Ghetto*. Northvale, N.J.: Jason Aronson, 1999.

——— "Miriam's Dance: Radical Egalitarianism in Hasidic Thought." *Modern Judaism* 12 (1992): 1–21.

——— "Sensitization to Holiness: The Life and Works of Rabbi Kalonymos Kalmish Shapiro." In *The Jewish Action Reader*, edited by Charlotte Friedland and Matis Greenblatt, 43–50. New York: Union of Orthodox Jewish Congregations of America, 1996.

——— "Where Heaven and Earth Touched: The Hebrew Works of Malkah Shapiro." *Jewish Action* 56, no. 2 (5756/1995): 30–32

Rabinowicz, Harry M. *The World of Hasidism*. Hartford: Hartmore House, 1970.

Rahel Hutner: Mukdash Le-Zikhrah ba-Yom ha-Shanah ha-Rishon le-Petiratah. Jerusalem: State of Israel Department of Social Services, 1967.

Ramer, Samuel C. "The Transformation of the Russian Feldsher, 1864–1914." In *Imperial Russia 1700–1917*, edited by Ezra Mendelsohn and Marshall S. Shatz, 136–160. De Kalb: Northern Illinois University Press, 1988.

——— "Who Was the Russian Feldsher?" *Bulletin of the History of Medicine* 50 (1976): 213–225.

Rapoport-Albert, Ada. "Hasidism after 1772: Structural Continuity and Change." In *Hasidism Reappraised*, edited by Ada Rapoport-Albert, 76–140. London: Littman Library, 1996.

—— "On Women in Hasidism, S. A. Horodecky and the Maid of Ludmir Tradition." In *Jewish History: Essays in Honour of Chimen Abramsky*, edited by Ada Rapoport-Albert and Steven J. Zipperstein, 495–525. London: P. Halban, 1988.

Ribalow, Menachem. *The Flowering of Modern Hebrew Literature*. Edited and translated by Judah Nadich. New York: Twayne, 1959.

Ringelblum, Emmanuel. "Samuel Zbitkower: An Economic and Social Leader in Poland at the Time of the Partition." *Zion*, n.s., 3 (1938): 246–266; 4 (1938): 337–355.

Roosevelt, Priscilla. *Life on the Russian Country Estate*. New Haven, Conn.: Yale University Press, 1995.

Rosenblatt, Samuel. *The History of the Mizrachi Movement*. New York: Mizrachi Organization of America, 1951.

Rosenstein, Neil. *The Unbroken Chain: Biographical Sketches and Genealogy of Illustrious Jewish Families from the 15th–20th Century*. 2 vols. Rev. ed. New York: CIS Publishers, 1990.

Schacter, Jacob J. "History and Memory of Self: The Autobiography of Rabbi Jacob Emden." In *Jewish History and Jewish Memory: Essays in Honor of Yosef Hayim Yerushalmi*, edited by Elisheva Carlebach, John M. Efron, and David N. Myers, 428–452. Hanover, N.H.: Brandeis University Press, 1998.

Schama, Simon. *Landscape and Memory*. New York: Vintage Books, 1995.

Scheindlin, Raymond P. "Review of A. B. Yehoshua, *A Journey to the End of the Millenium*." *Forward*, 15 January 1999, pp. 11–12.

Schoenfeld, Joachim. *Shtetl Memoirs: Jewish Life in Galicia under the Austro-Hungarian Empire and in the Reborn Poland 1898–1939*. Hoboken, N.J.: Ktav, 1985.

Scholem, Gershom. *Kabbalah*. Jerusalem: Keter, 1974.

—— *Major Trends in Jewish Mysticism*. New York: Schocken, 1971.

—— *The Messianic Idea in Judaism*. New York: Schocken, 1978.

—— *On the Mystical Shape of the Godhead*. Edited and revised by Jonathan Chipman. Translated by Joachim Neugroschel. New York: Schocken Books, 1991.

Schwartzchild, Steven. "Aesthetics." In *Contemporary Jewish Religious Thought*, edited by Arthur A. Cohen and Paul Mendes-Flohr, 1–6. New York: Free Press, 1987.

Seder Hadlakat Ner Hanukkah lefi Nusah Raboteinu ha-Kedoshim mi-Koidanov. Tel Aviv: Machon Siah Avot, 5755/1994.

Seeman, Don. "The Silence of Rayna Batya: Torah, Suffering, and Rabbi Barukh Epstein's 'Wisdom of Women.'" *The Torah u-Madda Journal* 6 (1995–1996): 91–128.

Seeman, Don and Kobrin, Rebecca. " 'Like One of the Whole Men': Learning, Gender and Autobiography in R. Barukh Epstein's *Mekor Barukh*." *Nashim: A Journal of Jewish Women's Studies and Gender Issues* 2 (1999): 52–94.

Segal, Samuel M. *Elijah: A Study in Jewish Folklore*. New York: Behrman's Jewish Book House, 1935.

Sered, Susan Starr. "Rachel's Tomb: The Development of a Cult," *Jewish Studies Quarterly* 2 (1995): 103–148.

—— "A Tale of Three Rachels, or the Cultural *Her*story of a Symbol." *Nashim* 1 (5758/1998): 5–41.

Shapira, Shalom Yosef. "Eleh Toledot Kfar Hasidim." In *Sefer ha-Tzioniut ha-Datit.* Vol. 2, edited by Rafael Shragai and S. Z. Shragai, 204–205. Jerusalem: Mossad Harav Kook, 1977.

Shapiro, Kalonymos Kalmish. *Conscious Community: A Guide to Inner Work.* Translated by Andrea Cohen-Kiener. Northvale, N.J.: Jason Aronson, 1996.

——— *Esh Kodesh.* Tel Aviv: Vaad Hasidei Piaseczno, 1960.

——— *Hakhsharat ha-Avreikhim.* Jerusalem: Vaad Hasidei Piaseczno, 1966.

Shapiro, Malkah. *Be-Lev Ha-Mistorin.* Tel Aviv: Netzah, 1955.

——— *Mi-Din le-Rahamim: Sippurim me-Hatzrot ha-Admorim.* Jerusalem: Mossad Harav Kook, 1969.

——— *Shneinu ba-Maginim.* Tel Aviv: Dvir/Association of Hebrew Writers, 1952.

Sharot, Stephen. *Messianism, Mysticism and Magic.* Chapel Hill: The University of North Carolina Press, 1982.

Shneur Zalman ben Barukh of Liady. *Likkutei Amarim [Tanya].* Bilingual ed. Translated by N. Mindel, N. Mangel, Z. Posner, and J. I. Schochet. London: Soncino Press, 1973.

Shneur Zalman ben Barukh of Liady. *Likkutei Torah.* Brooklyn: Kehot, 1995.

Shohet, Isaiah, of Odessa. *Sefer Tehilim . . . im Perush Asifat Amarim.* 1884. Reprint, New York: n.p., 1953.

Sholem Aleichem, *Tevyeh The Dairyman and the Railroad Stories.* Translated by Hillel Halkin. New York: Schocken, 1987.

Singer, Isaac Bashevis. *Love and Exile: An Autobiographical Trilogy.* New York: Farrar, Straus and Giroux, 1984.

Slonimski, Hayyim Selig. "Be'ur Nakhon be-Fei[rush] ha-Mishnah." *He-Asif* 1 (1884): 228–232.

——— "Ha-Bikoret ve-ha-Pilpul." *He-Asif* 4 (1887): 233–244.

——— "Moznei Zedek." *He-Asif* 3 (1886): 390–393.

Sokoloff, Naomi. "Modern Hebrew Literature: The Impact of Feminist Research." In *Feminist Perspectives on Jewish Studies,* edited by Lynn Davidman and Shelly Tenenbaum, 224–243. New Haven, Conn.: Yale University Press, 1994.

Sokolow, Nahum. "Henri Bergson's Old-Warsaw Lineage." In *The Golden Tradition: Jewish Life and Thought in Eastern Europe,* edited by Lucy S. Dawidowicz, 349–359. Boston: Beacon Press, 1967.

Spira, Zevi Elimelekh. *Bnei Yisaskhar.* New York: Hayyim u-Verakhah, 1975.

Stampfer, Shaul. "Gender Differentiation and Education of the Jewish Woman in Nineteenth-Century Eastern Europe," *Polin* 7 (1992): 63–87.

——— "Marital Patterns in Interwar Poland." In *The Jews of Poland between Two World Wars,* edited by Yisrael Gutman, Ezra Mendelsohn, Jehuda Reinharz, and Chone Shmeruk, 173–187. Hanover, N.H.: University Press of New England, 1989.

Stanislawski, Michael. *Psalms for the Tsar: A Minute-Book of a Psalms-Society in the Russian Army, 1864–1867.* New York: Yeshiva University Library, 1988.

Stillman, Yedida. "The Evil Eye in Morocco." *Hebrew University Folklore Research Center Studies* 1 (1970): 81–94.

Stryienski, Casimir, ed. *Memoirs of the Countess Potocka.* Translated by Lionel Strachey. New York: Doubleday & McClure, 1900.

Sutthon, Menashe. *Kenesia le-Shem Shamayim.* Jerusalem: Eliyahu and Moshe Sutthon, 1874.

Tikotski, Avraham Yehudah. *Ha-Mufla Be-Doro.* Jerusalem: Makhon Zekher Naftali, 1987.

Tishby, Isaiah. *The Wisdom of the Zohar.* 3 vols. Translated by David Goldstein. New York: Littman Library/Oxford University Press, 1989.

Twersky, Aharon David. *Sefer Ha-Yahas Mi-Chernobyl ve-Ruzhin.* 1938. Reprint, Brooklyn: Beit Hillel, 1990.

Ulam, Adam B. *Russia's Failed Revolutions.* New York: Basic Books, 1981.

Wandycz, Piotr S. *The Lands of Partitioned Poland: 1795–1918.* Seattle: University of Washington Press, 1996.

Waxman, Meir. "Heblei Mashiah." In *Messianism in the Talmudic Era,* edited by Leo Landman, 442–444. New York: Ktav, 1979.

Weinberg, David H. *Between Tradition and Modernity.* New York: Holmes & Meier, 1996.

Weiss, Jacob. "Torah Study in Early Hasidism." In *Studies in Eastern European Jewish Mysticism,* edited by David Goldstein, 56–68. Oxford, UK: Littman Library, 1985.

Weissler, Chava. *Voices of the Matriarchs: Listening to the Prayers of Early Modern Jewish Women.* Boston: Beacon Press, 1998.

Wengeroff, Pauline. *Rememberings: The World of a Russian-Jewish Woman in the Nineteenth Century.* Edited by Bernard D. Cooperman. Translated by Henny Wenkart. Bethesda: University Press of Maryland, 2000.

Wertheim, Aaron. *Law and Custom in Chassidism* (in Hebrew). Jerusalem: Mossad Harav Kook, 1960.

Wiener, Aharon. *The Prophet Elijah in the Development of Judaism.* London: Routledge and Kegan Paul, 1978.

Wolfson, Elliot R. "Left Contained in the Right: A Study in Zoharic Hermeneutics." *AJSReview* 11 (1986): 27–52.

——— "Walking as a Sacred Duty." In *Hasidism Reappraised,* edited by Ada Rapoport-Albert, 180–207. London: Littman Library, 1996.

Zierler, Wendy. " 'In What World?': Devorah Baron's Fiction of Exile." *Prooftexts* 19 (1999): 127–150.

——— "Yokheved Bat-Miriam's Female Personification of Erets Israel." *Prooftexts* 20 (2000): 117–118.

Zimmels, H. J. *Magicians, Theologians and Doctors.* London: Edward Goldstein, 1952.

INTERVIEWS

Drazin, Chava. Interview by author. Ramat-Gan, Israel. 31 July 1989.

Duvduvani, Rahel. Interview by author. Jerusalem, Israel. 7 August 1995.

Hutner, Rabbi Yehoshua. Interviews by author. Jerusalem, Israel. 16 and 17 July 1995.

Peli, Penina. Interview by author. Jerusalem, Israel. 12 July 1995.

Poker, Miriam. Interview by author. Bene-Brak, Israel. 30 July 1995.

Schechter, Sima. Interview by author. Jerusalem, Israel. 19 July 1995.

Silman, Devorah. Interview by author. Jerusalem, Israel. 12 July 1995.

Yonai, Arela. Interview by author. Kefar Hasidim, Israel. 8 August 1995.

Timeline

This timeline includes important dates in the Hapstein–Shapiro family history and the dates of selected events in Jewish and world history.*

1814	Death of the Maggid of Kozienice, Rabbi Yisrael ben Shabbetai Hapstein, founder of the Kozienice dynasty.
1844	Birth of Sarah Devorah Shapiro, great-great-granddaughter of the Maggid of Kozienice and grandmother of Malkah Shapiro.
1860	Birth of Yerahmiel Moshe Hapstein, father of Malkah Shapiro.
1861	Abolition of serfdom in Russia.
	Birth of Brachah Tzippora Gitl Twersky, wife of Yerahmiel Moshe Hapstein and mother of Malkah Shapiro.
1863	Polish insurrection against Russian imperial rule of Poland.
1874	Marriage of Yerahmiel Moshe Hapstein and Brachah Tzipporah Gitl Twersky. He is fourteen years old; she is thirteen.
1881	Tsar Alexander II of Russia is assassinated. Outbreak of pogroms. Beginning of mass emigration of Jews from Russia.
1885	Birth of Hannah Goldah Hapstein to Yerahmiel Moshe and Brachah Tzipporah Gitl.
1889	Birth of Aharon Yehiel Hapstein to Yerahmiel Moshe and Brachah Tzippora Gitl.
1890	Birth of Rahel Hayyah Miriam Hapstein to Yerahmiel Moshe and Brachah Tzippora Gitl.
1892	Birth of Asher Elimelekh Hapstein to Yerahmiel Moshe and Brachah Tzippora Gitl.
1894	Birth of Reizel Malkah (Bat-Zion) Hapstein (Malkah Shapiro) on April 27 to Yerahmiel Moshe and Brachah Tzippora Gitl. Author of *The Rebbe's Daughter*.
	Captain Alfred Dreyfus convicted of espionage, and sentenced to degradation and deportation.
1896	Birth of Avraham Elimelekh Shapiro of Grodzisk (husband of Malkah Shapiro).
	Birth of Havvah Hapstein to Yerahmiel Moshe and Brachah Tzippora Gitl.
1897	First Zionist Congress in Basel, Switzerland.
1898	Birth of Yisrael Elozor Hapstein to Yerahmiel Moshe and Brachah Tzippora Gitl.
1900	A fire in Kozienice destroys the Hapstein family mansion.
1903	Kishinev Pogrom arouses worldwide outrage against tsarist regime's anti-Semitic policies.
1904	Russo-Japanese war. Defeat of Russian forces exacerbates political tensions in Russian Empire.
1904–1905	The time period of *The Rebbe's Daughter*.
1905	The first Russian Revolution forces Tsar Nicholas II to promise basic freedoms and establish the Duma, a parliament.

1908	Marriage of Reizel Malkah Bat-Zion Hapstein to Avraham Elimelekh Shapiro on June 12 (13 Sivan).
1909	Death of Rabbi Yerahmiel Moshe Hapstein on August 30 (13 Elul).
1914	Outbreak of World War I.
1918	Russian Civil War begins. Tsar Nicholas II and his family killed by the Bolsheviks. End of World War I.
	Establishment of Second Polish Republic.
1921	Death of Sarah Devorah Shapiro on October 5 (3 Tishrei).
1924	Yisrael Elozor Hapstein emigrates to *Eretz Yisra'el* (Palestine) and founds settlement near Haifa called Avodat Yisrael (later to be called Kefar Hasidim).
1926	Malkah Shapiro emigrates to *Eretz Yisra'el* (Palestine); settles in Kefar Hasidim and later moves to Jerusalem.
1936	First publication of stories by Malkah Shapiro.
1939	Germany invades Poland. Beginning of World War II.
	Hannah Goldah Hapstein dies in the German bombardment of Warsaw on September 26.
1942	Death of Aharon Yehiel Hapstein in Nazi-occupied Poland.
1948	Establishment of the State of Israel.
1966	Death of Yisrael Elozor Hapstein.
	Death of Rahel Hutner, Malkah Shapiro's daughter.
1967	Six-Day War. Israel defeats Arab forces and captures Old City of Jerusalem.
	Death of Avraham Elimelekh Shapiro.
1969	Malkah Shapiro publishes *Mi-Din le-Rahamim*.
1971	Death of Malkah Shapiro.

* Dates are based on the best information available. Some pre-twentieth-century birth dates are variously reported and should be considered approximate.

Index

CPSIA information can be obtained at www.ICGtesting.com
Printed in the USA
LVOW120321090212

267835LV00004B/4/A